THE REPORTER AND THE LAW

Techniques of Covering the Courts

COMMUNICATION ARTS BOOKS

Related Title

THE ECONOMICS OF THE AMERICAN NEWSPAPER
by Jon G. Udell
& Contributing Authors

Publication sponsored by
American Newspapers Publishers
Association Foundation

THE REPORTER AND THE LAW

Techniques of Covering the Courts

by

Lyle W. Denniston

SPONSORED BY THE

AMERICAN BAR ASSOCIATION

AND THE

AMERICAN NEWSPAPER PUBLISHERS ASSOCIATION
FOUNDATION

COMMUNICATION ARTS BOOKS

HASTINGS HOUSE, PUBLISHERS

NEW YORK 10016

DISCLAIMER STATEMENT

LIBRARY OF CONGRESS CATALOGING IN PUBLICATION DATA

Denniston, Lyle W   The reporter and the law.

    (Communication arts books)
    Bibliography: p.
    Includes index.
    1. Press law—United States.   2. Newspaper court
reporting.   3. Free press and fair trial—United States.
4. Journalism, Legal—United States.   I. Title.
KF2750.D46   070.4'49'34705   79-24051
ISBN 0-8038-6341-1
ISBN 0-8038-6343-8 pbk.

Published simultaneously in Canada by Copp Clark, Ltd., Toronto
Printed in the United States of America

Contents

Introduction

Truth is the common pursuit of the professions of law and journalism. Each, of course, pursues it in its own way. But when either succeeds, the result is the same: a free and self-governing society's most basic interests are served.

Indeed, the establishment of truth often is the very achievement of justice. When the law succeeds in finding the truth, it gratifies the community's sense of right. That is justice. When journalism succeeds in disclosing the truth, it informs the community's capacity to function. That, too, can produce justice.

This common calling is a high one, and it has compelled the two professions to learn—slowly and still imperfectly, it is true, but determinedly—that they must approach each other with "the same turn of mind," as the Biblical injunction would have it. "There must be no room for rivalry and personal vanity among you. Look to each other's interest and not merely to your own."

This publication originated in that spirit, seeking to reach across the separations in habit and philosophy between law and journalism. Out of a mutual appreciation that we must know each other in order to work together, as often we are obliged to do, the professions are now committed to a process of reciprocal education.

This volume is meant to acquaint journalists with the law, and to assist them in reporting the law as news.

This work is but a part of a larger effort that has continued for more than a decade, growing in intensity and significance, to achieve a workable mutual understanding among lawyers and journalists. This began in what might be called, in shorthand form, the "free press versus fair trial" controversy.

As an American Bar Association committee has observed, "It has only been in the last half of the 20th Century that circumstances and events have combined to bring about the first serious efforts to resolve the questions of whether free press and fair trial really could co-exist in harmony, and if so, how."

The "circumstances and events" included the assassination of President John F. Kennedy, followed by the Warren Commission Report with its criticism of some of the press coverage immediately after the shooting. The Commission concluded that, if the assassin, Lee Harvey Oswald, had not been shot himself but had gone to trial, his "opportunity for a trial by 12 jurors free of preconception as to his guilt or innocence would have been seriously jeopardized by the premature disclosure and weighing of the evidence against him. . . . A major consequence of the hasty and at times inaccurate divulgence of evidence after the assassination was simply to give rise to groundless rumors and public confusion."

Among other developments at about the same time was a series of decisions by the U.S. Supreme Court—in 1961, 1962, 1965 and 1966—reversing criminal convictions because of publicity before or during the trials.

The bench and bar reacted, with the American Bar Association putting a special commission to work on a study of the "prejudicial publicity" issue. It produced the "Reardon Report" in 1966—named for the commission chairman, Justice Paul C. Reardon of Massachusetts' Supreme Judicial Court. The ABA itself adopted "Standards Relating to Fair Trial and Free Press" in 1968.

The controversy became, in time, a dialogue. In many communities, representatives of the two professions began to discuss joint approaches to the "free press-fair trial" issue. These often led to joint seminars and other formalized conferences and courses, and to agreements on voluntary "codes" or "guidelines" on the conduct of the press in handling newsworthy criminal cases.

Not surprisingly, the controversy also continued in the form of a legal dispute, resulting in an increasing number of cases in which courts, believing that the process of justice itself was in jeopardy, had imposed limits or controls on press coverage of court proceedings, particularly criminal trials.

At times, it appeared that this confrontation could so aggravate relations between the professions that the prior and continuing efforts at understanding would be frustrated or perhaps even ended.

However, this aspect of press-bar relations reached perhaps an ultimate in the "Nebraska Press" case in the Supreme Court in 1976, a case that produced one of the most important rulings on the constitutional dimensions of the free press-fair trial issue.

But the court refused to be drawn to extremes or absolutes, and instead instructed the two professions constitutionally on the need for common purpose. Chief Justice Warren E. Burger's opinion for the court said:

The authors of the Bill of Rights did not undertake to assign priorities as between First Amendment and Sixth Amendment rights, ranking one as superior to the other . . . It is not for us to rewrite the Constitution by undertaking what they declined.

The "ultimate" confrontation, then, illuminated a recognition that it was no longer appropriate—if it ever had been—to treat the relationship between the professions of law and journalism as a narrow contest confined within the phrase, "free press versus fair trial."

It is no longer accepted that there is an irreconcilable conflict between the press' mandate to inform the people so that they may govern responsibly, and the mandate of the bench and bar to do justice.

The process of accommodation remains a difficult one, nonetheless. Each profession, as much out of habit as out of purposeful intent, is enough absorbed in its own processes and ends that it is less than fully aware of the methods and the goals of the other.

It is the purpose of this publication to help produce that awareness within the profession of journalism. This work proceeds on the simple premise that the law is the public's business, and therefore it is the business of journalism to appreciate what law is and to convey that appreciation to the public at large.

This volume also proceeds on the assumption that much of the popular perception of law is fundamentally flawed, in considerable part because of the inattention or the ineptness of the press as a chronicler of the legal process.

For most people, the system of law and the process of justice become vivid only as seen in the news, on television, or in the theatre. The great "morality play" that works itself out in the courts of America, and in the private forums of the law in this society, is seen by the vast majority of people through the drama—the sometimes exaggerated drama—of a headline, a single photo, a fleeting television image, a stylized courtroom scene on the stage or the screen.

Comparatively few of America's citizens go to a real trial in the local courthouse very often. As a result, the way people *see* justice at work is usually not shaped by a direct, personal experience with the law. As "outsiders," in a practical sense, they may look upon the courts and law with their minds already partly influenced by what they have read, seen or heard outside the courtroom.

The shaping of those attitudes is part of the responsibility of the press as it covers the courts. Of course, a citizen's awareness of justice, such as it is, may come from any of the circles in which he moves: on the job, at home, in church, at a club or meeting, over lunch with a friend, in a classroom, over the back fence. Somewhere, in each of those encounters and independently of them, too, the press can have its influence.

The nature of that influence, of course, varies widely. The style, manner and result of legal reporting differs between and among the kinds of media, between cities and towns, probably even between regions; it differs in the minds and practices of reporters and editors; it differs from story to story. There are no commonly accepted standards; only rough custom acts as a guide.

There is one undeniable fact, however, that has shaped news about the law, and that will shape the continuing debates over the influence of news on the law and courts. That fact is that not all of law is news. Actually, very little of it may be. Whatever the press says about law and justice, therefore, may well be something of a caricature.

That is a point worth understanding at the very outset; it is also a point that news professionals should eagerly concede to judges, lawyers, and other professionals in the field of law. However closely news accounts may reflect the law as it truly is, those stories cannot and will not expound the law to the complete satisfaction of those who are trained in the law. Legal news at best is but a near approximation of the law in its formal sense.

But the responsibility to be accurate, to convey reliable and not faulty information about the functioning of the legal system, is a deep and compelling one—indeed, it is controlling. Accuracy in reporting the law can only proceed from a dependably accurate understanding of it.

If the citizen cannot, will not or simply does not watch the processes of the law for himself, he has every right to expect that the news media who watch in his place will be faithful to his interest in what takes place there. It is no exaggeration to suggest that most citizens will be able to monitor the quality of justice only if the press does it for them. The average citizen reads no court opinions, watches few proceedings in court, studies no law review articles, has no regular contact with judges or attorneys, and handles no legal problems himself. The press is his law reporter.

This publication is intended to be a practical and useful guide, for the student and for the working journalist, to the system of law as it exists now and to the press' role in covering that system. If it is successful, it will be so primarily as a reference work for every-day use, in the classroom or on the "courthouse beat."

In approach, this volume is meant to be both elementary and sophisticated. Its language is kept deliberately simple, and its analysis is intentionally uncomplicated. But it seeks to define with particularity how the journalist assigned to report on the law or to edit stories about the law can understand the basic system, can separate the mythology and the complexity of the law from its meaning in a popular or journalistic sense, and can appreciate the practical operation of the law at work. It offers some fundamental advice, on the basis of actual experience, regarding the methodology of the courthouse beat, including the selection of story material, the pursuit of legal news, and its presentation.

It is not a technical manual that, by itself, can acquaint every reporter and editor with the particular system of justice as he will find it in his own community or state. Legal and judicial structures vary widely, and practice and procedure will vary from place to place, from tribunal to tribunal, from judge to judge, from firm to firm, from lawyer to lawyer. It would be a task well beyond the scope of this publication to describe the system in all of its particulars. The individual journalist, then, will be obliged to discover and to know the technical detail of the law as he finds it locally. It will do him no good at all to appreciate the fundamentals of law without a full appreciation of the process by which law works itself out in his own area.

What the student and the news professional will find here is a reasonably full discussion and analysis of the language of the law, which is quite uniform regardless of the structure, a portrayal of the basic arrangement of most court systems, a description of the general paths of the law as they exist throughout the country today. These characteristics of the law are then traced through the process of legal reporting, to show the points at which law probably will make news and to illustrate how law that *is* newsworthy can be translated into news stories about the law.

The first four chapters of the book lay the foundation for the other 11 chapters. They include a brief survey of the basic philosophical and practical differences between the disciplines of law and journalism, an introductory look at the entire system of justice without regard to its news-producing potential, an opening review of the techniques of reporting on the law, with special emphasis on the methods of developing (and keeping) news sources, and a reasonably detailed analysis of legal problems that confront the press itself.

No doubt, there will be readers and users of this publication who will have little or no reason to dwell upon the opening four chapters. But there surely will be others who will be coming to the law afresh, either as students or as news professionals, and will require some introduction to fundamentals before proceeding into the details of covering the law.

The 11 chapters that form the bulk of the volume are the working tools of the journalist interested in the law. Using primarily a chronological method, they discuss how the various branches or specialities of the legal system operate, how and when they produce news, and what the journalist may or can do with the information. Those who sponsor this publication, and the author, expect that these chapters will be used most frequently, both as introductions and as ongoing reference materials for the legal journalist.

The publication contains a full index, and the chapter headings and subheadings are made deliberately detailed so that the table of contents itself serves as an index. An extensive glossary is included, and it is keyed to the textual material. When a legal word or phrase is first used or when it appears in a new context, it is in bold-face type. These are the words or phrases that are defined in the glossary. The definitions themselves are written in a form that may be used in actual news or feature stories about the law. As a general rule, no news or feature story should use a technical legal term without a simple definition of it; reporters and editors are urged to rely upon the glossary regularly for this purpose.

None of the text is footnoted. This is in keeping with the author's intention to make the publication complete within itself as a tool of practical utility for every-day use.

Although the literature that could be of assistance to the legal journalist is vast, this publication offers only a highly selective list of source materials. The items listed and briefly described in the reading list have been chosen to support the basic approach of this publication. Reporters or editors wishing to go further will have no difficulty finding other materials.

The reader will note the Sponsor's Preface, which stresses that the American Bar Association and the American Newspaper Publishers Association Foundation serve only as sponsors of this publication. The author is responsible for the contents. In no way may the ideas, advice or suggestions be attributed to either of the sponsoring organizations. There are a few references in the text to positions taken or statements made by the American Bar Association, but those are clearly and expressly identified. The views of the two organizations on the subjects covered in the publication should be sought directly from those organizations.

The author's feminist friends will notice throughout the text frequent use of the pronouns "he," "his" and "him." These were not meant to convey any assumptions about women in the professions of journalism and law or in society. The references were intended to be neutral. The author has only lately come to sensitivity on this point, and trusts that the tardiness of the conversion will in no way refute its sincerity.

Much of the material here represents the professional judgment of the author, based upon his own experience. Perhaps there will be many points at which the judgment will be deemed faulty or even erroneous. The author, obviously, assumes sole responsibility for what is said.

Nevertheless, the author has had the valuable help of many persons. In particular, the author is grateful to his principal editors, Arthur B. Hanson, for the American Newspaper Publishers Association, and Paul H. Roney, for the American Bar Association; to Stephen E. Palmedo of the ANPA Foundation and Harriet Ellis, formerly of the ABA, for their friendship as well as their assistance; to Joyce Homan, for genuine devotion to this project and for so many kinds of assistance, and to Judy Hines and Diane Savarese, for sharing—and easing—the final tribulations of publication. The author is indebted to Jack C. Landau, whose idea it was to bring this project and this author together.

This publication could not have been written without the continuing support of Beth Denniston and of Clark, Stuart and Alan.

Lyle W. Denniston
Washington, D.C.
January 1980

Sponsor's Preface

The American Newspaper Publishers Association Foundation and the American Bar Association are pleased to join together in presenting *The Reporter and the Law* as a resource and reference work for journalists covering the courts.

We expect that Lyle Denniston's clear, concise tour through the complexities of court reporting will contribute to a better understanding of an arena in which journalists, lawyers and judges all have a vital interest.

Beyond that purpose, and perhaps more important, the aim of the book is to bring the highest possible quality of information to a citizenry which bears the ultimate responsibility for maintenance of an effective judicial system within our democratic society. The reader will find that Denniston's first concern is for the newspaper and broadcast *audience*—to help them understand what is happening, and why, in their courts. This is as it should be.

Jerry W. Friedheim
Executive Vice President
ANPA Foundation

Norman P. Ramsey
Chairman
ABA Standing Committee on
    Association Communications

THE REPORTER AND THE LAW

Techniques of Covering the Courts

1

The Law and the Press

Law in America has a character about it, an atmosphere, that makes it a particularly challenging and desirable "beat" in journalism.

Many of the major conflicts in a community, in a state, in the nation work themselves out in lawsuits. Nearly a century and a half ago, Alexis de Tocqueville observed:

> Scarcely any question arises in the United States which does not become, sooner or later, a subject of judicial debate.

That becomes truer as time goes on. Resort to a legal contest now is often the first, not the final, tactic in seeking to settle significant controversy. American society has learned, particularly in the last generation, that the processes of law are more routinely available. Expanding access to the courts, indeed, may be the dominant feature of law in modern America. It has come about through the growth of new forms of legal representation, new interpretations of the "right" to sue, new laws conferring new legal right or responsibility, new levels of jurisdiction.

As a result, many of the issues of the day—major and minor—will arise on the legal reporter's beat.

In addition, the process of justice has much about it that will draw the attention, routinely, of most readers or listeners. It is often an arena of drama. It gets results, usually quite rapidly. Almost anyone can identify with it, even when the process is not completely understood. It operates in the open much of the time, and thus is highly visible. It is a center of power, even when its use of

3

power is quiet or subtle. And it is populated with fascinating personalities.

Of course, the system of law in a given community at a given time might have none of those qualities. But that is likely to be a rarity; sooner or later, law will again become a conspicuous arena of important or interesting public business.

Few other public institutions in this country, in fact, are equal to the courts as "peoples' tribunals"—that is, places where the people themselves, of modest as well as high station, can see issues of keen and direct interest to them being attended to.

The opportunity for the press, as partner to the people in witnessing what happens in the law, is an obvious one. But it is as much obligation as it is opportunity.

Justin A. Stanley, president of the American Bar Association in 1976, has offered a rationale for the role the press must play as an attentive monitor of the public business that is done in the legal system:

> Lawyers construct and conduct the cases that decide major points of law and policy for all citizens. In doing so they must be careful, competent and devoted to a spirit of commonwealth. An appreciation of their responsibility should be especially acute in lawyers themselves, for it is a truism that those to whom influence and power are accorded must account for their use of it.

There are several means by which those who hold influence and power in the law may account for its use: as holders of public office, as officers of the courts which oversee their practice, as members of a profession guided by ethical restraints and internal mechanisms of discipline, as agents of clients deeply aware of the trust they have placed upon their lawyers.

Each of those forms of potential control, as well as the lawyer's own professional sense of what is right, will serve in some measure as the monitor of the quality of justice in America.

But the press nevertheless retains its own obligation to provide a professional check upon the legal system, on behalf of the people. Law is, in essence, a function of government, and like all of government, it is subject to the probing scrutiny of the press. As the U.S. Supreme Court remarked in 1947:

> What transpires in the court room is public property. . . . There is no special perquisite of the judiciary which enables it, as distinguished from other institutions of democratic government, to suppress, edit, or censor events which transpire in proceedings before it.

The Court qualified its traditional view of the openness of criminal cases to public scrutiny when it ruled in 1979 (in the case of *Gannett v. DePasquale*) that the public, including the press, has no constitutional right to attend proceedings that a judge decides to close. Even so, that ruling can in no way limit the press' continuing obligation to discover and to report what has occurred in court, whether closed or open. That is an obligation that does not depend upon the state of constitutional law at any given time.

Of course, it is important to remember that not everything that happens in the law occurs in a court room, and not everything legal is public property. Law and legal disputes often involve intensely private matters, beyond the scrutiny of the press and the curious public. This is particularly true of *civil* law cases and controversies: that is, those legal disputes that arise when someone has failed to fulfill an obligation owed to someone else. *Criminal* law disputes—those that arise when someone violates a requirement of conduct that has been imposed to protect society itself—are always public business, whether or not conducted in open court.

But the distinction between civil and criminal law does not define the role of the press in monitoring the legal system. In both civil and criminal law, there is a wide universe of public activity, bearing importantly on the life of the community or nation. It is in this realm that the legal reporter functions and works. The legal profession, too, recognizes the press as a wholly legitimate observer in that realm.

This common recognition, however, hardly assures the absence of conflict and misunderstanding in relations between the professions of law and journalism. There is a wide separation between the perspectives of the lawyer and the journalist. It is a deep separation in philosophy, and just as deep in practice.

News about the law cannot always or even routinely speak to the courts, to judges, to attorneys, in a manner that meets their professional standards. The reporter covering the courts is sure to be told, sooner or later and perhaps often, that his story has missed the point of a legal event or development, or that he has gotten it wrong.

Obviously, there are some easy explanations for such criticism.

Stories about the law usually do not, and ordinarily they cannot, tell the full story of a case or controversy. Sometimes stories about the law may tell more than the full *legal* story. There is a process of inclusion and exclusion in journalism, and it is markedly different from the process of inclusion and exclusion in the law.

As Zechariah Chafee has observed,

> A journal does not merely print observed facts the way a cow is photographed through a plateglass window. As soon as the facts are set in their context, you have interpretations and you have selection, and editorial selection opens the way to editorial suppression.

Thus, what may be entirely acceptable as news may be much less (or much more) than would satisfy the legal professional's sense of completeness, objectivity, or relevance. It is no mere coincidence that news stories are not "competent evidence," as legal professionals understand those words. A news story may be absolutely right factually, and may be perfectly defensible in the inferences it draws from facts. But the facts and the inferences have not been subjected to the tests of legal credibility and competence, and that rules them out of court.

Beyond the surface explanations, there are deeper, more abiding sources of the differing judgments that lawyers and journalists might make about the performance of the press in covering the law.

To most journalists, the law often seems to be but a pragmatic tool, a social function that keeps order, adjusts grievances, punishes error—an instrument that supposedly makes the future more predictable by relying upon the continuity of the past, a method that converts "code words" and practiced rituals into binding or at least limiting controls. To many journalists, the law has been seen as a nearly closed society, elitist in habit of mind and quite unwilling to explain itself.

By contrast, most professionals in the law see theirs as a calling of dignity and reason, a discipline that keeps man's looser instincts in check—a process that develops the adhesive that holds a society together, a method for displacing disorder. To many lawyers, the law is a society of intellectuals especially gifted at achieving change through adjustment.

If the two professions look at law with such differing, even conflicting assumptions, there is no less difference in the ways they view journalism.

To the journalist, his own profession is the people's handmaiden, working best when it can force concentrated power to answer, suspicious of apparent privilege, anxious to know immediately what might be of no moment tomorrow, devoted to plain speaking as if utility of expression were a prime social value.

By contrast, as the legal profession sees the press, it often is a journal of superficial impression and petty horrors, addicted to imprecision and to exaggeration, gullible and yet inattentive, careless to the point of irresponsibility.

That, to be sure, states the differing perceptions in an extreme form. Clearly, there are those in the law who understand journalism and its premises better than that, and the same is true of some journalists about the law. But there is no doubt that there is and has been a considerable disparity in understanding between the two. Perhaps another good measure of that comes out of the differing methods of the two professions; the methods may be as much at odds as the philosophies.

The journalist will not (often he cannot) take the time that the lawyer *must* to know his subject before he acts. The lawyer will not risk the journalist's daring in drawing quick conclusions.

The journalist tells his story by moving from most significant to least. The lawyer often builds his case the other way around.

The journalist hopes for immediate impact with his audiences—and usually can expect it. The lawyer works toward a contemplative judgment from the courts—often, much later.

The journalist pursues the novel. The lawyer searches for the familiar.

The journalist is fascinated by the illogical. The lawyer reduces events and emotions to logic.

Obviously, then, when the journalist undertakes to cover the law and write about it, the potential for division and misunderstanding between reporter and sources is quite large.

That potential has seemed to be most evident in press coverage of criminal trials. In recent years, the legal profession has grown increasingly sensitive about the possible impact of publicity upon criminal proceedings. Publicity, particularly when it flows in heavy volume about a heinous crime that arouses a whole community, has been seen as a threat to the right of the accused to a fair trial before an impartial jury, the government's interest in assuring a fair trial, and the jury's obligation to judge an accused person solely upon the basis of evidence properly admitted in court. Reacting to those concerns, lawyers and judges have sought to encourage or to require restraint in news stories about crime and criminal cases.

Because the standards, methods and basic principles of the two professions have seemed so different, it was obvious that "restraint" deemed appropriate by one might well have been regarded as quite unsatisfactory by the other. In such differences arose the reality of legal conflict: the press insisting upon a First Amendment right to define for itself how (or even whether) to exercise restraint, the courts insisting upon the prerogative of taking such steps as were deemed necessary to protect the process of justice from disruption.

As a result, the press has become increasingly a litigant itself. That can be, and sometimes has been, an awkward position. Obliged to be a neutral in its coverage of the news, including the news of court activity, the press has discovered itself acting as a special pleader before those same courts.

As one attorney for the press, Floyd Abrams, has described the dilemma, the press' felt need to seek constitutional protection in court was likely to aggravate the conflict with the judiciary. Abrams has commented:

> When the courts make pronouncements as to what is newsworthy, they are acting as government and are to be feared and challenged precisely as the press would do if other branches of government were involved. . . .
>
> Judges are, of course, "public officials." They are, indeed, "government," the same government against which the First Amendment was designed to protect us all.

The reporter working at the courthouse, or elsewhere on the legal beat, is at or near the center of this problem. All or most of his sources will be persons who are involved directly in the process of justice. His own professional activity may become an issue before the courts. His newspaper, magazine, station or network may become a party to a lawsuit. And all of this could occur as he pursues what he and his editors believe to be the usual and regular obligations of covering legal news.

Perhaps nowhere else in a news organization does a reporter operate so close to potential sanction, including punishment, from the very persons and institutions from which he must get news. On other beats, displeasure may simply mean the closing off of a source. On the legal beat, the reaction could be far stronger.

Thus, the reporter's day-to-day work is immersed in a mixture of legal and ethical complications, with consequences possibly bearing immediately upon him, personally as well as professionally.

Moreover, not all of the hard choices he must make can be made for him or shared with him by his superiors. Yet, what the reporter does or fails to do may draw into legal difficulty the entire hierarchy of his organization.

This can put the journalist specializing in legal news under great pressure. The degree to which he succeeds as a journalist, particularly if he is an aggressive investigative reporter or one who works for a "crusading" news organization, may in fact dictate the amount of trouble he will encounter.

It is improper and inaccurate to assume, however, that judges, prosecutors and lawyers are insensitive to this journalistic dilemma. Many professionals in the law—perhaps most—are well aware of the press' role in society, and they support strenuously and sincerely the constitutional guarantee of press freedom.

They, too, are confronted with strong ethical concerns when they become associated with a court proceeding, especially a criminal case, in which the press displays a strong interest. The public's interest in and curiosity about the case is understood, and it is weighed against the demands of the process of justice, and the government's interest in assuring fair and impartial trials. Judges, prosecutors and lawyers are quite interested in accommodation, not confrontation. As Justice Harry A. Blackmun of the Supreme Court has observed regarding First Amendment cases:

> What is needed here is a weighing, upon properly developed standards, of the broad right of the press to print and of the very narrow right of the government to prevent.

Blackmun added: "Such standards are not yet developed."

At a minimum, however, the reporter on the legal beat may make an effort at accommodation on his own, even in the absence of agreed-upon standards about the proper roles of the press and of the system of justice. He can do that simply by knowing what he is doing on the legal beat.

Awareness of the techniques, the language, and the accustomed standard of behavior at the bar and on the bench is, of course, no guarantee that the legal journalist will stay out of trouble, or keep his organization out of trouble. But it is nearly certain that ignorance of the process *is* a guarantee of trouble, ethical if not legal.

In fact, the ethical problem might well be more compelling than the legal. There is no way that a reporter can make the courthouse beat sensible to a public unlearned in the law if he himself gets lost in its fine points. He also has no way of avoiding error and miscalculation. And he has no way of filtering the news out of the mass of legal minutiae that is not news. His sources' specialized knowledge of their field is no substitute for his own awareness of the law as news.

Moreover, the journalist has an abiding ethical obligation to avoid, wherever possible, adding complications to the process of justice. He, too, has an interest in seeing that the community and the institutions which it has chosen for dispensing justice have an opportunity to function to insure that the law is just.

A community cannot monitor its courts, judges, prosecutors, lawyers, and police if its information about the legal system is unreliable or inaccurate. The journalist and the legal professional, then, must work as partners not adversaries in the pursuit of this information. A legal reporter's information is no better than his sources, and there will be few good sources in the law for a reporter who is seen as a careless and uninformed adversary.

The reporter specializing in the law also must keep in mind another factor, a subtler phenomenon, about the way the community he serves will see his work.

It is difficult to describe, and even more difficult to appreciate fully, but there is a popular sense of mystery in America about the law and the system of justice. It is almost a mythology, a belief *in* the law. It is this thought that underlies the common suggestion, when a perceived wrong has occurred, to say, "There ought to be a law."

This seems to play a very large part in the generally high reputation that the courts, judges and lawyers enjoy with the public. It provides a basis for popular support even for judicial action that is itself quite unpopular.

That is the hidden dimension in the community's reaction to legal news. The reporter in handling stories about the courts will come to realize that he is handling something that a good many citizens quietly and deeply revere. It will be well to keep this mythological dimension in mind.

The day-to-day work of the legal journalist, though, dwells on the practical side of the law. Most of what is discussed in the main part of this volume—chapters 5 through 15—has to do with law in its practical dimension.

Before reaching the law in its particulars, the legal journalist should begin with some practical generalizations about the law. They will tell him, in fundamental ways, why the system of justice works as it does. They also will illustrate well how different the legal system is from the journalist's own professional world. Here are a few of the more significant of those basic characteristics:

- The law is, basically, predictable and orderly. It is not a spontaneous process, and it is not really a creative process in the sense of producing novelty or originality. Even the surprises within the system, and there are some, come within a range of expectations. The law has some shortcuts, but they, too, are used primarily for emergencies or compelling exigencies.

- The legal process, in almost all of its forms, is a contest of adversaries. Each side is expected to fight vigorously (though ethically) to win. Out of this **adversary system** is supposed to emerge the truth, or as near an approximation of the truth as is possible. The assumption that the truth will be achieved acts almost as an article of faith.
- As a system, the law operates through a hierarchy. The higher authorities speak to the lower, which listen—most of the time. Legal creativity and originality, when it exists, may start at the bottom, but it usually must await ratification up the ladder. (It is not true, necessarily or even routinely, that "federal law" is higher in the scale than "state law." More often than not, they operate in independent realms. When there is a conflict between state law and federal constitutional law, however, state law must give way.)
- In the law, the most compelling search is the search for authorities— something in the past, in reason, in argument, or in experience that will seem to lead or to compel a result, a decision. (As one consequence of this, legal scholarship—the development of new ideas in and about the law—often will originate outside the courts, and outside normal legal practice as such. This, too, however, is a form of authority which can and does guide the courts.)
- Procedure, in the law, is absolutely crucial, and frequently decisive. It can be ignored only at peril—by the journalist as much as by the professional in the law. The fact that legal procedure will seldom make a major news story does not protect the reporter who is unaware of its operation and meaning from falling into error or misunderstanding.
- Precedents in law are usually considered to be controlling. If a set of facts and legal relationships in a new case matches or approximately matches those of a prior ruling, that controls the result. It is often true that new cases will produce new variations, in fact or in legal relationship. Even then, precedent will be strongly persuasive. Only when a precedent simply will not fit does the judge or attorney feel truly free to strike out on a new path.
- Much that is not legal will find its way into the legal system. It is error to regard law as the mechanical application of strictly legal measures to an array of fact. Moral precepts, ideology, sociology, economics, political theory—and, occasionally, personal preference—can and do make a difference, albeit at times only a subtle one, in legal result. The trend in the law, for generations, has been to enlarge rather than to constrict the scope of knowledge that may attract "judicial notice." Even so, any "non-legal material" that finds its way into a case must be quite closely related to the legal issues at stake. The legal system is not a policymaking process, and

thus the range of information and philosophy that it may consider is not open-ended.

- A lawsuit is a self-contained unit, existing for its own purpose and in its own universe, despite the fact that it may figure in the larger universe of legal precedent and philosophy. It is limited to its own record, and thus to its own facts and to those specific legal questions which it poses. If it does become a mechanism through which law itself grows or changes, that is really quite incidental to its own purpose: that is, to get a result between its particular contestants.

Those, then, provide a beginning practical appreciation of the law. The legal journalist should keep them in mind as he looks at the structure and the processes of the legal system, and then views his role in relation to that system.

2

The Law: Structure and Process

LAW MIXES IN WITH MUCH OF AMERICAN SOCIETY and reflects public morality on many social and political issues. It interacts with many other institutions and, indeed, functions within those institutions, too. At the same time, law remains sufficiently apart that it may be analyzed as a system within itself.

As a system, it has a structure and a process. The law also exists in both public and private settings. It is too simplistic to suggest that structure and process are neatly confined parts of the law, or that public and private legal activity are separate and distinct. To the insider who knows the system as well as to the outsider who is largely unacquainted with it, law is an intricate and complicated phenomenon.

The legal journalist, however, must do what he can to make it intelligible to the outsiders, who include most of the reading and viewing public. It will be useful, then, for the reporter or editor to begin with an appreciation of the system in the simplest form in which it can be described. That is the function of this chapter.

It is important to remember, at the outset, that law is actually two systems, not one: civil law, involving the adjustment or resolution of legal conflict flowing from duties that people or institutions assume or have had imposed upon them, and criminal law, involving the enforcement of codes of behavior that society deems necessary for the protection of its citizens or of itself. There are some points at which the two systems occasionally merge or overlap, but the legal reporter most often will treat them as if they were separate. This publication treats them as if they were.

It is also important to remember that the legal reporter is on the *courthouse* beat: he is covering the courts, primarily, and not necessarily the legal system as a whole.

He must also know, of course, that most law is not practiced in the courts. Statistically speaking, most legal controversy is settled long before a court might become involved. Much of the time and energy of the profession is and must be spent in avoiding contests in court. That is as true in criminal law as it is in civil law. If that effort did not succeed most of the time, the courts could not possibly manage the workload they would have.

The journalist interested in the law must be as aware of the working of the legal process out of court as he is of the judicial process itself. Waiting to discover the law in a judicial setting will mean missing at least the preliminaries if not the whole of significant—that is, news-making—legal controversy. The news potential in any controversy develops early, and remains throughout.

Nevertheless, it remains true that the legal reporter more often than not will find that law becomes news only *after* the parties to a lawsuit resort to the courts.

Partly, that is due to the fact that many legal controversies simply will not become a matter of public notice or public record unless they do get into court. That is especially true of those that involve private law: the regime of law that surrounds individuals, families, organizations, businesses in their private dealings.

In addition, the process of law in general tends to go forward privately until it reaches the point of going to court for the formal recording of a legal settlement already made, if not actually for a trial or for the issuance of orders compelling a settlement.

To be sure, there will be many times that the reporter will hear about a particular legal dispute well before the powers of a court are invoked to deal with it. That is likely to be true, for example, in many criminal law matters. Police activity is often known to the press as it occurs, or soon after. The same is true of other legal controversies, including civil cases, that involve persons of public fame or notoriety.

Even in such situations, however, the journalist may have comparatively little opportunity to keep up with a controversy before it has entered the judicial process. A great deal of the legal preliminaries goes on outside the view of the public and the press. In criminal cases, for example, prosecutorial action, including that of grand juries, is conducted in private or even in conditions of enforced secrecy. The journalist may know that such activity is going on, but he will have difficulty—at best—knowing in detail what is occurring. Nevertheless, he must try to keep up with it as best he can.

There will be no such difficulty, generally speaking, when a case has gone into the courts. Then, the system of justice is most out in the open, and its patterns are more regular and predictable. The court is the place where, in fact, results are usually forthcoming. Thus, judicial activity frequently will provide the kind of conclusive or definitive development that will make news.

It is for all of these reasons that this publication, throughout, focuses primarily on covering the courts rather than the law in a more general sense. Even the parts of the discussion which deal with "non-court law" are developed in such a way as to relate them to their potential for producing court activity. Whether or not a given legal dispute is settled before it reaches the judicial stage, a resort to court at some point always remains possible. At the very least, even settled controversies will come to court if the understanding breaks down and there is a need for enforcement.

A. THE STRUCTURE OF COURTS

Basically, the courts of this country are organized by function, vertically and horizontally. The most common division is the vertical one, producing three layers of courts:

- Those where cases start, or "trial" courts
- Those where appeals are first heard, or "intermediate" courts
- Those with final judicial authority, or "supreme" courts.

Within each of those categories, there is almost baffling variety, from state to state, and between the state and federal systems.

In some states, there may be two or more layers of trial courts—some handling petty cases, others handling more serious or more financially significant cases, some handling special classes of cases regardless of their seriousness. There also may be two or more layers of intermediate courts—including, in some instances, courts that act as "trial" courts for cases that already have been tried once in courts on the first layer. Sometimes, the general intermediate courts are split into civil and criminal tribunals. In a few states, that is true at the supreme court level as well. The more common arrangement of a state supreme court, however, is to have a single court of last resort.

The federal system is basically simpler than that of most states. It has three layers of general courts, with a layer of special courts existing mainly at the intermediate level. (There are, however, some complexities within and between the layers.)

All courts in this country are organized as a hierarchy. Cases tend to move "up" to "higher" courts. What that means, in an oversimplified manner of speaking, is that a case may not be considered to be at its final stage until it has "gone all the way to the U.S. Supreme Court." But that is, in large part, illusion.

Out of the almost innumerable cases that are handled by all American courts, not more than 150 or so a year are given full-scale review by the U.S.

Supreme Court. Less than half of those, usually, are appeals from state supreme courts. Thus, many cases are final without ever having gone "all the
way."

More significantly, it has been estimated that trial courts dispose of perhaps
99 percent of all cases that get into courts. (Moreover, even that represents but
a small fraction of overall legal activity; for example, it is estimated that 90 percent of all criminal cases end with a guilty plea, and no trial. The proportion of
civil cases settled out of court is probably at least that high.)

Thus, not only do few cases go to the pinnacle of the American judicial
system, but also few ever move beyond the trial courts.

The focus of most legal reporters' efforts, then, will be on the "lowest" tier
of courts. These are the dominant part of the courthouse beat not only because
of their volume, but also because they are the only courts with which most
Americans are likely to come into contact. Roger Traynor, a former chief justice of California, has remarked:

> Trial courts of limited jurisdiction, including justice of the peace courts,
> have unlimited capacity to affect public attitudes toward law for better or
> worse. It is these courts, not the appellate courts, that the people generally
> know first hand. What they observe there of justice or injustice, of efficiency
> or bumbling, will determine whether they will look upon the courts with re-
> spect and pride or cynicism.

Trial Courts

State. Each state is free to determine its own particular kind of court structure, under its own constitution and laws. No two states have exactly the same
system. In every state, however, there are trial courts of one kind or another.
Some of them exist at the city or town level, others at a county or regional
level.

The phrase "inferior courts" is often used by specialists and scholars to
describe the trial courts dealing with the most minor lawsuits, civil or criminal.
(The phrase, of course, suggests their level in the system, not their importance
or significance. It is a phrase that a journalist probably should avoid using in
his stories.)

Usually, those courts will handle hearings or trials of cases that involve
"petty" or less serious crimes—that is, **misdemeanors,** those for which the
penalties are the lowest in fines or jail terms. They also will handle civil cases
involving "petty" money claims—for example, up to $500.

The names of these courts vary widely. Some get their names from the official title of the presiding judge: "magistrate courts" and "justice of the peace
courts," for example. Some are named because of the nature of their jurisdiction, like "traffic courts." Some have names that are quite misleading: "supe-

rior courts." Some have geographic but otherwise nondescript names: "district courts."

They exist all across a state, although sometimes in varying forms within a single state, according to local preference and custom.

Such courts often do not keep formal **transcripts** of their proceedings. That carries potential risks for the legal reporter, particularly if his stories get him into trouble, as in a libel suit. The chance of error is considerable, and the protection of a verbatim transcript is unavailable.

These courts use simplified, often quite informal procedures—such as exceedingly brief hearings (none at all, in some cases). In a "traffic court," for example, the entire case may be over in less than a minute, with the police officer reading a charge in formal or stilted language, a judge asking the accused for a plea and then passing sentence immediately.

Commonly, but not necessarily, the loser in those courts has a right—provided expressly by law or by prior court ruling—to appeal the result. Sometimes, the appeal right actually includes the right to a new trial in a separate, slightly "higher" trial court which has broader jurisdiction (technically, **trial de novo**). A "not guilty" verdict in the inferior court sometimes may be challenged in the next higher court by the prosecutor—something prosecutors seldom can do after "not guilty" verdicts in any other trial court.

In those states where the jurisdiction to conduct trials is divided into two tiers, the second or slightly "higher" of these courts is still, in all respects, a trial court. When it is conducting a **trial de novo,** this may seem like an appeal, since the same case had been tried previously in the next lower trial court. However, **trial de novo** is still a trial, since the case will be conducted as if nothing had happened in the next lower court.

This next group of courts goes by a variety of names: "district," "superior," or "circuit" courts, or "courts of common pleas." (In New York, they are even called "supreme courts.") Lawyers and judges refer to this group as "courts of record."

Customarily, these tribunals will have broader jurisdiction than the lowest-level trial court. They are said to have "general" jurisdiction, meaning—in most states—that they may try either civil or criminal cases. They often will try only the more serious criminal or more significant civil cases. But, in some states, they do conduct **trials de novo,** as indicated.

These courts often try cases with juries (sometimes with fewer than 12 members, but in no case may it be fewer than six), but the right to be tried by a jury may be waived by the accused person in a criminal case or by the parties in a civil case. Procedures in these courts usually are quite formal and technical, and they frequently will keep full records—including verbatim **transcripts**—of the proceedings both in open court and in closed proceedings with the judge.

Appeals by the losers (either party who loses in civil cases, only the accused who "loses" when he is convicted in criminal cases) usually will go to an "intermediate" court of appeals.

In some states, special trial courts exist to handle designated kinds of cases: for example, divorce cases, cases involving last wills and other "estate" law matters, child adoption or custody cases, juvenile crime cases, and so on. (Some of these are discussed briefly in Section F of this chapter, and more fully in Chapters 8 and 13.)

Federal. It is generally true that trials in federal courts are held in U.S. District Courts. That is the only name they have, wherever they sit, and they all are governed by the same Constitution and the same federal laws on their jurisdiction and the same federal rules on their basic procedure (although there are some slight variations for the U.S. District Courts that sit in Guam and Puerto Rico). District Courts may have some special local rules of procedure, peculiar to a particular district. (**Rules of procedure** control the manner in which a lawsuit is conducted in court, including pre-trial as well as trial proceedings.)

There are 94 federal judicial districts in the country. About half have jurisdiction that reaches statewide in a single state, and the remainder have jurisdiction in a district covering only part of a state. None has jurisdiction in more than one state.

Each district has a District Court, but most of them are multiple-judge districts. However, a single judge normally presides over the court when it is sitting as a regular District Court (but see the following paragraph regarding a special variation of the District Court). In some districts, there are 20 or more judges. Some of the duties that formerly could be carried out only by a district judge are now done by a U.S. magistrate, a sort of "parajudge" whose office was created to relieve district judges of routine procedural matters. Magistrates may hold various forms of hearings, and may try some types of cases involving more or less routine matters of federal law. They have the authority to decide whether to release an accused person on bond, whether there is sufficient evidence to keep a suspect in custody, and whether to issue an arrest or a search warrant. (The magistrate's use of his authority is discussed more fully in Chapter 5.)

While District Courts are customarily single-judge tribunals, the federal system until recently made frequent use of "three-judge District Courts" to handle lawsuits testing the constitutionality of federal or state laws or regulations. One judge from a U.S. Court of Appeals joined two District judges in such cases. Such courts often heard civil rights cases, for example. The theory behind the use of three federal judges was that the decision to strike down a law should be a more solemn, considered act. In 1976, Congress took away most of the remaining authority of three-judge District Courts, thus restoring the former practice of relying primarily upon single judges to try federal cases.

The District Courts have court reporters recording their proceedings, so that written **transcripts** may be made later if required. Often, however, the court will issue written opinions that will describe the factual and legal conclusions behind the decision—particularly when the cases are significant or complicated.

No District Court may handle a case unless there is **federal jurisdiction**—that is, express authority to decide a case. Not all cases in federal court involve federal law, however. If the parties in a case involving state law come from different states (**diversity of citizenship**), and their controversy is worth at least $10,000, one or the other of them may demand that the case be tried in U.S. District Court—but according to the law of the state where the case began. The theory is that the out-of-state party has a better chance for a fair trial in a federal forum. Some state civil rights cases may be transferred (the formal legal term is **removed**) to a U.S. District Court for trial if it can be shown that the state courts cannot or probably would not provide a fair trial because of arguable local prejudice or bias.

Appeals from rulings by single-judge District Courts go first to the Court of Appeals for that region of the country. There are, however, extremely rare situations where the Supreme Court will permit a party to by-pass the Court of Appeals and bring an especially significant case directly to the Supreme Court from the District Court. There are also a limited number of cases in which the normal appeal route is direct from the District Court to the Supreme Court: for example, appeals from District Court decisions enjoining the enforcement of a federal law because it has been found to be unconstitutional.

In addition, appeals from rulings by three-judge District Courts went directly to the Supreme Court, by-passing the Courts of Appeals. (Occasionally, however, the Supreme Court has sent an appeal brought to it from a three-judge District Court back to a Court of Appeals because the Supreme Court concluded that it did not have jurisdiction to hear a direct appeal in the particular case.)

There are only a few specialized trial courts in the federal system: the U.S. Tax Court, the U.S. Court of Claims, the U.S. Customs Court, and military "courts-martial." Appeals from their decisions are permitted, but the route of these appeals differs for each. Tax Court cases are appealed to the U.S. Courts of Appeals, Customs Court cases to the U.S. Court of Customs and Patent Appeals, and military court cases to the U.S. Court of Military Appeals. Further appeals in Tax Court, Claims Court and customs cases may be taken to the Supreme Court, with that court's permission. (These specialized courts are discussed more fully in Chapter 13.)

The "Intermediate" Appeals Courts

Appeals courts, in the state and federal systems alike, sit to review the results of trials held in "lower" courts. The appeals process is, generally, not one in which a case is given a fresh start; instead, the appeal is usually confined to the facts and the **record** of the case at the trial level. Customarily, that means that the appeals courts do not make their own, independent search for facts, and do not second-guess the facts as a jury or a trial judge found them to exist. (That, of course, is not true of intermediate courts given the function of conducting **trials de novo**—that is, afresh.)

The role of appeals courts is, primarily, to review the law. They are supposed to make sure that trial courts have followed the law correctly or fairly, and they are expected to develop the law themselves—that is, to say what it is supposed to mean. (Appeals courts, while not reviewing facts as such, do review the legal determinations which trial courts have drawn from issues involving the facts of a case and may review whether the facts were sufficient to justify the legal judgment.)

Trial judges may offer a new, fresh or distinctive interpretation of the law, but in doing so they are subject to review by the appeals courts.

In the state court systems, this formerly meant—at least in a majority of the states—that trial court rulings and interpretations were subject to review in the states' highest courts, the "supreme" courts. Most states simply did not have "intermediate" layers of courts to consider appeals. That was especially true of states with smaller populations. More recently, however, an intermediate court of appeals has been created in many more states. They were added either because of case congestion in the state supreme courts, or because of a belief that some issues of law were not of sufficient importance to take the time of the supreme courts but for which there ought to be an appeal to some court above the trial level.

The intermediate courts of appeals have existed in the federal system since 1891.

State. A loser in a trial court, as one of his first thoughts after the judgment against him is in, may think he ought to appeal. That, however, is not a guaranteed right, in all circumstances. There is no such thing as a federal constitutional right to appeal in state cases; the state legislature may say how and when—and even whether—appeals are permitted.

The states have used that discretion to limit the "right" to appeal. The choice as to whether to allow an appeal may be left, by the legislature, to the discretion of an intermediate court of appeals.

In structure, the state intermediate courts have more than one judge; multiple-judge appeals courts may have as few as three. The courts may sit in **panels**—that is, some number less than the whole membership of the court—or they may sit **en banc**—that is, all judges sitting jointly.

These courts differ, from state to state, in their placement in the hierarchy of courts and in the scope of their jurisdiction. Some are considered to be a branch of the trial court; others exist in a separate layer between the trial court and the state supreme court. Some may hear any kind of case that had gone through the trial courts; others are given a narrower mandate. Some may be by-passed, with the case going directly from trial court to state supreme court; others may not be by-passed under any circumstances.

It is not uncommon for these intermediate courts to be, in actuality, the **courts of last resort**—that is, the final court to review a case. That would result if a state supreme court used its discretion, which most of them have, to refuse to review cases sought to be appealed to it. This would have the practical effect of making the intermediate court decisions final and binding. (The discretion of supreme courts is discussed in the section below dealing with those courts.)

Federal. The "right" to appeal is considerably broader, as a general rule, in the federal system than in most state systems. Congress generally has opened these courts to hear at least one appeal by the "loser" in the District Courts—that is, the trial courts. (It is, however, a matter for Congress to decide; there is no constitutional right to appeal in federal cases.)

There are 11 intermediate courts of appeals in the federal system. There is one for each "circuit" (they are, in fact, called "circuit courts"). The circuits are set up geographically, with ten numbered circuits for various groupings of states, and one for the District of Columbia.

The number of judges varies, from a low of three to a high of 26.

Most of the time, the courts of appeals sit in **panels** of three judges. Upon a vote of a majority of all the judges, however, they may agree to sit **en banc.** They will do so for particularly significant cases. A decision by a panel, how-ever, is just as binding within the circuit as one by an en banc court. A decision in one circuit is not binding in any other; conflicts may be resolved only by the Supreme Court.

Although most of the work of these courts, numerically, comes in appeals from District Court decisions, they also get some of the most important cases on their docket directly from the agencies (such as the Federal Com-munications Commission, Federal Power Commission and National Labor Relations Board, for example). Regulatory agency cases do not go first to the District Courts. (Regulatory agencies are discussed more fully in Chapter 14.)

The jurisdiction of the courts of appeals is as broad as that of the District Courts (and broader, of course, for regulatory agency cases). The scope of their jurisdiction is a particularly technical matter, at least in the relationship be-tween these courts and the three-judge District Courts. At times—and the number of times is increasing—the appeals courts may be obliged to review decisions by the three-judge courts, even though the federal law provides that appeals from the three-judge courts normally would go directly to the Supreme Court.

There are three specialized intermediate courts of appeals in the federal system: the Court of Customs and Patent Appeals, which reviews decisions of the Customs Court, the Patent Office, and the Tariff Commission; the Court of Military Appeals, a tribunal of civilian judges which acts as something of a "supreme" court in the specialized system of courts for the armed services (although its decisions are subject to challenge, in some narrow instances, in the federal District Courts); and the Emergency Court of Appeals, a special tribunal set up to hear appeals only in cases involving federal economic regulation, such as price and energy controls. (The operations of some of these courts are discussed further in Chapter 13.)

The Supreme Courts

At the top—in every sense of the word—of every American court system is the **court of last resort,** the "supreme" court. In all state systems and in the federal system, that court has more power—and more discretion about the use of power—than any court below it.

Its power is due, mainly, to the fact that it is ultimate: within its own judiciary, it has the final say.

But its authority also stems from the fact that it is a supervisory court, as well as the final decision-maker. It monitors the performance of the courts below it, and controls them by rules, regulations, or special orders (such as **writs of mandamus** or **writs of prohibition**).

The supreme courts of the states lack ultimate power in only one respect: they may be reversed—but only on matters of federal constitutional or federal statutory interpretation—by the U.S. Supreme Court. That court may be "overruled" only by the passage of new laws, by an amendment to the U.S. Constitution, or, or course, by itself.

The trend, at both state and federal levels, is to increase the discretion of the supreme courts to control their own caseloads amid the growing volume of litigation. More and more, it is becoming true as a fact that there is no unqualified "right" to appeal to a supreme court, state or federal. An appeal may be filed, but the supreme court—state or federal—usually does not have to agree to hear it, at least in a full-scale review.

Nevertheless, because they retain the power to act ultimately, if they choose, they are still the **courts of last resort.**

State. The supreme courts of the 50 states do not "try" many cases, even though some few matters may be taken to those courts for original trial. Their function, in the main, is appellate—that is, reviewing the legal result of a decision in a court below them. (Some states have separate supreme courts for civil and criminal law.)

Generally, these courts, like the intermediate courts of appeals in most states, do not disturb or even reconsider the factual results of the cases they are reviewing. They exist to review the law.

There is one kind of state supreme court ruling that is as ultimate, and final, as any decision the U.S. Supreme Court may reach. That is a ruling on the meaning of a state law. Even when a state supreme court ruling is appealed to the U.S. Supreme Court, that tribunal is bound to accept the interpretation by the state court of the state law. The Supreme Court, of course, may strike down the law if it finds it violates the Constitution, or conflicts with a federal law on the same subject, but it may not re-interpret the state law to give it a new meaning.

The Supreme Court, however, usually will go a considerable way to avoid reversing a state supreme court decision. Should it find that the state court was wrong in its understanding or reading of the Constitution or federal law, the Supreme Court still will seek to discover an "adequate" rationale under state law to support the state ruling. In that event, it may simply overlook the conflict with the Constitution or federal law, and accept the state ruling as binding simply because the ruling is a binding interpretation of state law.

State supreme courts have a wide-ranging jurisdiction. They have authority, customarily, to review all types of cases. Since one of their more important functions is to "develop" the law—that is, give it a definite and final meaning, binding uniformly on lower state courts—the states' highest courts may deal with cases that range from the trivial to the profound in their legal issues.

The cases which a state supreme court sometimes has authority to "try" rather than to review on appeal are generally those that involve its supervisory authority, such as requests that it require a lower state court to act, or to prohibit it from taking some action. (This is its **original jurisdiction.**)

State supreme courts have as few as three members, but the more common number is seven. They sit together rather than in panels.

In most of the states, the supreme court is called that by name. There are a few variations, however, such as Massachusetts' Supreme Judicial Court, the Supreme Court of Appeals as in Virginia and West Virginia, and the Court of Appeals, as in Kentucky, Maryland, New York, and Texas. (The Texas Court of Appeals is actually two courts: one for civil, one for criminal.)

Federal. In America, there is only one court that *must* exist. It is the United States Supreme Court, the only tribunal specifically required by the Constitution. Congress is empowered by the Constitution to create, or abolish, any other federal court.

Most of the business of the Supreme Court—unlike its mere existence—depends upon Congress' will. The cases that it may hear on appeal (its **appellate jurisdiction**) are defined by laws passed by Congress. It also does have a class of cases which it alone tries—its **original jurisdiction**—and those are spelled out by the Constitution itself. As a matter of fact, however, the Supreme Court is likely to decide no more than one or two "original" cases in any of its annual terms.

Congress' habit, over almost all of America's history, has been to expand the court's reach. Only once, in fact, has a law been passed to deny the court authority to decide a case over which it had had jurisdiction. That was in 1868, depriving the court of an opportunity to rule upon the validity of the Reconstruction acts following the Civil War.

In addition, Congress' approach has been to give the Supreme Court an increasing amount of discretion to control its own caseload. Over much of history, the court had a class of cases in which there was a "right" to appeal; the justices had no discretion to decline to hear those.

Beginning in 1925, however, the court has steadily gained authority to deny any review to many kinds of cases, and to deny full-scale review to all others, even including "original" cases which the Constitution entrusts to it alone.

Thus, the justices themselves are now primarily responsible for shaping their docket. Moreover, they need answer to no one on their reasons for choosing not to decide any case.

In practice, the justices select about 150 cases for full-scale review during each nine-month sitting, or term. (Those are the cases it decides, with written opinions, after full briefing and a public hearing.) That has been a fairly constant figure, even though the general trend in recent years has been for the volume of cases sought to be reviewed to grow numerically.

Its jurisdiction, in terms of the kinds of cases it may elect to decide, is as wide as the federal court system allows for any court. There is no class of cases expressly withheld from it. Thus, it is, without limitation, the ultimate federal court.

The court has nine justices. (The figure is set by federal law; over the years, it has ranged from a low of six, at the beginning, to as high as ten, after the Civil War.) At least six of the nine justices must participate for the court to have a quorum to do any business. The justices of the court always sit together, never in panels. A single justice may, however, issue an emergency or procedural order. It takes the votes of only four justices to grant full review of a case. (See Chapters 7 and 12.)

B. THE LAWYER AND THE COURTS

It is literally true that the judicial process in America begins with the lawyer and his client. One of the lawyer's most significant functions is to decide when and, sometimes, where to go to court. Utah's Supreme Court has put it quite plainly:

> While doctors, plumbers, electricians, barbers, etc., may sell their time and skill to the public by virtue of their license from the state, the attorney alone has the right to set the judicial machinery in motion in behalf of another. . . .

That "right" is, of course, one shared by the attorney who is a public prosecutor, on behalf of the people, and by the attorney who is a private practitioner, on behalf of his client. As a general rule, it is not possible to begin a criminal case unless a lawyer—the prosecutor—elects to file it, and it is not possible to begin a civil case unless a lawyer—for a public or private client—implements a client's decision to file it. (However, there are a growing number of civil cases started by persons acting as their own attorneys—that is, **pro se**.)

But the attorney is supposed to start the judicial machinery for his client with care and caution. The attorney who thinks first of going to court may be acting, at least in some circumstances, in a way that will do his client no good, and may in fact harm his client's interests. As important as the role of "advocate" is for the legal professional, it is no more important than his role as counselor or negotiator. In performing those functions, the lawyer may—and often does—find that going to court is the very last thing he would want to do for his client.

His fundamental obligation is no different from that of anyone else involved in the nation's court system: to see that justice is done. It is justice for *his* client, of course, that he is obliged to seek. But that may not be obtainable, in a lawyer's professional judgment, by having the case go to court.

In a very real sense, he is obliged to stay out of court, not only because of his client's particular interests in a given case—including the cost of litigation—but also because of his duty as an attorney to avoid involving the courts in cases that use time and resources unnecessarily. (His view of what is an unnecessary or "frivolous" case in court and the view of a judge or court on that may well differ, but that does not diminish his duty to stay out of court if possible.)

The attorney whose case does get into court is, of course, a central figure in that process. Indeed, lawyers make up two-thirds of "a court," so to speak. The attorneys on the two sides of the case (prosecutor and defender in criminal cases, plaintiff's lawyer and respondent's lawyer in civil cases) may be as indispensable to the case as is the judge. (The precise functions that the lawyers perform in court are treated in later chapters.)

Advocacy and Ethics

It is when the lawyer appears in court that the somewhat dual nature of his profession becomes most evident—and, at times, most difficult to manage. While he is there to fight vigorously for his client's cause, he is also there to act as an officer of the court. He is obliged to assist the court in making the judicial process work, and yet to try—simultaneously—to insure that his client gets the best possible result from that process.

There is, in ideal terms at least, no reason why the attorney's duties toward the system of justice as a whole and his obligations toward his client must necessarily conflict. Indeed, the better he fulfills his function as a determined adversary, the more likely it will be that he serves justice in the general sense.

But the attorney who seeks to win "at all costs" may well find that he has gone too far, and will be found to have violated his ethical duties as an attorney and as an officer of the court. In fact, he may, in extreme cases, be punished for **contempt.** Still, he is entitled to proceed with his vigorous advocacy for a long way, even to the point of seeming to be quite uncooperative with the judge. This sometimes delicate balancing of duties is the essence of legal practice within the limits of professional ethics.

The task only seems the more challenging when one recalls that, in the American system of law, the basic function of the lawyer is in considerable part a constitutionally endowed one.

Legal Representation

In a criminal case, the accused person has an absolute constitutional right to have a lawyer if he wants one. One may not be forced upon him, however, if he wants to represent himself. (There is, and will continue to be, a debate about the specific stages of criminal proceedings where the right to a lawyer is to exist.)

In a civil case, there is no similar absolute right to a lawyer. There is, however, a constitutional guarantee that no person may be "injured," in a legal sense, without having had **due process**—basically, fair treatment. At least there would be serious questions of a lack of **due process** if a party in a civil case had to make do in court without a lawyer. (The courts have been engaged for many years in attempting to define the "right" to a lawyer in civil proceedings, particularly those that go on in forums other than courts.) The fact that more of the civil law process was opened to legal representation did not, by itself, guarantee that there would be sufficient legal manpower to provide the service.

"Pro bono" lawyers. It has long been true, however, that many attorneys have provided service on a gratis basis, and this has made a reality of the theoretical access to the law for those clients who had no money to purchase legal talent on their own. It is common for private attorneys to handle "**pro bono publico**" causes—that is, in literal translation, cases pursued "for the public good." The issue at stake in such cases often is of considerable public interest, but it would not have been carried to a decisive result had there not been free legal talent available.

Public interest lawyers. A more recent development, adding significantly to the pool of legal manpower available to provide representation as more and more social questions were put to the courts for resolution, has been the rise of the lawyer specializing in "**public interest**" law—that is, taking and pleading cases seeking to expand the frontiers of law by testing new issues, issues of wide "public interest." Ralph Nader's well-known legal teams are a classic example of this approach.

To be sure, the representation is much the same as in all legal practice: providing legal services to enable a client to win his case. But the fundamental goal of "public interest" law often has been to bring before the courts legal questions that may have been largely ignored, or to test new theories about new legal "rights" or "privileges."

The "public interest" lawyer may be a private attorney in a larger firm that offers a broad range of legal services, or in a smaller firm—perhaps a one-lawyer firm—that may do nothing but practice public interest law. At times, the lawyer in this field may be in a government agency, carrying on a more or less neutral role as a "public counsel" or "**ombudsman.**" A public interest lawyer sometimes works for a fee, other times for nothing.

(In its early development, public interest law focused heavily on cases involving minorities, the poor, women, and environmental issues. But it spread rapidly into a wide array of "new" branches of the law—for example, the rights of the mentally ill, or the rights of children.)

"Officers of the Court"

Beyond the contemporary developments in access to legal help, and beyond even the growth in the constitutional right to a lawyer, there is long-standing custom—indeed, some seven centuries of tradition—that places the attorney centrally in the process of justice. For all of that time, the attorney has been relied upon, to a greater or lesser degree, to share in the public duty of administering justice.

It is this deep involvement of lawyers with the court system that gives to the courts the almost unchallengeable authority to decide who practices law before them.

Legislatures may establish basic procedures for determining who is qualified to become a lawyer. But it is the courts, and no other part of the government, that ultimately controls the practice of law.

The reasons for this were stated by Nebraska's Supreme Court in 1937:

> The primary duty of courts is the proper and efficient administration of justice. Attorneys are officers of the court. . . . They are in effect an important part of the judicial system. . . . It is their duty honestly and ably to aid the courts in securing an efficient administration of justice. The practice of law is so intimately connected and bound up with the exercise of judicial power and the administration of justice that the right to define and regulate its practice naturally and logically belongs to the judicial department. . . .

"Officers of the court." It seems a peculiar description, for lawyers who are in private practice and especially for those who never set foot in a courtroom.

But it is a description—indeed, it is a role—that has applied for so long that it is beyond question.

Licensing and discipline. Attorneys are public officers. Significantly, they are first of all public officers of the *states*. In America, the states hold the authority to grant or deny licenses to practice law. Even an attorney who intends to or does practice during all of his career in the federal courts must begin with a state license. Admission to practice before any federal court, including the U.S. Supreme Court, depends upon a lawyer's prior admission to practice law in a state. If he loses that license, he is automatically denied the opportunity to carry on his career in the federal system. There is at present no such thing as a separate federal license, although that idea or some variation of it is discussed increasingly. (It should also be noted that some federal courts do impose special rules of admission to practice.)

State courts, of course, usually delegate to committees or associations of lawyers some of their authority to control entry into the profession, and to handle the disciplining of lawyers.

But the process does not thereby become a private one. The "bar" of every state is, ultimately, an arm of the state judiciary, and is thus a public agency— at least as long as it is exercising some aspect of the courts' public or governmental authority.

A fairly typical law showing the link between the professional control of lawyers' conduct and the state court system is the one in effect in Virginia, saying:

> The Supreme Court of Appeals may, from time to time, prescribe, adopt, promulgate and amend rules and regulations of organizing and governing the association known as the Virginia State Bar, composed of the attorneys at law of this state, to act as an administrative agency of the court for the purpose of investigating and reporting the violation of such rules and regulations as are adopted by the court under this article to a court of competent jurisdiction for such proceedings as may be necessary, and requiring all persons practicing law in this state to be members thereof in good standing.

(It should be noted that this is a law which establishes what is called an "**integrated bar**"—that is, an organized bar to which every lawyer in the state must belong, as a condition for practicing law. Not all state bars are "integrated" in this technical sense. But even where an attorney need not join a state bar in order to practice, he is still fully subject to the "rules and regulations" which spell out the kind of conduct required of those involved in any way in practicing law.)

The rules that control a lawyer's performance apply either at the time he enters the profession or after he is in practice. The entry rules are keyed to qualifications—particularly, formal legal education and basic personal behavior. The "disciplinary rules" are used to measure on-the-job ethics.

Like any other citizen with a right or privilege subject to withdrawal, the practicing attorney accused of breaking the rules is entitled to his "day in court." In other words, he can't lose his right to practice without first having a chance to tell his side of the story to someone or some group that is impartial.

Professional punishment of lawyers takes three basic forms. The mildest is a reprimand or "**censure.**" More severe than that is a **suspension**—that is, a temporary loss of the right to practice. Most severe is **disbarment**—the long-term or permanent loss of the right to practice.

Of course, if an attorney's misbehavior violates criminal laws, he may be prosecuted. If he is convicted, the chances are that he will also be punished separately as a lawyer by suspension or disbarment. In some states, conviction of some crimes leads to automatic disbarment.

Lawyers, like anyone else appearing in a courtroom, are subject to the power of judges or courts to punish for **contempt** for misconduct. Moreover, they, like other citizens, may risk contempt if their activity even outside the courtroom interferes in a significant way with the judicial process.

Finally, lawyers—like some other professionals—are subject to being sued for **malpractice** if the result of their professional performance brings harm or legal "injury" to their clients.

The record on discipline. Of all the forms of control over attorneys, the one that is most common (statistically) is disciplinary enforcement by courts or by bar associations which have been delegated that authority. That process, ideally, is the one that would insure that lawyers are fulfilling the trust of their public duty to administer justice.

But that has not been the reality. In fact, there has been a critical gap between the expectation that lawyers will be worthy of a public trust and the actual circumstance that many lawyers are not. An American Bar Association special committee chaired by retired Supreme Court Justice Tom C. Clark concluded in 1970 that the disciplinary process was a "scandalous situation."

Its conclusions, after three years of study, included these:

- Disbarred attorneys sometimes "are able to continue to practice in another locale."
- Lawyers convicted of federal income tax violations "are not disciplined."
- Lawyers "convicted of serious crimes are not disciplined until after appeals from their convictions have been concluded, often a matter of 3 or 4 years."
- "Even after disbarment, lawyers are reinstated as a matter of course."

Looking at the disciplinary machinery itself, the committee found that:

- Lawyers "will not appear or cooperate in proceedings against other lawyers but instead will exert their influence to stymie the proceedings."

- In communities with "a limited attorney population, disciplinary agencies will not proceed against prominent lawyers or law firms."
- State agencies that are supposed to do the disciplining "are undermanned and under-financed, many having no staff whatever for the investigation or prosecution of complaints."

The ABA has used the study as the impetus for a years-long effort to carry out, across the country, the reforms proposed by the special committee.

The "public" lawyer. The disciplinary process, in its basic form, does not vary as it applies to "public" lawyers compared to "private" attorneys. Those who practice law as part of the government—federal, state or local—are subject to being disciplined, too. Even if they do not actually practice law in their public positions, they still may be disciplined for misconduct.

However, there is the additional check upon them of direct public accountability for their service in office.

Lawyers who are appointed or elected to legal positions in government may be disciplined by being removed from office, either through some process of **impeachment, recall,** or dismissal, or by the failure of the voters to re-elect them. (That would be true, of course, whether or not a public officeholder was an attorney.)

The typical positions in government usually reserved (by law or custom) for candidates who are trained as lawyers include prosecutors at all levels, legal advisers—such as general counsel—to a variety of officers or agencies, and administrators of some agencies. (Judgeships also are most often filled only by lawyers; their selection and discipline is a different matter, treated separately later in this chapter.) It is quite common for persons who are lawyers to be elected to general positions in town, county, or state government, or to legislatures at the city, state or federal (congressional) level, but the fact that they are lawyers may have little or nothing to do with their service in such positions. Still, as attorneys, they would be subject to discipline for some forms of misconduct in office.

C. THE JUDGE AND THE COURTS

Just as the lawyer is, most of the time, the one who will get the process of justice started, the judge is, much of the time, the one who will determine its direction and destination. Justice Benjamin Cardozo has been quoted often on the theme: "In the long run, there is no guarantee of justice except the personality of the judge."

It is true that there are many checks or restraints upon the judge: precedent, custom, manners, ethics, appeals judges, legislators, the voters, the press. Still, the judge on the bench—and especially the trial judge—has a reach of authority that is exceedingly wide, and he usually has broad freedom to apply that power in practice.

Professor Harry W. Jones has written of "the inescapability of choice" that confronts the judge:

> We need not pause too long to dispose of the hoary fiction that judges have no discretion, no choices between alternative decisions, in "a government of laws and not of men." The notion that a judge merely pronounces results already preordained and fixed by the rules of the legal system is the long-discarded "slot machine" theory of the judicial process. . . .

The function of the judge is, in its simplest and yet most majestic form, the use of his judgment, making choices where there are "no clear mandates," as Professor Jones described them, requiring him to decide one way or the other.

There has been a good deal of special emphasis, in legal education (and, often, in journalism) upon the appeals courts and their function of "developing" the law through their reviewing authority over "lower" courts. But given the usually accepted statistic that only one in ten decisions of trial courts is appealed, and the fact that most trial court rulings that are appealed are upheld, it is clear that the judge on the trial bench is the key figure of the American judiciary.

There is another generalization that is compelling for the legal journalist: the only judge that most citizens—and, indeed, most reporters—will ever see or know at first hand is the trial judge. He is, in most communities, the embodiment of justice. It is his style, the tone of his performance, and the results that emerge from his courtroom that give the law its character and flavor. For most people, other judges and other courts are remote (and, quite commonly, of only passing interest, at most).

The Neutral Umpire

The role of the judge (and this is as true of appellate as of trial judges) is to be the umpire in the contest that every legal case becomes under the American system or **"adversary" justice.** It is assumed that the judge as umpire will be neutral. It is his obligation to be.

But the neutral umpire is not strictly confined to making simplistic judgments based on arbitrary rules for the legal contest. He can and often does intervene deeply and directly in the case itself, while it is in preparation or after it has gone to trial.

A significant part of his role is to keep the case in proper bounds, legally, by ruling on points of law and procedure. But just as important—more important, actually, for the trial judge—is the part he plays in seeing that the facts are brought out as fully as is necessary to make a legal judgment upon them.

The trial judge. When a judge tries a case without a jury (it occurs in civil cases much more often than in criminal cases), he is the sole "**fact-finder.**" It is he who determines the facts themselves, and the inferences to be drawn from those facts, that together form the basis for the legal **judgment.**

When a judge tries a case with a jury, he still has a major role in selecting the facts that may be offered to the jury for it to judge as to significance and credibility in reaching a verdict. The jury is the **fact-finder,** but it is left to "find" facts only from among those which the judge has allowed it to hear. Moreover, the judge can have a profound influence over jury fact-finding by the instructions he gives to the jury on the legal principles or rules that they must follow in weighing the facts.

The appellate judge. The body of facts that emerges from a trial court are, most often, beyond review or challenge in appellate courts. Appeals deal with the law that governed a verdict, not the facts upon which it was based. (Sometimes, appeals courts will examine the facts to see whether they do, indeed, support the legal findings made by the trial judge.)

The role of the appellate judge, then, is almost exclusively one of legal interpretation. He—acting alone or, on multi-member courts, with other appellate judges—sits primarily to review and if necessary to correct the judgments in law and procedure made by the trial judge.

In the process, the appellate judge or court shapes the meaning and scope of law, supposedly to make it consistent and uniform as a guide to the trial courts.

Rarely do appellate courts receive further evidence or testimony, from witnesses or by documents. (The exception is the appellate court that conducts **trials de novo,** as described briefly earlier in this chapter.) Rather, appeals courts do their work based upon argument—oral, written, or both—from lawyers and the judges' own knowledge and reading of the law and precedent.

The formal **record** of a case is, basically, the record made in the trial court. If new factual developments have occurred after trial that may affect a case importantly, those may be brought to an appeals court's attention. But if that occurs, chances are that the court will send the case back to the trial judge for his initial review of the new material.

Overall, the function of the appellate judge is more contemplative than that of the trial judge. Indeed, unlike the trial judge, the jurist on an appeals court seldom has to give his legal judgment without taking time to reflect upon it. The trial judge often makes rulings "on the spot" with, at most, only a brief recess for reflection and study.

Selection of Judges

Although the functions of trial and appellate judges differ quite markedly, the methods of selecting judges to serve at the various levels of the American judiciary do not necessarily differ. There is a very wide variety in the selection processes used in the states and at the federal level, and sometimes the process may have little or nothing to do with whether the chosen judge is to serve on a trial or appellate bench.

Over several generations, court reform groups and agencies have sought to make the process more regular, uniform and rational, but the results of that effort remain imperfect.

The choice of judges is, fundamentally, a political choice—in the broadest sense of the word political. Judgeships are governmental positions, and selecting persons to fill them is a public function which, presumably, should be accountable to the political will of the people.

But the reality is that, in most jurisdictions, even some of the most crucial steps in the process of judicial selection are not performed in any accountable way. If the final process of choice is an election, there nevertheless may be preliminary steps in that process—such as the selection of nominees—that are taken without any public scrutiny.

Moreover, there are no universally accepted standards on the qualities that a potential judge should have. It was only in 1962, for example, that anything approaching a model approach to judicial selection began being promoted nationwide. The campaign for court reform, including adoption of standards on selection, has gained since then.

Methods of selection. Judges are chosen in this country either by appointment or election, depending upon varying provisions of state and federal laws or constitutions. The U.S. Constitution controls only federal judicial appointments. All federal judges are appointed; nominations are made by the President, and the Senate accepts or rejects his nominees.

At the state and local level, the more common practice is to elect, rather than appoint, judges. The court reform movement has focused increasingly on making more judgeships appointive.

Basically, there are these forms of judicial selection in use in the states:
Appointment:

—nominated by a governor or some other executive officer, state or local, subject to legislative confirmation
—nominated and appointed by the governor or other executive, with no legislative review
—nominated and appointed by the state legislature or by a local legislative body
—nominated and appointed by a judge or court, with no legislative or executive review (This is a method usually used for quasi-judicial positions, such as magistrates with limited judicial authority.)

Election:

—nominated by partisan organizations or conventions, with popular election in general elections
—nominated by party primary election, elected by general election
—nominated in non-partisan primaries, elected by general election

Over the years, each of these methods has drawn criticism because of a supposed failure to select judicial candidates on the basis of merit. The appointment process has been challenged on the ground that it is part of the political "spoils" of partisan elections; a governor or other appointing authority uses judicial office to reward his supporters or friends. The election process has been challenged for supposedly relying upon mere political popularity, whether or not the process is partisan.

Beginning in 1913, with the development of a new plan by a law professor at Northwestern University, Albert M. Kales, there has been a continuing effort to make "merit" a part of the judicial selection process.

Kales' plan provided for a combination of appointment and election. But the elected official with the power of appointment could make his selections only from lists of candidates selected on the basis of qualification or merit by an "impartial" commission.

After judges put on the bench by this method had served for a specified period of time, their names would be put before the voters for a simple approval or disapproval vote. There would be no challenger on this ballot, only the sitting judge. If the voters rejected him, the appointment process would put another judge on the bench in his place.

The Kales plan is now known widely as "the **Missouri Plan,**" because it was first put into effect in that state in 1940. The nominating commissions in that state (there are separate commissions for appellate and for trial judges) are composed of judges, attorneys, and private citizens who are not lawyers.

In other states, where judges must seek the support of voters, the usual pattern is for them to be chosen for specified terms of office, with the right to seek re-election. Generally speaking, the terms of office are comparatively short— say, two or four years. (Some states, however, do have terms as long as 14 years.)

In some states, and for all judges on federal courts (except the Tax Court, where the terms are 15 years), judges hold their seats for life.

Disciplining judges. No matter how a judge got his seat at any level of government, he may be subject to discipline for serious misconduct, on or off the bench. This is usually true, at least on paper, even for judges who must submit themselves to the voters at specified times.

Judges may be disciplined by **impeachment** (filing of formal charges, followed by legislative trial, with removal after conviction), by a process known as **"address"** (filing of formal charges, followed by legislative trial, with request for dismissal by the executive), or by **recall** (a summons to go before the voters in a special referendum on a judge's right to retain office).

In recent years, there has been some movement toward new methods of judicial discipline, including the use of punishment short of removal from office. A common proposal is for the creation of an "impartial" commission, composed of judges, lawyers and some private citizens, with authority to investigate complaints against judges. Complaints could range from serious misconduct to physical or mental incapacity.

Such commissions would conduct investigations, and then either require or recommend that judges be censured,, suspended, involuntarily retired, or—in the most serious cases—dismissed from office.

If the commission were empowered on its own to discipline a judge, its action would be made subject to court review, perhaps by the state's highest court.

A similar approach has been studied at the federal level.

There are now provisions in a number of states that would accomplish removal of judges from the bench without discipline. Those provide for mandatory retirement at a specified age.

In many states and at the federal level, there are methods of challenging judges on the basis of alleged bias or prejudice, and thus to accomplish their disqualification from handling a given case. In addition, judges in most jurisdictions may choose on their own not to sit on a case because of some perceived or demonstrated conflict of interest.

D. THE CRIMINAL COURTS

The most visible court in America is the criminal trial court. It is watched with much interest, at times even anxiety, by the people. It provides an exhibition of the lengths to which society will go to protect itself or individuals from harm, and it offers a display of the degree to which society can or will act fairly toward those it believes to have broken its codes of behavior.

"Nowhere in the entire legal field," Professor Herbert Wechsler has remarked, "is more at stake for the community or for the individual." He added:

> If penal law is weak or ineffective, basic human interests are in jeopardy.
> If it is harsh or arbitrary in its impact, it works a gross injustice on those
> caught within its toils.

The very titles of criminal cases, "State against Jones," "United States against Smith," describe the interests at stake. The conflict of those interests is open, and it is direct. And yet, the criminal law process is supposed to reach a result that is acceptable on all sides: justice.

When a criminal trial is the arena where those interests come immediately into conflict, and where the public's perception of "justice" is on trial, it is a classic drama capturing the public's close attention. In America, there usually is a public audience for such occasions. The right to an open or public trial is guaranteed by the Constitution—but the Supreme Court has ruled that this is a right of the accused person, not the public's right.

The trial itself is only one step, and not the first one, in the criminal justice process. It should be understood as only a part, and not necessarily the most crucial part, of the entire system in which the government considers taking away the liberty of a person or otherwise punishing him.

The points at which this process produces news, and the response of the press to those developments, are discussed at length and in detail in later chapters. Here, the process is described in summary fashion to show its basic function and functioning.

Investigation and Case Preparation

A criminal case begins, of course, with an event or circumstance that does injury to an individual, an institution, or a community. Such an occurrence is a crime, however, only if society has decided beforehand that it should be forbidden, and sanctions against it should be imposed. That decision may have been made by a specific legislative act, or it may have come as a result of a long-standing social assumption acknowledged by the courts (that is, a **common law crime**).

The fact that a crime has been committed in fact does not mean, though, that it will be challenged or punished in law. It merely starts the criminal justice process to working.

First, there is the investigation. That may lead to an accusation. And that may be followed by prosecution.

Every level of government—federal, state, county, city, village—has law enforcement officers. These include not only the police, sheriffs, state troopers, and agents, but also the prosecutors. All of them may share in the investigative role. They may also share in the process of accusation.

In addition, some states and the federal system provide for a **grand jury.** (There is no federal constitutional requirement that criminal charges be brought by a grand jury at the state and local level. However, a grand jury is constitutionally required at the federal level for charging serious crimes.) The grand jury may have a role both in investigation and in accusation.

The prosecutorial function includes not only the choice as to whether to make or seek an accusation, or charge, but also the selection of a particular charge and the decision actually to go forward with that accusation once made. Here, again, the function is one that may be shared by several types of law enforcement officers, including prosecuting attorneys or sheriffs.

All of this precedes the trial—and, most of the time, will bring the criminal justice process in a given case to an end without a trial. The overwhelming proportion of criminal accusations produces guilty pleas, often as a result of **plea bargaining,** and only the formal offer of such a plea before a judge is done in court. A guilty plea is considered to be a "judicial confession," and that ends the matter. (Of course, there also are many criminal incidents that do not even result in accusations. Prosecutors simply decide not to pursue them.)

Pre-Trial and Trial

If a case does go to court for trial, there probably will be a series of pre-trial activities by the prosecution, the defense or both. These might include continued investigative activity by either side, or more formal legal maneuvering— such as filing of new or expanded charges by the prosecution, or defense requests to move the trial site, to suppress potential evidence, to get more information on the prosecution's case, and so on.

In addition, there no doubt will be pre-trial activity bearing upon the ultimate selection, at the trial, of a jury. This could include interviewing of potential jurors.

(The right to be tried by a jury is a constitutional guarantee in criminal cases—at least when the offense involved is a serious one. It is a right, however, that can be waived by the accused.)

Jury selection. The trial itself will begin with jury selection, a process in which the judge may take a greater or lesser part. Each side's lawyer will be able to try to shape the jury to his liking by the use of **challenges.** The number of such challenges varies widely, depending on the state and on the kind of case on trial. Each side probably will have a few **peremptory challenges**—the right to exclude a juror for no stated reason—and a greater or unlimited number of **challenges for cause**—the opportunity to exclude a juror for a stated reason, provided it is acceptable to the judge.

Argument and evidence. After jury selection, the case will begin with the presentation of **opening arguments**—where that is allowed. Not all states and not all judges, when they have discretion, permit opening statements to the jury.

Presentation of evidence—documentary **evidence,** and the **testimony** of witnesses—will follow, with each being subject to challenge by the other side, through the process of **cross-examination.** The **rules of evidence,** controlling what may and may not be offered, vary with every jurisdiction.

Evidence is offered by the lawyers for each side, but the judge may take a major role in determining which parts of the testimony or documentary materials are **admissible.**

(There are, basically, two kinds of evidence in criminal cases: **direct evidence,** such as testimony by eyewitnesses to the crime, or contraband materials or weapons; and **circumstantial evidence,** such as testimony or materials which create an impression or leave an implication of a crime.)

The prosecution presents its case first, followed by the defense. Usually, each side is then free to offer **rebuttal** evidence to try to undo the case that has been made by the other side. The prosecution must prove every part of its case **beyond a reasonable doubt** in order to overcome the **presumption of innocence** of the accused person.

At the close of evidence, each side may have an opportunity to file further or new legal motions—such as motions for a **directed verdict,** or a defense **motion to dismiss** the case.

Finally, each side has a right to make a **summation**—that is, a closing argument to the jury.

The jury function. The judge will then give the jury **instructions,** which will be his directions as to the jury's authority to determine the facts and to decide which inferences they may draw from the facts before they may reach a verdict—both within the limits of law. It should be stressed again that, where there is a jury, it is the sole judge of the facts; the judge is sole authority on the law governing the case. (Some variations of this exist in a few states.)

Finally, the jury will **retire** for secret deliberations, to reach its **verdict.** When it reaches a verdict, that will be announced in open court. The verdicts available to the jury will vary case by case, but usually will involve guilty or not guilty of the main offense charged, guilty or not guilty of any **lesser offenses** than the main offense. If the jury is unable to agree on a verdict (it need not be unanimous in all cases; however, verdicts in cases of the more serious crimes carrying more severe penalties may have to be unanimous), the jury is said to be a **hung jury,** and the judge very likely will declare a **mistrial.** That normally will free the prosecutor to prosecute again in a new trial, with a different jury.

Closing motions. Following the verdict—if it is guilty—the defense will probably make closing motions, including a **motion for a new trial,** or a **motion for a judgment of acquittal** despite the jury verdict. The judge may rule on those immediately, or postpone his decision until later.

Sentencing. In most classes of criminal cases, the role of imposing **sentence** is one exercised exclusively by the judge. The prosecutor, however, may recommend **leniency** and, in some cases, the jury may have a role in determining or recommending the sentence to be imposed.

Trials may range from very brief proceedings to very prolonged cases lasting weeks or months. The time used and the pacing of a trial may be determined largely by the trial judge, rather than by lawyers for the prosecution or defense.

Appeals

After the case is over, and sentence has been passed, the convicted person may seek to **appeal.** There is no such thing as a constitutional right to appeal a criminal conviction. It depends upon specific laws or court decisions in a given jurisdiction. Where a "right" to appeal is created by law or decision, it usually will be a right to appeal only once; the custom and practice is to discourage multiple appeals.

In a state case, the accused person has no right to take his case to federal court to challenge the verdict through the filing of a petition for a **writ of**

habeas corpus until after he has first **exhausted** all his **remedies** under state law in the state court system.

(Under some narrow circumstances, an accused person in a state criminal case may seek to have his case **removed**—that is, transferred—for trial in a federal court on grounds that he cannot get a fair trial in state courts. This, of course, would be done before a state trial had begun. When that is done, the federal court is bound to try the case under state law and procedure.)

When an appeal is taken after the verdict, either in state or federal cases, that is a **direct appeal.** If that fails, and a second appeal is tried, that is called a **collateral attack** on the conviction. Filing of a federal **habeas corpus** petition is **collateral.**

There is no automatic right to appeal either a state or a federal case to the U.S. Supreme Court. As noted earlier, the Supreme Court largely has discretion over its docket for review. The same is true of most state supreme courts.

Appeals in criminal cases, where they are allowed, are handled very much as any other appeals would be. The **record** for review is the one made in the trial court, and the scope of review is largely confined to legal questions (unless the intermediate appeals court is empowered to try the case **de novo**—a phenomenon that exists only in some state systems and not at all in the federal system). There may be some review of the factual evidence, to determine whether it was sufficient to convict.

The appeals courts need not always hold a hearing, and they need not always allow filing of new written briefs. It varies from state to state. When they have reached their decision, it is likely that it will be announced in a written opinion, though that is not universally true. It may be disposed of simply by a brief order, perhaps without much explanation.

Reversals and new trials. Appeals courts that decide to **reverse** convictions may be empowered to order new trials, to order dismissal of cases that have been tried, or—in fairly rare cases—to order new sentencing. The scope of remedies or judgments open to appeals courts varies widely across the country.

If a new trial is ordered, it very likely will be conducted much if not exactly as the original trial was conducted—with, of course, those changes necessary to satisfy the appeals court decision requiring a new trial.

Clemency

When all else fails, the person convicted of crime still has one possible "remedy" left: he may seek **executive clemency.** In other words, he may seek a reduction of his sentence ("**commutation**") or a **pardon,** which may go so far as to totally eliminate the conviction and make it impossible for the person to be re-tried for that crime. It may be surrounded with conditions. This is a power held by executive officers, such as governors and the President.

A power that has existed in practice for centuries, executive clemency is based on a theory that some public official must have the last-resort authority to grant mercy. As Alexander Hamilton expressed it in the Federalist Papers:

> The criminal code of every country partakes so much of necessary sever-
> ity, that without an easy access to exceptions in favor of unfortunate guilt, jus-
> tice would wear a countenance too sanguinary and cruel.

The power is unusually broad; it customarily is subject to limited review in court but sometimes not at all. It is a longstanding principle of American law that the pardoning power should be—again, as Hamilton put it—"as little as possible fettered or embarrassed."

It is a power that permits an executive official to override completely the entire process of criminal justice. In general, it is a power reserved for use in exceptional cases only. The pardoning of former President Richard M. Nixon illustrated vividly its use, and its rarity. State governors, however, do exercise the pardoning power more frequently than does the President.

E. THE CIVIL COURTS

The civil court in America is, no less than the criminal court, an arena for an **adversary contest** between two sides, each bent on winning. But, overall, civil law is more a process of adjustment or accommodation of relations between the two sides. It has, at least in appearance, a more genteel quality to it than criminal law.

True, many and perhaps most civil cases will begin as criminal cases do: there is a wrong done, actual or perceived. But, as the process works out in practice, it is basically remedial, not penal.

Society has a strong interest in seeing that the contests between those who seemingly owe each other an obligation are settled peaceably, whether those contests are major or minor. Civil courts provide a mechanism for resolution when agreement falters or relations break down.

Some civil cases do test major questions of broad social consequence, because the obligations that are at issue sweep broadly or cut deeply. For example, nearly all the major civil rights litigation, the conflicts over "one man, one vote" (legislative apportionment), the disputes about religion in public life, and contests over the rights of the poor and over equality of the sexes—those have been matters largely for the civil courts.

But there is much in civil law that will not involve large social interest; it deals also with those incidents that are confined, in fact at least, to two private parties going about their affairs in restricted realms.

The jurisdiction of civil courts, then, may range over nearly all facets of legal relationships. In finding remedies for the wrongs or the breaches in those relationships, civil law decisions may:

—require one party to fulfill his promises to another,
—restore to one party that which has been wrongly or unjustly taken from him by another,
—require one party to compensate another for harm or injury done,
—declare the rights of one party in his relations with another (rights of the person or rights of property),
—punish one party for past misconduct to another.

Civil cases often will seem—certainly to the non-lawyer, and at times even to the lawyer—to be highly technical, perhaps quite difficult to grasp. As a generalization, it is true that a criminal case is simplistic by comparison.

A civil lawsuit potentially may have in it very complex issues of **jurisdiction** (the court's power to hear it), the presence or absence of a **cause of action** (a legal basis for suing in the first place), the opportunity to sue not only on one's own behalf but on behalf of an entire **class** of persons, the inclusion or exclusion of other interested parties as **intervenors,** the possibility of **counterclaims** (the other side's rights or demands), a rich variety of pre-trial activity ranging from **temporary restraining orders** (often, to keep matters as they are until the issue can be decided) to **discovery** procedures (obtaining evidence and finding out in advance about the scope and content of the other side's case), and an equally rich variety of remedies at the close of trial ranging from **permanent injunctions** to awards of money **damages** to **declaratory judgments** (spelling out who has what right or rights).

For generations, at least in the traditions of Western civil law, procedures were exaggeratedly technical. A party could win or lose his or its case solely because of imperfections in the process of **pleading** without any regard whatever to the **merits** of either side's case. Since about the middle of the 19th century, however, the steady trend has been toward simplifying civil procedure so that cases would ultimately turn upon the substance of the dispute, not the manner of presenting or arguing it in court.

A civil case can be one wholly between private persons or companies or organizations, or between private parties and a federal, state or local government or governmental agency, or between governmental parties. It might be based upon a right to sue under a law (a **statutory** cause of action), under a **common law** tradition based upon no written statute but rather upon custom, under theories of **equity,** or under a constitutional provision (state or federal) provided that a court has jurisdiction to hear a constitutional claim.

Later chapters discuss the points at which a civil case produces news, and the response of the press. Here, as with the summary description of the criminal process, the progress of a civil case is described briefly and in its simplest form.

The Beginning and Pre-Trial

A civil case begins with the filing of a **complaint** or **petition.** It will state—sometimes quite simply, sometimes with great complexity—the issue or issues which the initiating party (the **plaintiff** or **petitioner**) wants resolved in its favor.

Its purpose is both to start the process (that is, by invoking a court's jurisdiction) and to notify the other side that a complaint or claim has been lodged against it. The complaint will be **served** on the other party by some form of formal notice, perhaps a **summons** issued by a court giving the other side a specified time period within which to **answer** or else lose by **default.**

The initial complaint or petition may be accompanied by some other opening requests to the court, such as a motion for a **temporary restraining order** (to preserve the status quo) or for a **preliminary injunction.**

Unlike criminal cases, which must move speedily because the Constitution guarantees that to the accused, civil cases may be subject to very long delays, occurring at most or all stages.

Before the case actually goes to trial, there may be a period—sometimes quite prolonged—when each side attempts to gather evidence and probe the other side's case. This **discovery** procedure may involve such things as **depositions** (testimony given under oath) or **interrogatories** (specific questions seeking specific answers).

In advance of trial there may also be one or more **pre-trial conferences**—often under a judge's direct supervision—seeking to narrow the issues that will be tried.

The Trial

A civil trial can occur before a judge alone or before a judge and a jury. The Constitution guarantees a right to a jury in civil cases in federal courts, but the practice there is to do without a jury unless a party specifically demands a jury trial. Every state provides for jury trials in at least some kinds of civil cases. There, too, it can be **waived.**

If there is to be a jury, the process of selection proceeds much as it does in a criminal case, with each side having opportunities to try to shape the trial jury by use of challenges.

A civil case may start with opening arguments by both sides, making the points that each side hopes to establish with the evidence that is to be forthcoming.

The first evidence to be offered is by the party with the **burden of proof,** that is, the suing party, usually. (The standard of proof in civil cases is somewhat less rigorous than it is in criminal cases; the suing party usually needs to establish its case only according to the **preponderance of the evidence** or **the greater weight of the evidence**—not beyond a reasonable doubt, as in criminal cases.)

As in criminal cases, each side may offer witnesses or documentary evidence, and each and all are subject to cross-examination by the other side.

When the party with the burden of proof has finished offering evidence, the other side may ask the judge by motion to dismiss the case. The judge ordinarily must, at that point, interpret the evidence so far before him in the way most favorable to the suing party. If, after viewing it that way, he finds that there is no realistic possibility that that side could win with that case, he will grant the motion and end the case. Otherwise, he will deny the motion, and the other side will then have to offer its case in reply.

At the close of evidence, the answering party may again seek to have the case dismissed. Either side may move for a directed verdict.

· As in a criminal case, if the case is submitted to the jury, the jurors will go into seclusion and deliberate, and then reach a verdict. In most civil cases, the verdict will be a **general verdict**—that is, one in which the jury finds for or against the plaintiff or petitioner, after determining the facts and weighing them according to instructions from the judge regarding the law. Sometimes, though quite rarely now, a jury may be asked to render only a **special verdict**—that is, one in which the jury simply determines the facts, perhaps in answer to specific questions put by the judge. It is then up to the judge to apply the law to those facts, and issue a **judgment.** The jury sometimes may fix money damages as part of its verdict.

After the verdict is in, either side may ask the judge to issue a judgment in favor of the losing party despite the verdict. The losing party may also file a motion for the judge to reduce the damages. Motions for a new trial also are allowed.

Appeals

Either party may file an appeal if it is dissatisfied with the result. The process of appeal is very much the same as in criminal cases, with the appellate court being obliged to take the facts as they come from the trial court jury, or the trial judge in non-jury cases. Sometimes, appeals courts may reduce the damages part of the verdict if it finds them to be "excessive."

While the loser in a criminal case may, because of the writ of habeas corpus, take his case to higher courts on appeal more than once, there is but one opportunity to appeal a given judgment in a civil case.

Again, the right of appeal is governed either by constitutional, statutory, or **"case" law** (case law is that established by court decisions).

F. SPECIAL TRIBUNALS

Every lawsuit in America is, in its own way, special—if for no other reason, because of the facts in each. But there are some legal actions which, over several generations or even from the beginning, have been or have become the special province of a court or tribunal created just to deal with that kind of case.

Some of these tribunals were created because of the identity of the persons who would come before them. They were thought, because of their condition or circumstance, to require special handling. That is true, for example, of courts for juveniles who get into trouble, or for married couples contemplating separation or divorce. It is also true of disciplinary panels for lawyers or commissions on judicial conduct.

Some exist to deal with a single branch of the law, sometimes not involving the usual adversary approach taken in regular courts. An example is the "probate court," or "orphans' court," which administers estates, either where there is a will or where there is not. Another example would be a commission or court to determine the value of property being taken for public use ("eminent domain" or "condemnation" cases). Another would be a labor arbitration panel or "court."

Some are created to deal with a mixture of legislative functions—that is, policy-making—and judicial functions—that is, rule-making. The most common example is the regulatory commission which oversees a public utility or a licensed private corporation or activity.

Some are created solely to handle lawsuits for money damages against the government, federal or state. These are the "claims" courts.

Some come into being to handle simple and low-value money or property disputes between private parties. An example would be a "small claims" court.

Finally, some exist as an arm or function of a legislature. That would be, for example, a legislative body with power to punish, directly, for contempt of its processes. It also could be a legislative committee, or an entire legislative chamber, created to handle impeachment of public officials.

It is generally true of these special tribunals that they are part of the civil law system. Many of them are empowered to impose sanctions, but they are not penal tribunals as such. Most of them will function according to some concept of procedural **due process,** but many of them are not courts, as such. They may be considered, however, to be a part of the judicial system because even where they are not courts, they may be subject to some form of judicial review. The one clear exception—and even it is not a universal one—is the legislative process of impeachment.

For purposes of summary treatment of the functioning of these tribunals, they may be grouped into three broad categories: courts of special jurisdiction, regulatory agencies, and legislative bodies.

Courts of Special Jurisdiction

Family courts. The best known branches of "family law" are domestic relations—that is, divorce or marital separation and including issues of child custody—and problems of juveniles.

It is becoming increasingly common to have the legal relationships of the family assigned to a single court, to accommodate the integrated approach that is more often taken to the "law of the family." A family court may, however, be no more than one part of an "inferior" civil court in which judges rotate between the various types of proceedings within that tribunal's jurisdiction.

Customarily, proceedings in family courts will emphasize negotiations, reconciliation, and "treatment" in order to try to avert more serious difficulty.

They also will, however, have available trial-type procedures for use if a truly **adversary contest** develops. The normal pattern of civil procedure usually will be followed. Family courts, however, do not use juries; their proceedings are before judges alone.

In dealing with issues of domestic relations, family courts are empowered not only to arrange or supervise separation agreements, but also to grant divorces that bring marriages to an end. In granting **decrees of divorce,** the courts will customarily make awards of alimony, child support, and child custody.

In dealing with problems of juveniles, these courts may seek to rely upon highly informal advisory or counseling sessions, or may use more formal procedures that will have some of the aspects of a criminal trial. In some jurisdictions, family courts are empowered to issue orders requiring that juveniles be tried as adults in regular criminal courts. Decrees or judgments from family courts in juvenile cases may actually lead to forms of imprisonment in specialized institutions, but the stress is always (at least in theory) upon treatment rather than punishment.

Proceedings in family courts customarily are secret, to protect familial privacy and juvenile reputations. It is not uncommon, however, for some divorce proceedings to be open.

Probate courts. The courts that administer estates are known by such names as "probate court" or "orphans' court." It is their task to interpret last wills or testaments (where the dead person had made one—technically, a person who has died **testate**) in the event of uncertainty or conflict over their meaning, or to determine rights to an estate (where the dead person has died **intestate,** or without a will).

Procedures in these courts may be very brief or summary in form, or they may develop into full-scale **adversary proceedings.** Some wills are self-executing, and the probate court need only review them in summary fashion to determine their legal sufficiency and authenticity.

Probate courts are judge-only tribunals.

Condemnation courts. The tribunals which determine the value of private property being "**condemned**" for public use may be either courts or commissions. They will have a presiding officer and, in some jurisdictions, they may use a jury.

Normally, the process of "**eminent domain**" begins with the filing of a notice of condemnation. That is served upon the owner of the property, who customarily is advised of the procedure for challenging the order of condemnation or at least for determining the value to be paid.

Hearings are held at which there may be oral or written testimony, and the proceeding concludes with a **condemnation award**—that is, a declaration of the value to be paid. These awards may reflect several variables of value: current market price, replacement value, value of intangible characteristics, and so on.

"Claims" courts. In some states, and at the federal level, special tribunals are authorized to hear and determine claims for money damages against government agencies.

They are a form of civil court that, by use of conventional procedures, will determine whether a person or company doing business with the government, or a person employed by government, has been wronged in that relationship, and is entitled to recover damages.

In some jurisdictions, "claims" courts have the authority to require the reinstatement of a public employe whose discharge has been ruled illegal.

"Small claims" courts. Generally, a "small claims" court is something of a miniature, or simplified, general civil court. Commonly, it is created in order to relieve persons with little means from going to the expense of a regular civil lawsuit in order to pursue their claim.

The claim may involve a dispute over money or over property, provided that the amount in dispute is below a specified figure.

These courts usually are conducted without attorneys for either side. The judge, acting alone (there is no jury), will seek to determine whether there is a just claim, and if so, how much it is to be. The process is, at least in design, highly informal.

Regulatory Agencies

There is a wide—and still growing—variety of regulatory or "administrative" agencies, sometimes considered a "fourth branch of government."

In form, function and purpose, they are likely to be somewhere between a legislative and a judicial institution, but they also have some resemblance to executive agencies.

Before Felix Frankfurter became a Supreme Court justice—while he was serving as professor of administrative law at Harvard Law School—he wrote an article analyzing what he called "perhaps the most striking contemporary tendency of the Anglo-American legal order." He was describing the widening area of regulatory authority:

> These administrative complements are euphemistically called "filling in the details" of a policy set forth in the statutes. But the "details" are of the essence; they give meaning and content to vague contours.
>
> The control of banking, insurance, public utilities, finance, industry, the professions, health and morals—in sum, the manifold response of government to the forces and needs of modern society, is building up a body of laws not written by legislatures, and of adjudications not made by courts and not subject to their revision. These powers are lodged in a vast congeries of agencies.

Some of the special tribunals mentioned at the opening of this section are regulatory agencies: labor arbitration panels, lawyer disciplinary committees or panels, commissions on judicial conduct.

But the variety stretches much further: it includes state public utility commissions; medical, architectural and pharmacological licensing boards; contract administration boards; civil service review boards; and an almost astonishing array of federal agencies: the National Labor Relations Board, the Federal Power Commission, Federal Trade Commission, Federal Election Commission, Federal Communications Commission, Federal Aviation Agency, Federal Railroad Administration, Interstate Commerce Commission, Civil Aeronautics Board, Federal Maritime Commission, and on and on.

With some few exceptions, regulatory agencies—at the state-and-local and federal levels—generally are assigned the task of monitoring the performance of persons or businesses which have been granted special licenses or privileges. (Labor-management panels are an exception, and so are consumer-protection or business-regulation agencies such as the Federal Trade Commission.)

Whether they are regulating a licensed activity, or monitoring a private activity that some legislature has thought to be in need of public regulation, the administrative agencies typically operate under basic laws that set outer limits on their authority. Those laws may be very broad and general, or they may be quite specific.

The function of the agencies is, more often than not, split between the fashioning of specific regulations, and the implementation of those regulations on a case-by-case basis. Thus, they are quasi-legislative, quasi-judicial, and quasi-executive.

Judicial review. It is quite common for their decisions to be subject only to limited judicial review. The standard that most often applies is that reviewing courts will overturn a regulatory agency decision only if it has been "arbitrary" or "capricious." Under that standard, courts are typically bound to accept the factual **findings** of the agency if the evidence supports those, and may review only the legal dimensions of the agency ruling.

Modes of operation. When they are developing general policy or spelling out specific regulations, these agencies often will publish their policy regulations in proposed form, and invite public reaction. They may hold hearings before issuing a policy statement or a regulation in final form.

It is quite customary for them to hold hearings when they are implementing policy regulations on a case-by-case basis. Those hearings will have many of the same attributes of a civil court proceeding, although the kinds of testimony that may be offered may be quite closely limited. Hearings may, at times, involve witnesses.

Some regulatory agencies (particularly at the federal level) will refer their cases to subordinate officials or panels for preliminary decisions, which then are subject to approval, disapproval, or modification by the parent agency.

Their decisions will be written, with findings and conclusions of law. The content of those decisions may range from the setting of rates to be charged for a service to a determination of the specific mode and manner of conducting a business (including the way it is required to keep its books) to awards of licenses or privileges, and to punishment for violation of laws and regulations.

Many of these agencies operate in public much of the time. Some, however, almost never do (such as lawyer disciplinary panels). It is typical of many of them to provide public reference or docket rooms for public inspection of their records and decisions.

Legislative Bodies

Contempt. Legislatures, including Congress and the state legislatures, generally rely quite heavily upon the regular courts to deal with the problems of **legislative contempt**—that is, disrupting or interfering with the legislative process. That is a crime punishable by fine or imprisonment, and it is prosecuted virtually as any other crime would be.

There are, however, provisions that are now rarely used for direct punishment of contempts by legislative bodies. In formal language, this may involve bringing a person charged with contempt "before the bar of the house," and imposing some sanction if the person is found guilty of contempt. This may even include imprisonment, although at the congressional level, legislative orders of imprisonment may be in effect only through the length of the session imposing them.

When exercising their direct contempt power, legislatures are more or less beyond judicial review. If, however, they wish to invoke the regular criminal process to deal with a person they seek to have charged with contempt, that process follows regular court procedures and controlling court precedents.

Disciplining members. Legislatures may also hold some power to punish their own members for misconduct. That may be limited to expulsion or suspension, but in some instances, the sanction may be stronger.

In using such direct powers, a legislative body typically will act much as if it were a court, with lawyers participating and evidence being offered to try to shape the judgment that will result.

Impeachment. A legislature acts most like a court when it is exercising its powers of **impeachment.** This is the process by which public officials *outside* the legislative branch are tried for crimes related to their public offices, and, if convicted, are forced to leave office. The punishment for impeachment cannot go beyond removal from office and a prohibition upon holding public office in the future. (It is generally true, however, that the fact that an official has been convicted of an impeachable offense does not immunize him from being tried separately and convicted of a criminal offense growing out of the same conduct.)

The process of impeachment begins with filing of charges, sometimes (as at the federal level) called "articles of impeachment." These are formal statements of the offense the accused official is alleged to have committed.

Approval of articles of impeachment generally follows an investigation that may be quite like a grand jury or other prosecutorial investigation.

The official or officials charged in the articles is then put to trial. Customarily, the trial will be conducted very much as any criminal trial would be, with participation of prosecution and defense attorneys, the submission of evidence (documentary and oral), and oral arguments by the lawyers, followed by a judgment or verdict of guilty or not guilty.

All of this process, however, is strictly legislative. It is judicial only in appearance. There is considerable question as to whether any judicial review may follow an impeachment; if so, it would likely be quite limited. There may be no specific assurance—constitutional or otherwise—that an officer facing impeachment be assured of **due process,** that is, procedural fairness.

Impeachment, though, is a grave act of government, and thus there is little possibility—for political reasons, if no other—that the process would be conducted without at least minimal fairness to the accused.

3

Legal Reporting

IF JOURNALISM IS THE CONTEMPORARY HISTORY OF CONFLICT, and often it is, the courtroom can and will be a place of intense fascination to the journalist. Whatever else law may be, when it is at work in court it is conflict—done up in gentleman's garb, perhaps, but conflict nonetheless. That, at least, is the way the legal reporter will find himself treating it most of the time.

Supreme Court Justice William O. Douglas, intending no doubt to be disparaging rather than analytical, once described the perspective of the legal reporter colorfully:

> Journalists are primarily interested in the story of one judge letting the air out of another judge's tire or when he throws an inkwell.

There is some truth in that, as well as color. The reporter on the courthouse beat will get into the habit of looking for conflict on the bench, partly because it is his job to do so and partly because that is his habitual perspective.

The conflicts that are being worked out in the process of justice are real and they are live. Indeed, there is no room (and no jurisdiction) in the courts for the frivolous conflict in which the parties' interests are not really adverse and thus there is no genuine legal controversy between them.

In a court of law, because there is true conflict, there are winners and losers, and it is the daily or periodic task of legal reporting to tell who won or lost. Of course, it is also part of the task to describe how the process went, and—if at all possible—how the ultimate result was reached.

There is another element of truth to Douglas' characterization of the journalist observing the courts: the reporter's view of the process often seems superficial and quite simplistic.

But that is not a concession that should be deeply troubling to him. That moment when a reporter holds the attention of his larger audience is a fleeting one, no matter how important the subject of his story and no matter how long he has taken to prepare it (or to be prepared *for* it). He is driven, therefore, to offer that which tells the most newsworthy facet of a legal or judicial development, and to do it quite briskly, simply and understandably.

In a very real way, the writing or broadcasting of a story about the law must be almost conventional, in language that will provide meaning and understanding even to the reader or listener who is unlearned in the law. It is well to remember that, as the journalist must see it, the court is a peoples' tribunal that helps to teach a community about basic right and wrong, and its processes and results must be conveyed well beyond the courthouse.

But it would be a mistake to assume, therefore, that the journalist may bring with him into the courthouse nothing more than the language of the street or of daily conversational commerce, and the lack of specialized learning that would go with that, and be able to do his work.

To be able to write simply, any journalist—on the court beat or elsewhere—must understand penetratingly. The language of the law and its processes can be excruciatingly precise and arcane. It is an accomplishment of major dimensions to translate it into the popular vernacular, and to lose nothing of consequence in the translation.

Simplicity in legal reporting does not, need not, should not, depend upon inaccuracy or misconception. If the result of a case in court is precise and definite—and it will be, whatever qualifications and limitations surround it—then the journalist has no business conveying something other than that result. His audience, whether it has greater or lesser awareness of the intricacies of the law, is entitled not to be misled.

To be sure, a given court case may, even while producing a legal result, not produce news. In those situations, the reporter may have no story at all to convey, or he may have a story indicating that (from a news perspective, at least) there was no significant result. These situations usually will arise when the result is one based on technical procedural considerations, not the merits of the legal dispute.

It is only a statement of the obvious that the legal journalist must know the difference between the varieties of results that emerge in court proceedings, or else he will be unable to tell what is significant and what is not.

But it is far from obvious what this may mean about the particular preparation a journalist ought to have before he attempts to cover the law or the court beat. There is a debate about that, not ever likely to be resolved fully.

A. PREPARATION FOR THE BEAT

There are those, including many legal professionals, who would insist upon a formal legal education, perhaps leading to a law degree, for the journalist who would cover the law. Short of that, it is suggested, there ought at least to be some fairly lengthy exposure to law in an academic setting—say, a year or so of "auditing" selected courses in the law school curriculum.

The journalist who is truly trained in the law—capable, perhaps, of being an attorney himself—will have an unusual capacity to solve the puzzles of the legal process as they occur before him. He will be quite fully accepted, most of the time, by his sources on the beat. He may be a good deal more efficient in getting to the core of legal or judicial developments.

There is, however, another view. It is that the journalist assigned to cover the law will not need to be a fully trained legal professional himself—and perhaps ought not to be. What he needs to know, with specificity, about the law, he will be able to pick up along the way. In fact, it would be part of his obligation to get the answers from those professionals who are part of the system of justice.

According to this view, the journalist is very much like most of his audience: he sees the law not in terms of its refined and special nature, but in terms of its broad social utility. He will be a better observer, on behalf of his larger audience, if he does not forget the perspective that that audience will bring to his stories about the courts.

There is, of course, a middle ground between the legal reporter who is knowledgeable in the law because of a pre-determined choice to be educated professionally, and the legal reporter whose knowledge is, at best, his vicarious accumulation of lore from his contacts with the system and with legal professionals.

Reading and Study

The journalist who approaches the court beat seriously should want to study and read widely in the law, at least in the popular treatments of it. He also would be well advised to know, with some intimacy, history and political science and economics. The consequences of the legal process will be reflected in those fields, as the law will be but an instrument for making things happen that have meaning in history, political science, and economics.

It is a bit over-stated, but a letter by Supreme Court Justice Felix Frankfurter to a 12-year-old "interested in going into law as a career" does offer a beginning goal for the journalist approaching the law in his profession:

No one can be a truly competent lawyer unless he is a cultivated man. If I were you, I would forget all about any technical preparation for the law. The best way to prepare for the law is to come to the study of law as a well-read person. Thus alone can one acquire the capacity to use the English language on paper and in speech and with the habits of clear thinking which only a truly liberal education can give. . . . Stock your mind with the deposit of much good reading. . . .

The journalist, if he begins with that kind of base, still will need to add to it an appreciation of the law as a discipline of its own. Perhaps he can come to that by daily exposure to the legal process, especially if he insists, step by step, on understanding what it is that he is observing. But he also could make it easier for himself by doing some directed reading—directed by a practicing attorney or an academic in the law. This, of course, could go on simultaneously with his actual coverage of the law.

For the journalist who attends college, opportunities very likely could be arranged for some course work or at least occasional study at the law school. Again, it should be directed or supervised.

Special Problems in Writing Legal News

Ultimately, the reporter will have to work at his craft: there is no better way to become efficient in covering the law than doing it, day by day. Then his understanding of the law as a discipline will have to be made usable, in a very practical sense, in an atmosphere of deadline pressure, simplicity and brevity of expression, and severe selectivity in content.

There is a great deal that must be left out in legal reporting. That is perhaps the most rigorous aspect of this specialty. For any given story, news or feature that a courthouse reporter will write, he will or should know a great deal more in detail and breadth than he can expect to convey to his audience.

The facts are as important as the legal principles. The personalities or institutions involved are as important as the legal results. But, still, it is *the law* that one is dealing with, and it must be the core of any story originating on the legal beat.

After the burden of selectivity, the obligation to write simply is the next most taxing. It will not do, for a general audience, for a reporter to allow himself to use formal language of the law without at least explaining it as it is used. It is not an unreasonable task to avoid all legal terms of art and substitute for them lay expressions that say the same thing.

Hypothetical example. An illustration of the dual problem of selectivity and simplicity may be useful. Suppose that there is a case in State Supreme Court in which a lower court judge's removal from the bench is sought because of his supposed bias. Very likely, this would be a "writ of prohibition" case as it comes to State Supreme Court.

The clerk of that Court may tell reporters, orally or in writing, something like this: "The Court has entered an order granting leave to docket an original action for a writ of prohibition in No. 12345, Jones v. Smith."

What is there of law in that, and what is there of news?

In law, there is the fact of the State Supreme Court's exercise of its discretion to hear or not to hear a matter; there is a reference to the fact that it is an "original" matter that is not within the jurisdiction of any lower court; there is the character of the action, the use of the Supreme Court's supervisory power to require a judge subject to its authority to do or not to do something; there is the docket number, always crucial in legal proceedings; there is the cryptic identity of the parties. In addition, no doubt, there is a **record** in the case that will add facts and include legal argument, pro and con.

What is the news? It can be stated in a typical news "lead":

"The State Supreme Court today agreed to consider a demand that County Judge Joseph X. Smith be forbidden to try the civil rights case of Paul Y. Jones."

It is unnecessary to discuss the scope of the State Supreme Court's jurisdiction. It is similarly unnecessary to discuss the fact that this is a "prohibition" matter rather than, say, a "mandamus" action. And it need not be said that the Supreme Court had acted only procedurally, by granting "leave" to proceed. Each of those elements, however, is crucial to the case in law.

The news is in the nature of the issues at stake: Was the Supreme Court willing to move into this controversy? Is Jones making headway in his challenge to the judge? What kind of case could produce such a clash?

It should be noted immediately, of course, that the legal reporter will have had to have done his reporting and research in advance, if he is to be able to move speedily to get his story out. A cryptic order by a court official often will not tell him much about the background and issues and facts. It also cannot fill in the legal lore that the reporter must have to help him decide whether he has a story at all. There may not be time to consult a lawyer or a professor.

Basic ingredients of legal news-writing. The basic professional needs of the reporter, and his basic approach, will be the same no matter what kind of legal proceeding he is covering. He always will need to know facts (some of which he may not find in the court **record** and thus must be obtained by reporting beyond the courthouse), the legal issues, the authority of the judge and/or court involved (including some awareness of the range of possible results that may emerge), the procedure to be followed, the schedule for proceeding, and the significance of it all.

B. FINDING THE STORY

He begins where reporters always must: with the discovery that there is a case potentially of news interest. Although the parties involved, or their attorneys, often will volunteer to the news media the fact that they have a case, this is not a routinely dependable source of discovering cases initially.

Sources

More dependable will be the reporter's routine checks of court **dockets** and **calendars,** as well as his routine informal checks with court clerks, law clerks, judges, prosecutors, lawyers. Among his best sources in the courthouse will be the court clerk and his assistants. They will know what is going on and very often they will have a keen sense of what is newsworthy. The reporter who feels the clerk is unimportant or unworthy of being cultivated as a source will be quite seriously handicapped.

It is not common, in most American courts, to have "press officers" or "public information officers." That is, sometimes, a blessing. If the function of such a court official is to "promote" his court or to seek to garner favorable publicity for it, he probably will be of little value to the journalist, and may be a nuisance. If his function is to assist the reporter in gaining access to dockets, exhibits, court officials and judges, he could be a definite asset.

Perhaps there are few beats, at least in reporting about public affairs, where the reporter should feel as deeply obliged to do his own direct research and reporting. The chance of error or misunderstanding is especially great. It simply will not be possible for a substitute, whether it is a press officer or other court official, to describe to the reporter what he must have. There is no substitute for the documents and the principals themselves.

Fortunately for the reporter, most documents associated with a case in court are "matters of public record"—that is, they are open to public inspection.

The record. After "discovering" a case that interests him the legal reporter should go promptly to the **record.** That may be abundant, or it may be meager. (If the reporter is dealing with a case newly filed, the most that may be available immediately will be the complaint or petition that sets the case in motion. If there is time, he should attempt to contact the other side before he does his story for publication or broadcast. He should, in fact, try to make the time for that.)

C. NEWS AND FEATURE STORIES

The mere filing of a case, naturally, can produce news. Along the way, there may be immediate stories upon the filing of replies or answers, announcement of court dates, the occurrence of pre-trial preliminaries, the various stages of trial, the release of a verdict or judgment, and the filing and pursuit of appeals. (See later chapters.)

In addition, along the way there may be feature stories which are not related directly to any immediate development in a case. It is a reasonable rule of thumb that a feature story about the law can be better told if it is done with a specific case or cases in mind. For the journalist as for the legal professional, law comes alive in particular controversies affecting identifiable persons or institutions. Even if the feature is a personality piece about a judge or attorney, it is likely to be stronger if the personality is related to particular lawsuits.

The courthouse reporter ought also to be on the watch for what may be called "institutional" stories: how the courts work, the interrelationship between courts, the movements for court reform, the interaction between courts and other arms of government, and the process of justice as an issue beyond the courthouse—say, in political campaigns.

Investigative Reporting

There is likely to be occasional opportunity on the court beat for the investigative reporter who is assigned to develop stories about the undisclosed facets of public business.

There is, in the judicial system, much that goes on beyond the courtroom that is of immense public importance. It will be difficult, at best, for even the most enterprising reporter to monitor the closed deliberations of courts. But that wholly legitimate use of authority is not the object of the investigative reporter's attention. He will be interested, rather, in the discovery of questionable and perhaps illegal conduct, and professionals within the legal system will be as interested as the reporter in seeing that the courts are free from illicit or compromising influences, from within or from without.

The courts are public institutions, and the reporter covering them regularly or on special, perhaps investigative, assignment has as much obligation to learn about them as has the reporter dealing with any other agency of government.

D. LEGAL ETHICS: A SPECIAL RESTRAINT

The reporter on any kind of legal news assignment is sure to become familiar with a problem quite peculiar to the court beat. The arm of government that he is covering is restrained from participating in public discussion of its business. From the reporter's point of view, that restraint sometimes seems to be a severe one. But it has a very compelling source: professional ethics.

A judge, aides of the court, and attorneys are required by legal ethics to avoid any form of interference with the processes of the law and justice. They are obliged to perform their professional functions *within* the system, according to its rules, procedures and limitations. A lawsuit is to be pursued in a forum where each side is to have an opportunity to respond to every thrust of the other side, before a neutral judge and in a setting where attention is focused precisely. The reporter's professional sources, then, will avoid generating publicity about their cases or adding to existing publicity if doing so would compromise their commitment to try the case in court. In popular terms, it may be said that they must avoid "trying their case in the newspapers."

Unlike elected officials in the legislature or in executive offices, judges and lawyers do not regularly or routinely rely upon publicity in the performance of their duties. They understand that they will be held accountable on the basis of the official records of their performance, not any contemporary press account of it.

Moreover, judges, lawyers and court aides are no more free ethically to discuss the internal workings of the judicial process than they are the merits of the cases that are pending in court.

Obviously, this poses an ethical problem of another kind for the journalist. His strong commitment to the monitoring role of the press requires him to observe as fully as he can the acts of government, including judicial acts. He cannot hope to do that without very considerable assistance from legal professionals, on and off the bench.

He must seek, then, to keep open lines of communication to his professional sources, but he must deal with those sources with a well-honed appreciation of the ethical limits within which they must and usually will function. The remainder of this chapter discusses some of the means by which this quite delicate process might be made to work for the reporter.

E. RELATIONS WITH LAWYERS

The lawyer is, naturally, one of the prime sources of the legal reporter. He knows his case better than anyone, including his client. But the lawyer does much of his work confidentially.

There will be times, and they may recur often, when the attorney will actively seek to avoid publicity of any kind about his case. If one of the fundamental aims of legal practice is to stay out of court, the art of negotiating in private for settlement may be an attorney's most important professional technique. Publicity, the lawyer may conclude, could harden each side's position, complicating if not frustrating negotiation.

When the matter is one involving private persons or institutions, the lawyer will be moved by an additional consideration: protecting his client's privacy at least until going to court is no longer avoidable or postponable. This factor, of course, will be most significant when the client is involved in a criminal case.

Beyond his professional reasons for choosing to avoid publicity, the lawyer often will feel obliged by his ethical code—and sometimes required by court order—to avoid commenting on pending or developing cases.

These are generalizations; there may be circumstances where an attorney concludes that he is free to make at least limited revelations about his client's case. Even these, however, very likely will be confined to what is in the public record about the case.

Specific Suggestions

Each reporter, no doubt, will find his own technique for dealing with lawyers. But some suggestions may be helpful:

- A reputation for objectivity may be a reporter's most important asset. Lawyers are not likely to accept a continuing relationship with a reporter if they have doubts that he will hear and consider what they have to say fairly and openly. A "prosecution-oriented" legal reporter, for example, will find his relations with defense counsel difficult—and the opposite, of course, is as true.
- A reporter, even if he is well educated in the law, should always let his attorney-source describe, as far as he will, what his case is about legally. The lawyer's theories or strategies are what will count, and they may vary, perhaps considerably, from a reporter's assumptions about the "norms" for supposedly similar situations.
- It is most useful for the reporter to try to get the lawyer to discuss his case as much as possible in lay language. Not only will that help the reporter in writing his story, but also it will reduce the risk of error in translation to journalistic prose.
- Occasionally, some attorneys will discuss their case on a "background" basis—that is, they will not be speaking for publication and will be talking to the reporter to guide his understanding of the legal issues at stake.
- Wherever and whenever possible, a reporter should try to rely upon documents in dealing with lawyers—that is, he should seek access to the formal, printed materials upon which the lawyer will be relying in court. Again, this reduces the risk of error, and it very likely will enhance basic understanding. Legal reporters, like legal professionals, will want to rely upon **the record.**
- A reporter's relationship with a lawyer, as with any source, should always be at arm's length. The attorney, after all, is on only one side of an adversarial contest. Moreover, the attorney is an officer of the court, limited in his freedom to deal candidly with the press.
- When a reporter is working on a case that is being handled by several attorneys in a law firm or in a prosecutor's office, he should try to deal directly with the lawyer or lawyers most intimately involved with the case. A senior or "name" partner in the firm or the chief prosecutor in the office will not necessarily know the matter well enough.

- Most of the time, a reporter who wants to contact a lawyer's client should do so with the lawyer's knowledge. There may, however, be times when a reporter will want to, or must, contact a client without the attorney's presence or awareness. That should not be done routinely. It is a situation potentially troublesome in ethical as well as legal terms, and it no doubt will threaten the reporter's relationship with the attorney.

- Obviously, lawyers can be of real help in keeping a reporter informed about developments in their case. They usually will know about dates and filings before they are publicly available. They also may know of a judge's decision on a procedural issue or on the merits of a case before it becomes publicly available. If a reporter knows when a court decision is expected, he should arrange in advance to talk to attorneys for both sides afterward in case an immediate response is needed for his story. Prompt post-decision contact with lawyers in the case, in fact, should be made routinely.

- A reporter is entitled to assume as a general rule that a lawyer in a public position will be more accessible to him, and more willing to go "on the record" with him, than an attorney in private practice. The fact that a lawyer is a government official himself, however, does not relieve him of the ethical restraints to which all lawyers are subject.

- There may be special problems, and special opportunitites, too, for the reporter in dealing with "public interest" lawyers—those involved regularly in the kind of advocacy that seeks to extend the frontiers of law through court cases. They may be more attached personally to the causes they pursue, and thus they may be more energetic in "promoting" their cases with the press. That has both advantages and disadvantages, and those are obvious.

- A reporter should maintain continuing contact with lawyers' organizations, such as bar associations. They make news, and they also hold seminars and conventions at which a reporter may add to his knowledge of the law as a discipline.

F. RELATIONS WITH COURT AIDES

A court cannot get along without its staff—clerks and other administrative officers, legal research aides, court reporters and bailiffs. A reporter covering the courthouse cannot do his work without help from them.

Their obligation, and their loyalty, is to the court, of course. In most courthouses, the staff will be directly subordinate to the judge or, on a multi-judge court, the presiding judge. It is a mistake to assume that they will be freely accessible to anyone else; they, too, are "officers of the court" in the truest sense.

Thus, a reporter is likely to find that court aides, of all persons in the process of justice, will be the most uninterested in being quoted publicly. They will show the reporter the way and provide almost innumerable tips and support along the way, but this is not a kind of assistance upon which a reporter may insist by demanding. Diplomacy, in other words, may be the critical factor in this relationship.

Court clerks sometimes are elected officials and will be subject to a measure of public accountability. At the same time, even they will feel that their first obligation is to the court they serve.

It is true generally that most of the records a reporter will need to use around the courthouse are public records. The reporter, like any other citizen, is free to inspect them and copy from them. That makes them available by right, but not necessarily in fact. A reporter still must arrange for access as a practical matter, and this, too, is a process substantially aided by diplomacy.

Forms of Help

Some of the forms of assistance a reporter may seek from court officials or employes are:

- Court clerks: They will be able to provide information on new case filings, records in cases, names and addresses—perhaps telephone numbers, too—of attorneys involved in cases, data on schedules and assignments of judges, data on schedules of hearings and trial dates, copies of or access to originals of exhibits, tips or direct information on expected decisions by the court, tips on new cases about to be filed, information about court operations and finances.
- Court "administrators" or "executives": Where these officers exist, they probably will handle budgetary, personnel and operational matters for the court. They also may handle some public relations duties.
- Judges' clerks or research assistants: Again, these kinds of staff positions do not exist universally. Where they do, law clerks or assistants may be of major help in keeping up with the judges' schedules and in helping to understand the legal meaning of their actions or decisions.
- Court reporters: Their responsibility is to keep verbatim transcripts of court proceedings. (Not all proceedings are "**record**" proceedings, however. This is particularly true in the so-called "inferior" trial courts.) From them, a legal journalist may get substantial help in ensuring accuracy in his own coverage. Arrangements for access to and copies of transcripts vary widely; a reporter will have to deter-

mine locally what is or will be available to him. Not infrequently, court reporters are hired from outside the court process, and they sell their transcripts independently. As a general rule, transcripts are quite expensive, and will be beyond the financial means—and, in fact, the practical needs—of many newspapers, magazines or stations.

- Bailiffs: These are the court officers usually in charge of security and decorum in the courtroom. Often, they will have a significant role in determining where and how the press is to be accommodated physically in the courtroom and elsewhere in the courthouse. Sometimes, bailiffs are employes directly of the court; sometimes, they are officers of the sheriff's department or police department detailed to the courts. A reporter should take care to understand in advance just how far their independent authority in controlling the courtroom goes and how far it is subject to the ultimate authority of the judge. (See Chapter 6.)

G. RELATIONS WITH JUDGES

In the courthouse, the judge is singularly eminent. That has to do with his authority and, usually, his personality. He is the figure of consequence with whom all who enter the courthouse must contend—including the press. He may be the most valuable source a reporter can have there.

Judges dominate courts, with varying degrees of finesse. A reporter cannot function on the law beat until and unless he finds a way to deal with judges easily, regularly and satisfactorily. And because the personality and style of each judge is in some ways unique, a reporter will have to be unusually adaptable and perhaps even clever in his approaches to the judge or judges on his beat.

Over the years, some court critics have dealt harshly with what they have called "the cult of the robe." By that they tend to mean, among other things, the judges' sometimes exaggerated sense of self-importance and the deference which they expect. But whether or not a judge allows himself to commit what has been called "the sin of arrogance," the mere fact of judicial authority and independence puts the judge in the center of attention in the courthouse and the courtroom. He is as important to the reporter as he is to the whole process of justice.

The reporter's relations with the judge may be shaped, at the outset, by the way in which the judge came to his position and the degree to which he is formally held accountable after he is on the bench. If a judge is chosen by election, he very likely will have developed fairly close communication with the press as he campaigned for office. That could carry over into a strong relationship after he has taken office.

Where an elected judge has a fixed and fairly short term of office, he may well "court" the press as a part of his effort to ensure his own re-election, if he desires to run again. Moreover, he should expect to be held more openly accountable if he is to ask the voters again for their support.

There may be something of the same force at work where a judge is subject to some kind of fitness review process, at least where it goes beyond the normal monitoring of legal ethics by disciplinary committees of the bar. Again, the difference results from a known sense of having to account for his performance.

The degree of access and accountability may be materially different if the judge holds his seat for life, or for a quite extended, even though fixed, term of office. Then there may be no developed habit of maintaining close ties with the press or no strong interest in being accessible to the press. In those circumstances, the reporter is faced with the challenge of cultivating the judge as a source.

Specific Suggestions

A reporter will have to find his own methods for reaching and associating with the individual judges he is assigned to cover. But, again, some suggestions may be helpful:

- Many judges, perhaps most of them, will be reluctant to be interviewed by reporters. Even more of them will be firmly opposed to holding press conferences as such. Some, however, will be willing, at least occasionally, to provide "background" information or "guidance" for the reporter.
- A reporter who has no regular and continuing contact with a judge, to discuss the business of his court and the decisions which the judge himself reaches, will be handicapped seriously. The judge usually assumes that he has explained himself adequately in his formal, public declarations and decisions. But the chances are that a reporter will need some assistance in understanding as well as "translating" the judicial product into news stories. The judge, naturally, would be the best source of such help, and some will provide it.
- Contact with judges, and resulting good relations, also can have an impact on the reporter's ability to work with court personnel. It would be awkward to try to deal with the judge's subordinates if they felt, rightly or wrongly, that they would be "subverting" a judge by dealing with a reporter. Moreover, a judge can be of help in settling problems with uncooperative court aides.

- In working directly with a judge's decisions, a reporter should seek access to written opinions or orders wherever possible. There are serious risks in working with oral decisions—risks, of course, which must be taken when there is no time to await the written version, or when there is going to be no written version. A reporter is in no position to insist that a judge do his work in writing, but he should do what he can to encourage that.
- A reporter covering a multi-judge court may develop problems when he becomes aware of conflict among the judges. Of course, he is obliged to report that. It is, however, not uncommon for judges to believe that their internal conflicts are not fit subjects for publicity. A reporter, therefore, may have to live with some loss of sources or worsening of relations if he is obliged to disclose to his readers or listeners troubles within a court. (The same may be true when the conflict is between a judge and courthouse personnel, rather than with other judges.)
- A somewhat related problem could arise in a reporter's monitoring—which he must do—of a judge's relations with attorneys who practice in his court. Again, many judges feel that that should not be publicized. But it may affect materially how well a given court operates, and how a particular case may come out, so it is proper material for news stories. A reporter should simply know of the risks to his access to the judge about whom he reports critical news.
- The most difficult problem of this kind may arise in a reporter's monitoring of a judge's off-the-bench activity. There are some parts of a judge's non-judicial life that are, beyond any question, purely private. But many facets of a judge's private life may have a bearing upon his public work, and a reporter should pay close attention to them. These would include any formal business activities. They could include his activities in bar associations or even in non-legal organizations, such as charities. There is a significant potential for some of these contacts to develop into conflicts of interest with the judge's public duties. It is not enough for a reporter to assume that the normal disciplinary procedures that exist will monitor closely a judge's non-judicial conduct. This will be an investigative obligation of the press, and perhaps of the reporter on the court beat.

The difficulties that a reporter may encounter if he does write critically of a judge may not be limited to a denial of access to the judge. In extreme situations, he may experience problems in the courtroom pursuing normal coverage. A judge, as has been indicated, is plainly in charge of his courtroom and he can, subtly as well as blatantly, complicate the reporter's task by denying him access to which he may have become accustomed.

There would appear to be little if any risk that a reporter would face contempt charges for writing about the judge's out-of-court activity. (Contempt problems are discussed in the next chapter.)

It is clear, then, that there is a considerable variety of circumstances that may test the day-to-day relations of the press and the bench. Neither side, of course, need expect trouble with the other and the potential for difficulty between them can be reduced if reporter and judge begin with good relations based on mutual understanding. Each should consider it his obligation to do so.

4

The Press as Adversary

FEW ISSUES IN COURT ARE AS LIKELY TO STIR JUDGES to rhapsody about the American system as a test of the First Amendment's guarantee of a free press. Yet no issue is as likely to be troublesome to the reporter on the court beat.

The courts have become the arena in which the spreading conflict over the performance of the press often is worked out. And, even assuming that the rhapsody over the First Amendment still will be heard there, the legal journalist must hear it two ways: as reporter and as adversary.

His own profession is the "party in interest," one side of these cases. Perhaps the courthouse reporter's own professional rights are at stake. (The reporter himself may be a party, and he may be appearing before a judge whom he normally covers.) But these are still cases in court and must be covered. Obviously, objectivity and credibility are very much on trial.

A reporter should never cover his own case in court. But he should have no hesitation whatever to report on a "press case" in which he is not personally involved, even though his own news outlet is. First Amendment cases are very important for the community, and their outcome may significantly affect public access to information about public business. To ignore such cases would be irresponsible and unethical.

As the opening chapter suggested, courts are part of government, and the press has a duty to monitor them—in press cases, too.

The Supreme Court, in one of those rhapsodies about the press, has suggested:

The press has been a mighty catalyst in awakening interest in governmental affairs, exposing corruption among public officers and employes and generally informing the citizenry of public events and occurrences.

The court also has said:

The press does not simply publish information about trials but guards against the miscarriage of justice by subjecting the police, prosecutors and judicial processes to extensive public scrutiny and criticism.

And it has been even more pointed:

What transpires in the courtroom is public property. . . . Those who see and hear what transpired can report it with impunity. There is no special perquisite of the judiciary which enables it, as distinguished from other institutions of democratic government, to suppress, edit or censor events which transpire in proceedings before it.

Even so, the relationship between the press and the courts becomes more difficult when the press itself is in court as a party. It then is asking for something from the court, and it is thus under a legal obligation to accept what it gets or does not get.

At one meeting where the press and judges came together to talk over their relations, this dependent position of the press was described vividly by an important judge (who could not be quoted by name):

Where, ladies and gentlemen of the press, do you think these great constitutional rights that you are so vehemently asserting and that you were so conspicuously wallowing in yesterday, where do you think they come from? The stork did not bring them. These come from the judges of the country . . . that's where they come from. . . . It's the courts that protected you and that's where all these constitutional rights come from.

Chief Justice Warren E. Burger has made the same point, somewhat more subtly, in a speech to a group of editors:

Who, then, under our system, has the power to enforce the great freedoms of the Constitution, including press freedom? . . . You can assert and demand, but you cannot enforce. When the chips are down on great rights under our system, whatever those rights may be, there are ultimately two forces that really count, because the final battle moves to the arena in which the ultimate decision is made. That arena is a court where the key people are lawyers and judges. At that point you may be parties or witnesses, but your fate depends on competent, courageous lawyers and competent, independent judges.

Courts derive their authority from the Constitution and, ultimately, from the people. Thus the press, seeking to vindicate its freedom under the Constitution, may wind up in court in its own behalf. But like any other party, it may find that going to court should be its last resort, not its first, in a legal dispute.

A. TECHNIQUES OF ADVOCACY

Until about the middle of the 20th century, the press seemed to have one significant legal problem: libel. It usually went to court with that problem, not by choice, but of necessity: the other side sued.

But the pressures of life in an urban society, the emergence of civil rights as a control on power centers in society, and the rise of the aggressive investigative reporter—in combination, those influences made new and novel legal problems for the press.

In response to that, the press began pursuing remedies on its own, in a determined way. The press took on an advocate's role, on its own behalf.

Legislation

One technique of advocacy has been to seek legislation. Before state legislatures and before Congress, the press has sought protective legislation, including such measures as so-called "shield laws"—laws to protect reporters and media when they refuse to disclose, under court or administrative orders, the identities of news sources or information gathered but not published. Another form of protective legislation more recently sought is a limitation on the authority of police to search newsrooms or a news organization's files.

In addition, the press has sought legislation that would aid the newsgathering function directly: "sunshine laws" or "open meeting" laws, requiring the organs of government to meet and act in public session, and "freedom of information" laws, providing access to data in confidential or otherwise restricted public files.

Press-Bar-Bench Efforts

Another technique of advocacy has been joint effort: newsmen work with lawyers, with judges, or with legal organizations to draft voluntary approaches to press restraint, particularly in reporting crime news and criminal court proceedings.

An example of this approach was the drafting, with the advice of news organizations, of the American Bar Association's "Proposed Court Procedure for Fair Trial-Free Press Judicial Restrictive Orders"—an attempt to deal with issues involving the impact of pre-trial publicity on the trial of criminal cases. The ABA, on its own, has gone further, by drafting new codes of ethics for judges and lawyers in the form of "Standards Relating to Fair Trial and Free Press." Those were first adopted in 1968 and then substantially revised—and liberalized—in 1978.

Another example is a series of jointly drawn "guidelines" on press coverage of the criminal justice process, from arrest to appeal, suggesting the types of publicity that could or should be avoided. Those have been shaped, in large part, by the ABA Standards as initially developed in 1968.

Finally, the technique of going to court, on the initiative of the press, began to be used with growing frequency. The issues raised are discussed in more detail in the last part of this chapter.

B. ADVOCATES FOR THE PRESS

As the legal problems of the press deepened, the need for a legal "specialization" in the field became more evident.

For many years, there had been specialists in some branches of "communications law." This was largely limited to libel law, however, and to the practice of law before the regulatory agency for the broadcast industry, the Federal Communications Commission.

There had been little movement toward a First Amendment specialty— that is, a broadening legal practice dealing with freedom of the press in all the forums and in all the varieties of conflict over that freedom.

Gradually at first, then more rapidly, a First Amendment specialty began to emerge. The volume of court cases alone, rising markedly, encouraged the development. So did the sensitivity of the press generally to what it perceived as a threat of significant dimensions.

Lawyers for the press exist, basically, in three categories, and there are freedom-of-the-press specialists in each.

"House Counsel"

A lawyer on the staff of a company, corporation or other organization is said to be "house counsel." He will be a part of the legal, or general counsel's, department or division.

If he is practicing regularly in the press freedom area, he may be used by those who are making editorial policy and selection as a close and regular adviser on the likely legal consequences of publishing sensitive stories. If he is not active or well-versed in that area, he may be used as a legal counselor to the editorial policymaker only as a specific legal threat arises or seems likely to arise. He may call in other attorneys from outside the organization for help on a specific case, or he may seek to handle it himself or with his associates in the organization's legal department.

The advantage of having a "house counsel" is that he will be routinely available, he will know organization policy with some certainty, he probably will be quite well acquainted with those who make editorial policy, and he may be experienced in dealing with the editorial staff itself. Of course, there also may be a saving in legal fees for the organization.

Depending upon the size of the legal department, lawyers on an organization's staff may have such a variety of legal duties that they are unable to focus very closely upon press-freedom law. Another potential disadvantage, at least to the reporter on the staff, is that their primary obligation is to represent the organization, and it is possible that, on a given press-freedom issue, the reporter's interests may differ from or conflict with those of his employer, thus suggesting the need for his own lawyer from outside.

Outside Counsel

A lawyer brought in from a law firm outside an organization—the more common experience for the press in America—may be able to bring to bear immediately a wider array of legal talent and experience than house counsel would be able to offer.

If outside counsel does in fact specialize in First Amendment law, then the variety of legal experience in that area will be noticeably broader. One news organization is not likely to have had the range of legal challenges or threats that would have occurred with several. A true specialist will have seen most kinds of challenge before, and thus may have some advantage, particularly in dealing with a matter of immediate moment.

A lawyer from outside the organization, in addition, may be able to call upon associates and a supporting staff that will permit a more penetrating response to a legal challenge.

In some circumstances, an outside counsel will be fully aware of a given organization's policy and past legal experience, because counsel will have been on a "retainer"—that is, on call to handle all of the organization's legal problems in his area of specialization.

Generally, however, he will be less acquainted with the editorial staff, particularly at the reporter's level, and that could be a disadvantage. There may be, perhaps, a problem of availability. And, of course, there will be the consideration of the level of fees.

Legal Aid and Assistance

Some forms of support during a news medium's legal troubles have become available, although the development of First Amendment law as a subject for "public interest" law firms has been slow.

In general, a reporter or his organization have had to provide their own legal representation at their own expense.

The increasing challenge to the press, however, has produced some forms of legal assistance—sometimes free—from organizations that have a particular interest in defending the First Amendment.

One such organization, for reporters and editors, is the Reporters Committee for Freedom of the Press, based in Washington, D.C. It operates a "legal defense and research fund" whose activities include some free legal aid—particularly in emergency situations.

Press organizations or media may also receive some support from legal counsel for groups such as the American Newspaper Publishers Association, the American Society of Newspaper Editors, the National Association of Broadcasters, the National Newspaper Association, the Radio-Television News Directors Association, and the Society of Professional Journalists (Sigma Delta Chi). At a minimum, those organizations can add considerable weight to a "test case" on First Amendment issues by agreeing to join in as friends-of-the-court (**"amici curiae"** or just plain **"amici"**). They have done so frequently.

C. THE VARIETIES OF LEGAL CHALLENGE

First Amendment cases, so called because they usually involve ultimately a challenge to the freedom of the press to gather and report the news, come in many forms. Special emphasis is given in the final part of this chapter to three of those forms: libel, privacy claims and contempt-of-court citations. But there are many others, and the number and novelty is increasing notably.

This book is in no way a casebook on press-freedom decisions. The reporter or editor who undertakes to guide his own legal destiny is like the lawyer who takes his own case: he has a fool for a client. Any journalist who gets into trouble with the law owes it to himself to get legal help of a professional kind.

Thus, the following is simply a summary treatment of the forms of legal challenge that may confront a reporter or his medium. The methods of responding to these challenges should be shaped in consultation with a lawyer, because responses will vary with the peculiar facts and the local circumstances, procedurally, substantively and institutionally.

Legal challenges may occur at all stages in the news-gathering and publishing process: limits on the initial process of gathering news, direct or indirect restraints on news publication *before* a story is published, and controls or sanctions *after* publication. Any one of these may involve significant First Amendment questions, and many may lead to lawsuits.

Limitations on News-Gathering

- Denial of reporter access to official proceedings, such as hearings in court, the taking of pre-trial evidence by deposition in civil cases, and conferences or meetings of official judicial bodies or professional organizations exercising public duties.
- Sealing of various official records, such as evidence in criminal proceedings, police records of arrest, government personnel files, official documents bearing upon private individuals.

- Direct court orders imposing obligations of silence on attorneys, witnesses, court personnel and jurors in criminal cases—before, during or after trial.
- Legislation restricting public and press access to official documents, including materials that are not protected by classifications of secrecy for "national security" purposes.
- Monitoring of news media toll ("long distance") telephone calls by investigative agencies, with permission of the telephone company.
- Direct investigation of reporters known to be pursuing stories that might bear upon suspected criminal activity.
- Direct court orders implementing, with the power of contempt, "guidelines" restricting coverage of the criminal justice process. (See contempt discussion below.)
- Subpoenas or other forms of compulsory disclosure seeking to force a reporter to reveal his sources or to disclose information he has obtained but not published.
- Controls or prohibitions upon reporter access to inmates in jails or prisons.
- Indirect limitations on broadcast news content, through imposition of a requirement to permit "answering" or "reply" broadcasts.
- Slander lawsuits against investigative reporters for remarks made during interviews.

"Prior Restraints" and Other Pre-publication Controls

- Direct court orders forbidding publication of evidence in criminal cases, in the pre-trial period or during trial, where the evidence is part of the public record of a case.
- Direct court orders forbidding publication of potential evidence in criminal cases, at least until after a jury is seated and **sequestered,** if the evidence is not admitted in open court.
- Limitations on the content of advertisements.
- Regulation of the manner in which evidence, such as tape recordings, may be used in broadcasts even after the recordings have been admitted in open court as evidence.
- Limitations on distribution of publications in controlled settings.

Post-publication Penalties, Restraints

- Libel lawsuits (see below).
- Right-of-privacy lawsuits (see below).
- Contempt threats/prosecutions (see below).
- Subpoenas or other forms of compulsory disclosure seeking to force a reporter to reveal his sources for published stories, or to disclose added details of materials not published.

- Police searches of news organizations' files.
- Arrest of reporters/editors on criminal suspicion following publication of stories describing witnessed crime.
- Criminal prosecution of reporters/editors.
- Threats of damage lawsuits for refusal to publish information. including advertisements.
- Withdrawal of credentials or other "access" documents.
- Limitations on sale of publications because of content.

D. THE SPECIAL PROBLEMS OF LIBEL

A central consideration in the work, indeed the daily work, of a legal reporter is the risk of a libel lawsuit against him and/or his news organization.

Libel lawsuits claim damage to one's reputation, and much of the matter with which the legal reporter deals could be injurious to someone's reputation. That may be truer of the news grist of the courthouse beat than of any other. A considerable part of courthouse news comes from criminal cases, and the potential for defaming someone with information out of such cases is obvious. But even civil lawsuits often contain material that has a high potential for defamation.

To be sure, there are a variety of protections in the law of libel for the reporter. But the best defense is not built upon after-the-fact protections. Rather, it is built upon care and diligence in reporting before-the-fact—professional obligations the reporter should feel anyway.

The Scope of Libel

Libel deals with false facts. It is quite clear that published truth, where truth can be proven, is not libelous, except that in some states good motives and/or justifiable ends must be shown. The truth of any given fact may not be self-evident, and merely because a fact came from a supposedly knowledgeable source or an apparently authoritative document may not settle the matter.

The law, however, does seem to make some allowance for straying a bit from the truth. Supreme Court Justice Lewis F. Powell, Jr. has written:

> Although the erroneous statement of fact is not worthy of constitutional protection, it is nevertheless inevitable in free debate. . . . Allowing the media to avoid liability only by proving the truth of all injurious statements does not accord adequate protection to First Amendment liberties. . . . The First Amendment requires that we protect some falsehood in order to protect speech that matters.

The matter of fault. The journalist should not be lulled by assurances like that from Justice Powell. Falsehood, if published, is libelous if it defames someone's character or reputation and if the one who published it is found to be at fault. The kind of fault that matters will vary from state to state, but it will usually turn on some notion of negligence by the reporter or editor. It may vary, perhaps, according to the public or private character of the person who claims to have been defamed.

The basic theory behind libel laws, whatever their particular scope, is that those who have suffered "wrongful injury" to their reputation or standing in their community are entitled to have that injury "redressed" by some form of compensation. Obviously, then, the key questions always have been: what is injury and what is wrongful?

The question of injury. For a time, beginning in 1964 and continuing in the decade afterward, it had appeared that there would develop a general standard applying nationwide to guide the courts in libel cases. This began with the Supreme Court classification of public officials—those in government posts—as the least likely to suffer "wrongful" injury to their reputations, because they voluntarily put their reputations into the public domain. Gradually, this moved closer and closer to a sweeping protection of the press even when the person claiming to be defamed was a private individual, caught up involuntarily in a newsworthy event. "Wrongful" injury—that is, the kind of negligence that would demonstrate the wrongfulness of letting the injurious falsehood get into print—grew very narrow in scope.

But this developing process ended, however, and the Supreme Court made at least a partial return to the long-standing circumstance that each state had discretion to fashion its own theories of liability for "defamatory falsehoods," at least where private individuals were involved.

Varying Approaches to Libel

Some attempt at guiding state legislatures and state courts in this responsibility has gone on for a number of years in various institutions and organizations—notably, the American Law Institute, as part of its study of **"torts."** (Torts are wrongs which can be remedied by a legal decree.) If past experience is followed, some states will adopt some or all of these formulations, and others will ignore them, going their own way.

It has been quite common for the states to develop their standards of libel through case-by-case court decisions rather than specific legislation of statewide application.

Therefore, the reporter on the courthouse beat may be able to observe this process of development firsthand. He has an obligation, in fact, to report newsworthy libel cases as fully as he would any other lawsuit of news significance. There is simply no excuse for failing to report a libel lawsuit merely because it involves the reporter's own organization. (He should leave the matter to another reporter on the staff if he, himself, is involved directly in the suit.)

Libel Proceedings and Results

In form, the proceeding in a libel case is like a standard civil case. The most significant evidence in it is likely to be the testimony of reporters and editors who were involved with the selection and publication of the challenged news. (Much of that evidence may be gathered before trial, in the **discovery** phase of the case—when the lawyer for the suing party may ask probing and wide-ranging questions about how a story was gathered, reported and written.) The judge's instructions to the jury will be crucial in defining the law that is to govern the jury's reaction to the facts. A verdict by the jury, in favor of the person who sued, may involve one or all of three kinds of money damages: **"compensatory"** or **general damages,** to seek to offset the harm to reputation; **"special" damages,** to recover actual "out of pocket" costs or losses; and **"punitive" damages,** to seek to punish the publication or its staff and to deter them from such error in the future.

The Reporter's Obligation

The reporter, in seeking to avoid libel threats that would involve him directly, will have to depend heavily upon his own performance. There is no way that a supervising editor can protect him from reporting false facts and getting into trouble for it, if the reporter himself is cavalier about gathering facts or is content to write recklessly about facts even though he is uncertain about their truth. Intentional use of falsehoods, or careless error in the use of facts, may make the case for the other side. Sometimes, there can be no undoing once the publication is out.

A reporter will have to work out with his own editors the process by which a libel problem is to be handled. It might be advisable, however, for him to draft a thoroughly detailed memo describing how the story developed step by step and where the problem seems to have entered that process. He should avoid trying to build a defense on his own by going back to his sources in hopes of encouraging confirmation of his story, at least until after he has talked it over with his superiors and legal advice has been obtained.

E. THE SPECIAL PROBLEMS OF PRIVACY

A legal reporter very often must write about private individuals, persons whose lives have been drawn into the public realm of the system of justice. It may seem, logically, that once they are in a public forum with their problems, individuals have less of a "right to privacy." But that is not necessarily so, legally, and the burgeoning of privacy litigation confronts the courthouse reporter as much as it does any other journalist.

It perhaps was inevitable that there would be a deep conflict, some day, between the right to publish and the right to be let alone. As the nation crowded more and more into cities, and life became more impacted, and as the press changed its tastes and habits—or had them changed for it—so that the "zone of privacy" grew ever narrower, the makings of a confrontation over the right of privacy were at hand.

Trends in the Law

In 1967, the first right-of-privacy case involving the media went to the Supreme Court. As was true regarding libel law, the initial result of that case seemed to be the start of a trend toward a severely restricted right to sue the press.

But something different was happening, even then. The theories that lay behind privacy lawsuits were not of long standing, unlike those behind libel litigation. Privacy was a right that was only beginning to expand, as a legal and constitutional phenomenon. The Supreme Court was not even sure where it came from in the Constitution, but it was found to exist.

As Supreme Court Justice Byron R. White remarked:

> Powerful arguments can be made, and have been made, that however it may be ultimately defined, there *is* a zone of privacy surrounding every individual, a zone within which the State may protect him from intrusion by the press, with all its attendant publicity.

The origin. To understand why this "zone" exists, it may be useful to go back to a law review article written in 1890, one of the first compelling pleas for the development of a legally enforceable right of privacy.

Louis Brandeis and Charles Warren wrote:

> The intensity and complexity of life, attendant upon advancing civilization, have rendered necessary some retreat from the world, and man, under the refining influence of culture, has become more sensitive to publicity, so that solitude and privacy have become more essential to the individual; but modern enterprise and invention have, through invasions upon his privacy, subjected him to mental pain and distress, far greater than could be inflicted by mere bodily injury.

Translated into a legal concept, these thoughts provide a theory of injury and provide a basis for compensation for those found to be injured. Unlike the field of libel, where the injury is harm or real threat of harm to one's reputation, the field of privacy recognizes an injury that may result from unwanted publicity. Therefore, it is not at all certain that publication even of true facts is insulated from challenge in a privacy case.

Theories of injury. Among the theories upon which privacy damage awards have been based, there is injury that results from:

- Publicity that puts a private person in a "false light" in public—that is, something which subjects him to unfounded ridicule.
- Publicity that directly intrudes into purely private affairs.
- Publicity that discloses, in a sensational manner, private facts that are true but are embarrassing to the person or persons involved.
- Commercial exploitation in the media of a person's identity—as in the unauthorized use of his picture.

It is clear, then, that the right of privacy takes into account not only the bare fact content of what is said about a private individual, but the manner and the context in which it is said.

While intentional lies or falsehood about a private person clearly are subject to legal challenge for invasion of privacy, unwanted publicity that does not involve falsity as such also may be legally risky for the media.

The Constitutional Basis

One of the difficulties in knowing the scope of the problem is that the Supreme Court has only recently developed the constitutional basis upon which to build notions of a "right to privacy."

On the one hand, it has been suggested that it might be covered by a loose collection of parts of the Bill of Rights and might emerge as the "penumbra," the partial shadow that is cast by several of those amendments. On the other hand, it has been argued that it is part of the "concept of personal liberty and restrictions upon state action" that lie in the Fourteenth Amendment's protection of rights, privileges and **due process.**

Sources of the right. In any event, there is now a "right of privacy" of some form recognized in every state and at the federal level, and articulated in a growing series of court decisions. The privacy laws at the state level are, in some instances, written statutes. In others, the right to sue for an invasion of privacy is based on a "common law" recognition of such a right. Either way, they may exercise a significant restraint on publicity and the press.

Even though the Supreme Court moved into the area constitutionally in 1967, and is destined to remain in it, it still is true that the right of privacy in relation to publicity will be developed primarily in lawsuits in state courts.

Again, therefore, the legal reporter will be a day-to-day observer of its development. Since this is largely a "frontier" area of the law, it will make news because of its novelty. It also will be news of wide interest, since nearly everyone has some sense that he is entitled to privacy regarding at least some aspects of his life.

Privacy Proceedings and Results

In form, a privacy case is like a civil damage case. The evidence to be watched most closely by the legal reporter will be that which bears on the methods of obtaining the news of private affairs, the testimony on the way in which it was said in the press, and the evidence on the alleged injury resulting from the unwanted publicity. As in a libel case, the judge's instructions will be a key to the case, legally and journalistically. A verdict by the jury holding that there was an invasion and an injury resulting from it may take the form of money **damages,** either **compensatory** or **punitive,** as in libel cases.

The direct legal risk for the reporter on the courthouse beat in covering news about private individuals is considerably reduced (but it is still present) when he is reporting facts that emerge in public records that are open and available for public inspection or in testimony given in open court. For the reporter whose story goes beyond the testimony, or interprets that testimony too freely, the legal risk heightens considerably.

The manner of gathering news that may be challenged on privacy grounds can be crucial. The right of privacy seems clearly to include protection from physical intrusion—that is, going onto or into someone's private property, without permission, to get information. (This could include telephone wiretapping or other forms of electronic eavesdropping.) The right might also apply even if the reporter himself did not make a physical intrusion but someone else did and passed on the information he had obtained to the reporter for use as news.

For the reporter sued for invasion of privacy, as with the one sued for libel, it makes sense to prepare a detailed memo for his superiors and for the lawyer on how the story was gathered and why it was written as it was.

F. THE SPECIAL PROBLEMS OF CONTEMPT

If there is one kind of case that can be said to be the most sobering to those who regularly observe the law—including the legal reporter—it is the contempt-of-court case.

Nothing else comes close to it as an occasion for the use of overwhelming judicial power, at times raw judicial power. The contempt power is as nearly unlimited as any authority held by any branch of government. The reporter who witnesses its use—particularly, the one who feels its sting himself—will know well what the basic independence of the judiciary truly means.

The value behind the power to punish for contempt is deeply honored in Western traditions of law and government. Affronts to the system of justice, serious enough that they threaten to undermine the capacity of the courts to dispense justice, are offensive to the very idea of government and must be dealt with promptly and severely. If an independent judiciary is necessary to do justice, the courts must remain open and operating, and the contempt power can go far to assure that they will be. That is the theory behind it, and the value it serves.

More than two centuries ago, an English jurist, Lord Hardwicke, said it eloquently:

> There cannot be anything of greater consequence than to keep the streams of justice clear and pure, that parties may proceed with safety both to themselves and their characters.

Source and Scope of Contempt Power

The contempt power is awesome, at least in concept if not in every instance of its practical use, simply because it is a power that the courts hold inherently. In America, the power does not need to be provided by legislation; the courts simply have it, derived from the **common law.**

There are some safeguards to be observed—imposed, primarily, by the courts themselves. Legislatures, as part of their authority to control the jurisdiction of courts, have sometimes sought to curb the excessive use of the contempt power. It is also possible that arbitrary use of the power could lead to some form of discipline, perhaps removal or impeachment, of a specific judge.

Summary contempt. The safeguards which have come through judicial decision generally deal with the timing and procedure governing the use of contempt power. If a judge is forced to act immediately in order to make it possible for his court to continue functioning in the face of a disruption or a serious threat of disruption, he usually may act summarily: on the spot, without any hearing or discussion. Summary action may even include an order for immediate jailing of the **"contemnor"**—the person found guilty of contempt.

Other contempts. If there is time, the judge is obliged to hold a hearing so that the person accused of contemptuous conduct may seek to defend himself. If the judge presiding at the time of the alleged contempt became deeply embroiled in the incident personally, he may not be allowed to preside over the delayed contempt case.

It remains unclear whether a person accused of contempt has a right to have the case tried by a jury.

Contempts as News

Use of the contempt power, of course, almost always will make news. It is difficult to imagine a use of the power that would not make a news story. Presumably, in publishing such a story, the legal reporter would run no risks of being held in contempt himself merely for distributing to the public the factual information of how the judge had used his authority.

Threat to Reporters

But there are circumstances where the reporter himself could be cited for contempt, and the Supreme Court seems to have left no doubt of that:

A newspaper or a journalist may be punished for contempt of court, in appropriate circumstances.

There have been very few cases of nationwide value as precedents spelling out what circumstances would be "appropriate" for such punishment of the press.

But with the rising frequency of judicial orders seeking to limit what the press may publish, particularly about criminal cases or trials, the prospect of direct conflict over the contempt power increases.

The risk is probably greatest in that area because a reporter would be more inclined to defy a court order of that kind than any other, since such an order goes directly to his basic obligation to report the news. He cannot defy such an order without inviting possible contempt action.

For the courthouse reporter, however, there may be other situations where the possibility of contempt will exist. The judge's almost complete control of his courtroom, and his wide authority over the proceedings before him, may lead to orders that severely restrict the journalist's operating freedom in covering a case. Violations of those orders could result in severe and immediate punishment. Some judges have consulted the press, in advance, before issuing orders that limit the physical and substantive opportunities of reporters to cover cases (see Chapter 6). A reporter should welcome such consultations and join in them, to reduce the possibility of later misunderstanding or confrontation.

A reporter who does get into trouble for alleged contempt badly needs a lawyer. There is no apparent value in going it alone, hoping to talk the judge out of taking any action. In seeking a lawyer, a reporter should seriously consider having one entirely of his own choosing, rather than one selected or retained by his news organization. The journalist's personal liberty is at stake, and he should allow no other considerations to affect the legal representation he will need.

5

Covering Criminal Cases: The Beginning

CRIME IS THE MAIN STAPLE OF LEGAL REPORTING. Of course, crime alone does not make all the news on the court beat. But it does dominate the beat, so much so that it often is but an extension of the police beat. This will be almost as true for the reporter covering the appeals courts as it is for the one assigned to the trial courts.

Criminal law is simply more "newsworthy" than civil law. More often, a criminal case will have in it the ingredients of human interest, public policy and clearcut controversy that make news. At a more fundamental level, criminal law provides the most vivid test of a community's sense of justice and morality. Moreover, every criminal case can involve the basic guarantees of the Bill of Rights of the Constitution, at nearly every step.

For the legal reporter, there is another reason for preoccupation with the criminal side of his beat: he is likely to experience more difficulty with it not only because key steps in the process are secret but also because the legal risks for the reporter himself are the greatest. Covering criminal cases always brings a reporter close to the edge of libel, and it may bring him in direct confrontation with judges and prosecutors over what may be published.

There is another general consideration: a reporter covering criminal cases must focus, and focus very closely, upon details. The least detail in any of the stages of the criminal justice system—from the point of arrest to the moment of conviction—can make the difference in the ultimate outcome of a case. It is a legal axiom that when a person's liberty is at stake, the smallest details of his case can and often do count significantly. To be sure, a criminal case does not have to be handled perfectly to be considered legally fair. But there is no certainty about what if any lapses from perfection may be allowed before a case will be found to be legally wanting.

It is as important for the legal reporter to know the specific facts about a criminal case as it is for him to know the legal principles that will govern that case. Those facts begin to accumulate from the very beginning. As they develop, the facts will shape the entire case.

But it is the law that converts those facts into matters of consequence in a criminal case. So, the legal journalist also will need at least a basic appreciation of the theory and practice of criminal law to be able to tell where a case may be going legally.

Because this chapter focuses on the beginning, it will deal with the first encounters of the police with a suspect, and the earliest encounters of the suspect with the courts.

Following the over-all theme of this publication, the pre-trial activity of police and prosecutors will be treated as a prelude to court action. Each step in the process is examined for its potential to raise an issue that later will be a factor if the case goes to trial.

In some circumstances, the reporter who is assigned to cover the court beat is also the one who must cover the police beat. Thus, he needs to focus on police news itself; the considerations may vary from those that will govern police news as a prelude to a court case.

It would be well to remember throughout that most police work does *not* produce a court case. Rather, the criminal justice process may come to an end in the police station or in the prosecutor's office, and the courts will have been involved little if at all.

In those instances where the courts *do* become involved, and that may be more likely for the most newsworthy crimes, all that has gone on before could and usually will be significant. This chapter and the next two will treat news developments in a criminal case chronologically.

A. NEWS AND THE POLICE

Sources of Police Information

News about police may begin with a crime, or a mere suspicion that a crime has been committed. The reporter on the police beat normally will learn about police activity in one of three ways: from the police "**blotter**," the police radio or his own police contacts and sources. As a general rule, a reporter seldom will be a witness to crime himself. He may be contacted, however, by a witness or perhaps a victim, even before the police become involved. There will be some occasions, perhaps rare, when a reporter will accompany police on an investigation or to witness a crime that the police know will occur because of a tip from an **informer**; there are special risks for a reporter in such situations since he may be summoned later as a witness.

The reporter on the court beat may learn about police activity long after it has occurred—that is, as it arises as an issue in initial court appearances or the trial itself. Nevertheless, he will make some use of the same sources of police information as the police reporter.

The police "blotter." At most police stations, some kind of written record will be kept of activity that occurs during the day or during a shift. The nature of that record varies widely, from a scanty list of times and notations to an extensive file of sometimes copious notes and official documents detailing police activity. For convenience in discussion here, any such record will be called a **"blotter."**

Reporters who report on police news will seldom find that all the kinds of information of interest to them are located in one convenient file or record. Indeed, in the larger cities they may find that parts of what they need are widely scattered among police jurisdictions and locations.

Moreover, once a reporter has located the source of information he needs, he may not always have access to it. For example, there may be a local practice of withholding from public and press disclosure some types of information (even, at times, such basic data as a record of persons arrested). Some standards are emerging in this area through police administrative action and test cases by the press.

The reporter's access will depend, most of the time, on the nature of his relations with his police sources. In some circumstances, the reporter and his supervisors may decide that some formal legal action may have to be taken to obtain access to police records. This should be a last resort; it has obvious potential for converting a highly useful, informal understanding into a formalized arrangement that may result in diminished access.

Police records often will be of less use to a police reporter if he sees them hours or days after they were made. A fight over access may result in that kind of delay. Thus the reporter should work diligently with police sources to be assured of early and complete availability of "blotter" information. Sometimes this will depend upon a reporter having an authorized police credential or "press pass," providing access that may be materially greater than is accorded to the general public.

The "blotter," in a general sense, is the record of the first encounters of police with a crime or a suspected crime.

It should show, among other information, the sources of the initial police awareness of a crime or suspected crime: that is, a citizen complaint, given with or without taking an oath; routine police patroling or beat monitoring; tips from informers.

That kind of information may also be important to the courthouse reporter because it may show the presence—or absence—of a justifiable police belief that a crime has been or was being committed. That belief is what is called "**probable cause.**" Sometimes, an officer may make an **arrest** or a **search** without a court order or "**warrant**" if he can show that he had "probable cause" for his action.

A police officer will be considered to have had "probable cause" for an arrest or a search *without* a warrant if he can show that he did believe that a crime had been committed but that he did not have time to get a warrant because, among other reasons, he feared the suspect would flee or that criminal evidence would be destroyed or lost. If the officer has time to seek a warrant, he usually is obliged to do so. To obtain a warrant, an officer must convince a judge or magistrate that there is "probable cause" to justify the proposed arrest or search. In this sense, "probable cause" means a well-founded belief that the person or evidence being sought will, in fact, be at the place the police determine is a site for an arrest or for a search.

Police "blotter" data also should reflect arrests and searches made by officers, and should show whether any given arrest or search was made with or without a **warrant.** (A **warrant** is a specific form of court authorization for police action.) Later, in court, the presence or absence of a warrant may make a difference in whether an arrest is to be sustained, or whether a search is to be upheld.

If police made an arrest even though they lacked "probable cause" to do so, or made an arrest not specifically authorized by a warrant, the whole case may fall. Any evidence gathered by the police as a result of an unlawful arrest might be barred from the case—in legal terms, "suppressed." (Evidence that is excluded from a case before trial is said to be "suppressed." If such illegally obtained evidence has been used at the trial, the so-called "**exclusionary rule**" may be invoked: that is, a conviction based upon such evidence will be overturned, and the evidence will be excluded from use in any re-trial.)

The same could be true if police made a search without authority—that is, without "probable cause" or without a warrant. Sometimes, it should be noted, police may have sufficient authority ("probable cause") to make a search without a warrant if they do so right at the time they make an arrest, and in the same location. This is called, in technical terms, a "**search incident to an arrest.**"

A "blotter" should indicate some reference to a formal document used to support the request for a warrant, either an arrest warrant or a search warrant. This document is an **affidavit,** a sworn statement by an officer seeking to justify a request for court permission to make an arrest or a search by showing "**probable cause.**" A reporter should seek access to the affidavit itself. It could become crucial in determining whether the warrant was justified—and, thus, whether police evidence resulting from an arrest or search may be used to prosecute the accused.

Another form of police activity that should show on "blotters" are "stop-and-frisk" encounters. These are considered, in law, to be less formal and less intrusive forms of police arrest or search. Therefore, the police may engage in a "stop-and-frisk" of a person without having either "probable cause" to do so or a warrant specifically authorizing such an encounter. Usually, this action will take the form of a brief arrest of a person for limited questioning, and perhaps for a "pat-down" or "frisk" of the person, in search of weapons or "instruments of crime" such as burglary tools or the "fruits of crime" such as stolen goods.

When any action is taken by police under a warrant, there should be a record—legally, a **"return"**—showing the results. This would include a report of the person or persons arrested, including a description of the circumstances of the arrest, or a report of the place or area searched, including a description of the circumstances of the search and a list of the items seized by police.

Even when an arrest or search is made without a warrant, police generally are obliged to make some record later of the event. This could figure importantly in a future court case.

Most of these records and documents will be of immediate help to the reporter on the police beat. Indeed, much of the time, because of the imminence of deadlines, a reporter on that beat may have to rely entirely on "blotter" information because there will be no opportunity for him to verify that information himself. He would be well advised, therefore, to treat it with caution. The only way he can test its strength is by questioning police officers as closely as he can before he writes or dictates his story. It will be obvious that some of the data will have been gathered directly by an officer, perhaps witnessed by him. But some will be only the officer's second-hand account of what he had been told by others.

The reporter on the courthouse beat, by comparison, probably will have time to check out quite thoroughly the information that is available to him from police station records. Generally, he will become aware of this information as part of his reporting in preparing for a trial in a criminal case. By then, however, he may have some difficulty obtaining access to those records, particularly if a prosecutor has put those records into his files as *he* prepares for the trial.

When a criminal case moves to the trial stage, its dimension may be determined in considerable part by the actions of police in the investigative stages of that case. Thus, the "blotter" is as much a key source for the legal reporter as for the police reporter.

The police radio. Many news media, particularly in larger cities, will have radios that are capable of monitoring the frequencies upon which the police communicate. In general, this source of information will be helpful to the reporter primarily as a tip to ongoing police investigations or other activity, enabling the reporter to go to the scene.

Normally, the "traffic" that one overhears on a police radio is much more limited in form and content than the data that is recorded on the "blotter" or is otherwise on file at the police station.

The courthouse reporter very likely will have little need to monitor the police radio. If recordings of it are kept, they may—at some future point in a case—have some bearing on the question of "probable cause," thus perhaps affecting the legality of an arrest or search.

Other sources of police information. As is true on any beat, the legal reporter may have a variety of informal relationships with his sources, all of which may produce usable information for his story or stories. He will interview, or merely converse casually, with a variety of police officers and other investigators. He also may cover press conferences held by ranking police officers, particularly in cases of spectacular crimes or widespread civil disturbances, such as riots.

Information from these sources may be cited, when a case goes to trial, as indications of "prejudicial publicity"—that is, pre-trial disclosures to and by the news media, helping to shape the community's attitude about a developing criminal case and perhaps influencing the opportunity to assemble an unbiased jury.

A reporter's own enterprise in reporting may also have a bearing on that issue, should it develop in a given case. Publicity of any kind about a case— particularly one that becomes notorious in a community—may affect that issue. (See Chapter 6.)

Police Tactics and Conduct

Many of the issues in criminal law—certainly some of the most difficult— arise because of the actions of the police. Much of the time those issues will develop because of the wide discretion that policemen necessarily have in doing their work. Chief Justice Warren E. Burger once commented:

> No public officials in the entire range of modern government are given such wide discretion on matters dealing with the daily lives of citizens as are police officers. . . . The policeman on the beat, or in the patrol car, makes more decisions and exercises broader discretion affecting the daily lives of people, every day and to a greater extent, in many respects, than a judge will ordinarily exercise in a week.

That discretion is exercised by policemen of widely varying degrees of training and sophistication, yet each is controlled—ultimately—by the same rules of law. Thus the thousands of decisions made by policemen in thousands of different situations are bound to turn up an almost endless array of legal issues.

As the preceding section on sources of police information has shown, the officer may be engaged in anything from an informal, perhaps even haphazard "stop-and-frisk" situation to a formal arrest and a broad search for evidence, and each carries with it the potential for creating a legal question that later will influence the prosecution for crime.

At this point, it will be useful to go through each of the steps of police action prior to trial to show how the legal questions are created and shaped, and how they may be treated as news.

Initial complaint or incident. At the beginning, of course, there is police discovery of a crime or a suspected crime. That may come through routine patroling or beat work, or through a call or tip to police by someone who knows of or suspects the commission of a crime.

The initial report of crime very likely will make "spot" news, something that is immediately newsworthy. One or more policemen in the very act of responding to a criminal incident will also begin to make news that will be of continuing importance as the case develops. They will question witnesses, perhaps suspects, and they will look for or seize evidence.

The way an officer handles witnesses or suspects at the scene may create issues of unauthorized detention or arrest, excessive use of force, loss or diminution of police credibility, unreliability of police evidence, involuntary confessions or damaging admissions, and "prejudicial" publicity.

The methods used to gather physical evidence at or near a scene may create issues of unauthorized search or seizure, loss, compromise or even destruction of vital evidence, and general or specific unreliability of evidence because of the way it was collected, marked and handled.

From the moment the police arrive on the scene, their investigation has begun, and a potential criminal prosecution begins to build. If the crime or the circumstances they encounter are not simple, then a continuing series of more intense and complex police actions will follow.

The objective of a quick, on-the-spot inquiry by police will be the same as if a prolonged, in-depth investigation were undertaken: that is, to determine to the satisfaction of police or a prosecutor whether a crime has been committed and if so, who did it.

A police reporter who goes to the scene is not bound to limit his reporting to the activities of police. He may feel obliged to question witnesses or suspects independently, and he may feel he must examine the scene without doing so under the eye of a policeman. He must be aware, however, that any actions he takes are likely to be subject to police control at that point. Moreover, it is fundamentally important that he not intrude into the event itself, to the extent that he may disturb evidence or compromise testimony. He is there to get the story, and perhaps the most significant part of the story for him may be how the police handle their duties. Their actions, then, should be the primary focus of his reporting.

Usually, the courthouse reporter will not be on the scene at the time police begin their investigation. By the time the legal reporter gets to the case, it probably will have developed into an ongoing criminal prosecution, and his view of the actions of police will be after the fact. By that time, perhaps, police activity itself will have become a focus of the prosecution or defense investigation prior to trial.

Investigation and arrest. Assuming that the police do not close a case—that is, get everything they need—in their initial response to the crime, they will investigate further. This may come either before or after an arrest of a suspect or suspects.

It is impossible to go beyond general guidance on the norms of police investigatory activity. That will vary with each case. It may be as simple as having a single officer do a few more interviews than he had been able to conduct on the scene. It may be as complex as having dozens of officers, police scientists, prosecutors and grand juries drawn into a steadily widening inquiry that may last for months.

It may be assumed, as a general rule, that the simpler the case, the more discretion there will be for the policemen assigned to the case. With increasing complexity, more of the activity will come under some form of neutral scrutiny by a judge or a lesser judicial officer such as a **magistrate.** This certainly applies to the searches that will be made (including electronic "searches" through wiretaps or hidden listening devices), and it applies to the questioning of persons who are targets of the investigation.

Police are not free, at least in theory, to take any action just because it occurs to them. The standard that is supposed to guide their conduct, always, is that they have "probable cause" to believe a crime has been committed before they take actions which would interfere with a person's freedom or otherwise intrude upon his rights. They also must have "probable cause" in order to obtain an arrest or search warrant.

In the simplest cases, it will not be difficult for the police to establish "probable cause" justifying them to detain a person for a brief period, or detain him long enough to have accomplished his arrest—in other words, to have taken him into custody so that it is clear he is not free to go. It also will not be difficult in the simplest cases to establish "probable cause" for conducting limited searches for evidence. (No "probable cause" is needed if police ask for and obtain consent to enter private property and conduct a search.) If police have "probable cause" for making an arrest, this is sufficient to justify a simultaneous search—at least of the arrested person's body and clothing, and of the area close at hand or within the officer's view.

As a general rule, police should obtain warrants before they make arrests or searches. They are supposed to rely upon the detached judgment of a judicial officer, not their own.

The officers will be obliged to prepare affidavits showing the basis of their belief that an arrest or a search will be justified—in other words, showing that they have enough evidence to establish "probable cause." If the judge or magistrate is persuaded, he will issue an arrest warrant or a search warrant. Reporters usually will not become aware of the filing of affidavits by police seeking warrants until after warrants have been issued; they may not even become aware until after the arrest or search has been made under a warrant. The process of obtaining a warrant is seldom, if ever, a public proceeding with an open hearing. This process, technically, is an **ex parte** proceeding—that is, a proceeding in which only one side is represented, the police.

The judicial officer will expect to be informed of the results of the warrants he has issued. The reporter often will learn of these results, sooner or later, because they become a part of the public record in the case file.

The police do not need warrants to authorize questioning of witnesses or other persons believed to have information relating to a crime. They also do not need warrants to conduct scientific tests on evidence—provided that the evidence was lawfully obtained. In general, reporters will not become aware of the results of this kind of questioning or testing until those results are revealed in court as evidence.

Once an investigation has turned up enough information to support an arrest (and it should be remembered that police often make arrests on the spot, at least in the more clear-cut, simpler cases and where it is impractical to seek a warrant), they very likely will take a suspect into custody. That means the person becomes subject, at least for a brief interval, to the complete control of police officers. A person may be detained at the scene, or at a police station or police headquarters—in other words, in some more formal detention facility.

The entire process of arrest and detention is surrounded by basic constitutional limitations and safeguards, and these reach not only the length of time an arrested person may be held, but also the scope of police authority to deal with that person.

Because police have arrested a person does not mean that they or prosecutors have enough proof to convict that person of a crime. But the arrest is supposed to be justifiable only if police have a strong basis for believing that that person has committed a crime or has information about a crime that has been committed. Arrests based solely on idle suspicion are suspect, in law. But often, police do make arrests and detain persons for questioning when the officers are far from certain that those persons are linked directly to a crime. They also make arrests of persons with known criminal records when new crimes of a similar nature have occurred and police are looking for suspects.

In most police jurisdictions, a person who is placed "under arrest" will be brought to a police facility for "processing." That may include some form of **"booking"**—that is, entering the person's name, address and other personal details in an arrest record, with some indication of the possible criminal violation for which the person has been detained, plus the name of the arresting officer.

It also may include more elaborate procedures, such as fingerprinting, photographing, placing in a police **lineup** for possible identification by crime victims or witnesses, and taking voice or handwriting samples. Depending upon how each of those procedures is handled by police, a legal issue may arise. At a minimum, each such step might be challenged on grounds of unreliability. Lineup identification is particularly vulnerable to that kind of challenge.

Immediately after booking, an arrested person may be subjected to questioning by police, or may be jailed promptly with interrogation coming later, if at all. Any questioning must be done within strict constitutional limits, including respect for the person's right not to be forced to incriminate himself.

The jailing of a person is usually recorded, although it may be no more than the record that was made in the "booking" process.

Not every person who is arrested is actually placed in a jail cell and held. In fact, most will be released after a brief time—perhaps after some questioning. Those who are detained very likely will be suspects against whom the evidence appears to be strong, or those considered too dangerous to be set free, or thought likely to flee if released. In some police jurisdictions, arrangements for release on bond may be made immediately at the police station, with the arrested person posting, or having paid for him, a comparatively small sum of money on bond. At times, however, release on bond is a more complex process (see below).

If a person is detained for longer than a short period, he may not necessarily remain in the same jail. It is quite common for police at the local level to hold a jailed suspect for only a few days at most. After that, the arrested person is likely to be transferred to a more secure facility, such as a county jail or a state prison institution. The procedure of transfer is highly informal, and is likely to vary in practice from place to place. No judicial authority usually is required for such transfers to more secure jails or prisons.

A reporter on the police beat may or may not learn of a person's arrest, or of the details of his detention, including possible transfers from jail to jail. There will be times, of course, when police will disclose publicly that they have made an arrest, and at that time, they may disclose the name and some identification of the person arrested. As a general rule they are not obliged to do so, however. In particular, if a person has been held by police for only a brief period, that person may come and go before the police reporter will even know that he has been brought in—if, in fact, the reporter ever learns.

If police choose to withhold the fact of an arrest, the reporter may learn of it only after a person has been taken into court for what is called an "**initial appearance**" before a judge or magistrate (See below). Arrest records, while kept, are not uniformly available for public inspection by reporters or others.

It should be clear, then, that the entire period of investigation by police is surrounded by uncertainty of access to information for the police reporter or the legal reporter. Access will depend, here as in so many other situations in the criminal justice process, upon the relationships that an individual reporter will have built up in his own community with his sources.

Obviously, every step of an investigation, and certainly the process of arresting and detaining persons, is capable of producing news—either news of a "spot" variety for the police beat reporter, or news of legal significance for the courthouse reporter. Both should remember that police activity does not always produce unquestionably true facts or allegations, so the problem of libel is always present. The reporter's capacity for, and interest in, testing the strength of his police information often will make the difference not only in the soundness of his story, but also in its immunity to legal attack.

B. NEWS AND THE PROSECUTION

It is somewhat arbitrary to select a point at which police activity supposedly ceases and the prosecution takes over. The police often, perhaps regularly, are involved in supporting the prosecutor's work, and the prosecutor very likely will be involved, perhaps deeply, in managing or superintending the policeman's work. All are law enforcement officers, routinely reinforcing each other's particular tasks.

A reporter on the police beat probably will be covering the prosecutor's office. That will be especially true when the prosecutor is the local chief of police or the county sheriff. In larger jurisdictions, the prosecutor often will be an official who operates outside of the police or sheriff's department. More often than not he will be an elected public official, holding a title such as city, county, district or commonwealth's attorney. In some jurisdictions where there is a city or county attorney, there also may be a district attorney or "solicitor" who acts as the prosecutor.

Sources of Prosecutorial Information

As a general rule a legal reporter will have more continuing professional contact with the prosecutor—whatever title or particular position he holds— than with the policeman who works directly on case investigations. Prosecutors hold a public office, and thus should be accessible to the press and to the public so that they are accountable for their performance and that of the police. Moreover, the prosecutor usually will control the release of information.

It is not likely that a reporter will have regular or routine personal access to the case files of the prosecution. Sometimes, the information in those files—or some of it, at least—will be released in a press conference, press releases, or periodic official reports. Although the reporter should always seek to learn what he can from those files, he will find that release of the information is largely within the prosecutor's discretion and thus the reporter may learn many of the specific details of a case only when evidence comes out in court, in a preliminary proceeding or at trial.

Because the prosecutor's basic functions are to decide whether and when to charge a person with a crime, and then to go forward with the actual prosecution of that case, his whole approach is geared rather largely to the needs he will confront when he gets to court.

Thus, the prosecutor is very likely to be most concerned about developing evidence that will be **admissible** in court—that is, evidence which will be accepted by the judge as legitimate for use at the trial.

It is true, of course, that a prosecutor often will have or will obtain information that cannot be used in court. The fact that it is not admissible, however, should not necessarily mean that the reporter has no interest in it. The way in which such information was gathered may tell the reporter a good deal about the methods of police or other investigating officers. It also may tell much about the quality of police investigative sources.

A reporter, however, ordinarily will have difficulty gaining access to that kind of information, because a prosecutor will be reluctant at best to have that material open to public discussion or scrutiny. It could compromise his case by fostering what he will consider to be "prejudice" of potential jurors toward the accused person. The reporter may also have libel problems with this information.

The formal **indictment** or "**information**" by which a prosecutor charges a crime, and the actual evidence he introduces or seeks to offer at trial, will be the best and most reliable sources of prosecutorial information for the reporter.

Prosecution Tactics and Conduct

Except for the crime of contempt and some crimes which may lead to an official's impeachment (that is, removal from office), a charge of crime normally will be made by a prosecutor. He is a part of the executive branch, not the judiciary, and it customarily is a matter within his discretion whether to initiate a criminal case. If he chooses not to press a charge, that—in most situations—is the end of it.

It is a truism, and one that is simply stated, that "the duty of the prosecutor is to seek justice, not merely to convict," as the American Bar Association Criminal Justice Standards phrased it. Thus, it lies within his choice to decide *against* prosecution as well as *for* it. In the criminal justice system, he speaks for the state, deciding when the power of the state is to be focused on those believed to have violated its laws. Both the rights of the accused and the rights of the public are, in very real part, in his care.

Nevertheless, it often is true that the very actions of the prosecutor may produce legal issues in the criminal justice process. This emerges clearly as the prosecution is followed step by step, and as each step is analyzed for its news potential.

Investigation and filing of charges. As has been indicated, the role of the prosecutor does not begin only after police have finished their tasks. It is, in fact, a major part of the prosecutor's duty to conduct investigations so that he may satisfy himself whether to charge a person with crime, to close a case without filing any charge, or to close a case after charges have been brought but before trial.

A key element in the investigative phase of his work is the **grand jury,** where that exists in law or custom. Use of a grand jury is not required constitutionally for the states, and about half of the states do not have it at all. Others which have the grand jury may not always make use of it. In the federal system, grand juries are required by the Constitution in cases of serious crime. (The grand jury's role in charging a crime is discussed later in this section.)

A grand jury is an arm of the court, not a prosecution agency as such. Its historic function has been to provide a layer of citizen review between the state and the person believed to have committed a crime. Thus, it is supposed to sit in independent judgment of the way in which the prosecutor carries out his duties.

It is true, however, that the grand jury can become the main means by which a prosecutor gathers evidence against a criminal suspect. The grand jury usually has broad **subpoena** powers, and its review of potential evidence is not limited to that which would be admissible in court. The purpose behind this wide-ranging investigative authority is to inform the grand jury fully before it decides whether the prosecutor may go forward. A secondary purpose, of course, is to provide a check upon police and prosecution conduct.

Sometimes, in fulfilling its "inquisitorial" role, the grand jury will have the authority to issue pronouncements on the misdeeds of those charged with enforcing the law. These so-called **"presentments"** will not charge a crime, but will merely expose a condition that the grand jury felt should be brought to public attention.

A grand jury usually will not make news until it takes some form of public action at the conclusion of its work. Customarily, all grand jury proceedings are secret. Reporters may seek to learn from witnesses going into and coming out of a grand jury session what the scope of its inquiry is. But that may be the limit of access to the grand jury.

There may be news in the process of selection of the grand jurors because that usually is not a secret matter. Moreover, the means by which a grand jury has been chosen may itself become a legal issue to be tested at the trial; the composition of a grand jury panel may be subject to challenge on the ground that it is not representative of the community at large.

A prosecutor need not rely solely upon a grand jury in making his investigation. He may use police or other law enforcement personnel to continue the investigation well past the point of initial complaint and arrest. Moreover, the prosecutor's own staff may be directly involved in the investigation.

At some point in the investigative chain, the prosecutor will decide, when he thinks the evidence justifies it, that a charge does not necessarily bring investigation to an end; the inquiry may continue, formally or informally, right up to the time of trial, and perhaps even while the trial is being conducted.

The decision to charge, or not to charge, is largely within the discretion of the prosecutor. In ordinary circumstances, he may not be forced to go forward with a prosecution if, in his judgment, a case should be closed without a charge. In other words, his use of "prosecutorial discretion" is not subject to review by the courts. In an extreme situation, the absence of prosecution may be considered a failure to perform his duty, and that conceivably could lead to charges against *him* or to his removal from office.

A prosecutor usually will press charges in one of two ways. First, he may file them on his own, in the form of a **criminal information**—a document formally accusing a person of a crime. An information may also provide the basis for making an arrest, since it does constitute "probable cause" that a crime has been committed. Second, the prosecutor may take his case before a grand jury, and seek an **indictment**—a formal accusation by the grand jury of a crime.

It is impossible to generalize about the timing of the actual filing of a charge. It may come right after a person has been arrested, after a person has had an initial appearance in court, or after a grand jury has been assembled to inquire into possible crime by a person who already is in custody on suspicion of crime.

Whenever it comes, the charge could easily make news. This is the point at which a criminal case may be said to begin, at least in a formal way. It more or less commits the prosecutor either to go forward toward a trial, or to enter negotiations—**"plea bargaining"**—to attempt to obtain a guilty plea, and thus close the case without a trial.

If the charge is made by a grand jury, it may not be released to the news media immediately upon the jury's decision to indict. In many jurisdictions, a grand jury charge does not become a formal charge until the prosecutor agrees to authorize it, by signing it himself. (It is highly unusual, but there have been instances of **"runaway" grand juries,** seeking to indict despite the contrary wishes of the prosecutor.)

Charges need not be and ordinarily are not filed in a formal court proceeding. They are filed with the formal entry of a charging document ("information" or indictment) with a court, usually the clerk. A judge or magistrate need not take any action on the mere filing.

Procedure after arrest. The prosecutor's role may be initiated formally in a criminal case within a short period after a person has been arrested. At an early point after a person is detained, that person is supposed to be taken before a neutral judicial officer—a judge or magistrate—for a decision on whether his continued detention is to be allowed. This is a duty for the prosecutor, not the police.

This first encounter of the suspect with a court may be called, for convenience, an **initial appearance.** In some areas it is called a **"preliminary hearing,"** in others an **"arraignment."** The terms are somewhat confusing, because in some jurisdictions they are used for a later stage of the criminal justice process, after the initial appearances.

In this opening encounter, the arrested person usually is advised of the nature of the crime for which he has been arrested, is told of his legal rights, including the right to a lawyer if he wants one, and may have his bail set.

At that proceeding, the suspect normally will *not* be asked to enter a plea. The main function of the initial appearance, aside from apprising the suspect of his rights and warning him of the possible consequences of what he has been accused of doing, is to determine whether there is "probable cause" to justify either detaining the person further or of sending his case to trial. The proof needed to demonstrate "probable cause" will be materially less than is needed to convict of a crime. The standard of proof at the preliminary hearing is whether the evidence seems to point, clearly and convincingly, to the arrested person as one who has committed a crime. At the trial, of course, proof must establish guilt "beyond a reasonable doubt" in order to convict.

In some areas, the initial appearance also is the point at which a date for a "preliminary hearing" is set.

A preliminary hearing may be the occasion for a suspect actually to enter a plea to a charge against him, or it may be a more formalized kind of initial appearance in which charges are explained and rights are defined.

A bail hearing may sometimes be held as a separate proceeding, although it is more common for the bail issue to be dealt with at the initial appearance or the preliminary hearing. There is no universal requirement that an arrested person be released on bail. This is usually in the discretion of a judge or magistrate. The primary purpose behind the imposition of bail is to insure that a suspect who has been released will not flee to avoid prosecution.

Bail may take the form of cash, put up by the suspect himself or his friends, or by a bail bondsman who is willing—for a fee—to deposit a bond with the court. When money bail is required, the suspect or his bondsman sometimes will not be required to put up the entire amount of the bail; rather, some portion of it—perhaps as little as 10 percent—may have to be posted. Sometimes, a person will be released **"on his own recognizance"**—that is, without paying any money but with a promise to be on hand for trial.

At some point following an initial appearance or preliminary hearing, and definitely after a formal charge has been made, the accused person will be **arraigned.** An arraignment generally is the proceeding at which the accused is asked to plead to the charge against him.

The accused person may plead guilty, **"no contest"** (formally, **nolo contendere**), or not guilty. A plea of guilty ends the case at that point, assuming the plea is accepted by the court. (A judge may reject a guilty plea if he concludes that the accused person did not make it voluntarily, or did not fully understand what he was doing.) A plea of "no contest" also ends the case; however, it is not considered an admission of guilt, and thus does not constitute a formal conviction. The plea is simply a means of bringing the case to an end, and setting the stage for sentencing, without the need for a trial. The judge may accept or reject a guilty plea at his discretion. A plea of not guilty requires that the case go to trial.

It is considered quite acceptable for prosecutors and defense lawyers to "bargain" over the kind of plea that a suspect may offer. The purpose, of course, is to determine whether a trial might be avoided, and a just result reached, by encouraging a person whose guilt is not in serious doubt to plead guilty or "no contest." This is called **"plea bargaining"** because the prosecutor usually will offer to give up something in return for a plea—for example, he may agree to reduce the charge to a lesser offense, or perhaps to dismiss some charges. The terms of a plea bargain ordinarily will have to be disclosed in open court, and usually will be subject to some inquiry by the judge as to the advisability of the bargain. The suspect will be asked whether he agreed to the bargain without being coerced. Any promises made to him, for reduced sentence or other benefit, to induce him to plead guilty or "no contest" must be disclosed to the court.

Obviously, any one of these proceedings—initial appearance, preliminary hearing, arraignment—could produce some news.

At the initial appearance, some indication of the scope of a prosecutor's case will emerge. At the preliminary hearing, the prosecutor may lay out much of the evidence he has, or at least he will show enough of it to indicate what his strategy of prosecution is likely to be. At the arraignment, the entry of a plea could be news of prime significance.

Moreover, the way in which each of these proceedings is conducted may provide a legal issue that will figure in the trial. For example, there may arise a question as to whether the person was illegally detained, whether his bail was wrongly denied or was set too high (the Constitution forbids "excessive" bail), whether the evidence brought out was insufficient to detain him further or to hold him for trial, whether any plea was voluntarily, intelligently and knowingly made.

There is no guarantee, in most jurisdictions, that all of these opening parts of the criminal court process will be open to the press and public. Indeed, it sometimes is expressly provided by court order that some of these proceedings are to be closed. In addition, many of these proceedings are held without a formal transcript being kept.

Thus, there may be a twofold difficulty for the courthouse reporter in covering the initial appearance, the preliminary hearing, and, if it is separate, the bail hearing. Not only may the reporter be unaware that such a proceeding has been held, but also he may be unable to find out exactly what happened later when he does discover that the proceeding did occur. Again, the reporter is obliged to arrange his relations with police, prosecutors and court personnel so that they will share with him, as fully as possible, information about these activities in court.

More often than not, the arraignment—the point at which a plea is entered—will be a public matter, and the press and the general public will be allowed to witness it. It also is likely to be recorded, on tape or by stenographic transcript. That will not be true, of course, in cases of petty offenses, such as traffic violations. Those proceedings are highly informal, and may be completely disposed of in a few minutes at the most.

It should be remembered that not every criminal case will go through these preliminaries to arraignment. It is not uncommon for a prosecutor to decide, along the way, not to press forward with a case even though a charge has been filed formally.

A prosecutor may simply decide to end a case outright, by filing a motion of **nolle prosequi**—that is, "I do not choose to prosecute"—or he may make a motion in court to dismiss charges. In some jurisdictions a prosecutor may need a court's permission to "nolle pros" a case. A motion to dismiss, however, may be within the discretion of the judge to grant or deny.

A courthouse reporter should expect to have knowledge of and access to either kind of motion, whether they are merely filed with a court or are made in an open hearing before the court.

Another form of pre-trial prosecutorial activity that may make news on the legal beat is an attempt by a prosecutor to force a reluctant witness to testify before a grand jury. If the witness is merely stubborn, without having a compelling reason for his refusal to testify, a prosecutor may seek to have the witness held in contempt of court. If the witness is refusing to testify out of fear of giving criminal evidence against himself, the prosecutor may seek to have a court grant legal immunity from prosecution in return for that person's testimony. The immunity generally protects the witness only from a prosecution based directly on the evidence he gives, or on clear leads from that evidence. A prosecutor who has independent evidence that the witness has committed a crime may rely upon that in charging the witness with crime. If a witness is granted immunity, and still refuses to testify, he may then be held in contempt of court and imprisoned for a considerable period or until he agrees to testify.

Immunity hearings generally are open, so the press may expect to cover them.

Pre-trial "discovery." From time to time throughout the period before trial, there may be some legal maneuvering between the prosecutor and the defense lawyer as each prepares his case. There may be some close professional contact between them, perhaps a great deal of it. This usually will be part of the process that goes by the name of "**discovery**." Used in this way, discovery means the pursuit by each side of information held by the other that can or will make a significant difference to the outcome of each side's case.

The process may be highly informal, or it may follow very strict procedural rituals. In some jurisdictions, discovery is not encouraged at all. In only a few is the process well developed.

Legal reformers, however, are working increasingly to broaden the scope of each side's "discovery." With a series of major Supreme Court rulings expanding the rights of the criminally accused, there appeared to be a real threat that the complexities even of preparing for trial would get out of hand.

By encouraging each side to engage in discovery, pre-trial preparations may be simplified, the trial itself may be shortened and made more efficient, and the prospect of surprise—potentially a major complication when it occurs in mid-trial—is reduced.

Discovery has become a constitutional issue of its own in criminal law. The prosecution now has a constitutional duty to share with the defense any information held by the prosecution that might be **exculpatory**—that is, evidence that might help the accused demonstrate or prove his innocence. Failure to disclose such information may result in reversal of a conviction.

Among the other data that the prosecutor may be obliged to disclose to the defense are the names of prosecution witnesses and copies of statements they have made. The prosecutor may also have to disclose any statements—written or oral—that the accused has made, portions of grand jury minutes, data or statements supplied by expert witnesses, books, records, photographs and other physical evidence that the prosecution intends to use, facts about possible wiretapping or other electronic surveillance, results of searches, and past criminal records of prosecution witnesses.

The defense does not have as broad a disclosure requirement as the prosecution, but there are forms of discovery *to* the prosecutor that may have to be followed. For example, an accused may have to give fingerprints or samples of writing, hair, blood or voice, and may have to appear in a lineup, or pose for pictures. A judge may also order some medical or psychiatric examinations, and results of those probably will have to be turned over to the prosecution.

Legal reformers have recommended that discovery procedure be made quite regular, beginning with initial exploration of what the other side may have, followed by whatever hearings or courtroom appearances are needed to obtain rulings on discovery, and concluding with conferences where the issues to be tried are sorted out.

Although such regularity is not now widely practiced, there are pre-trial proceedings in many criminal cases—particularly, major cases—that do serve the same function. Some of these are discussed more fully below, in the section dealing with pre-trial activity by the defense.

Discovery procedures could make news, particularly if they occur in open court. The reporter, however, is not legally entitled to know about every exchange of information between the prosecution and the defense, and indeed may not learn of some of the more meaningful exchanges until evidence or testimony comes out at the trial. Generally, however, if a reporter's sources within the prosecution or defense team are good and reliable, he will be able to learn about major revelations almost as soon as they have been made. This may depend upon the degree to which either side in the case is interested in publicity as a matter of trial strategy.

C. NEWS AND THE DEFENSE

The defense lawyer usually will be the last of the principal figures to join a criminal case. Much will have happened to his client before the lawyer is even summoned: the crime will have been committed, an arrest very often will have been made, police processing may have been completed, and a charge may have been leveled.

Even so, the defense lawyer may become one of the legal reporter's most significant sources. When a criminal case goes forward, it is a process that focuses directly on a particular accused: it is that person's conduct, or suspected conduct, that is the core of the case. The news, too, will focus heavily upon the accused. There is no way to cover the accused except by covering the defense function in the case.

The prosecutor, of course, determines almost alone whether there will be a case at all. But the defense lawyer will be singularly important in the decision as to whether the case goes to trial. His advice to his client about the plea is as crucial a matter to the case as is the prosecutor's choice about filing a charge. Moreover, at many stages along the way, the tactics chosen by the defense may do much to shape the nature and pace of the proceeding.

There is another factor, quite amorphous, that tends to enhance the value of the defense lawyer as a news source. While experience will vary from case to case, it is generally true that defense lawyers will be quite accessible to reporters. There is an almost indefinable affinity between them.

A partial explanation for that may be that, with all the forces of the state arrayed against his client, the defense lawyer may see the press as a potential ally of real value. If the press' role in monitoring the conduct of the prosecution and the police is carried out effectively, it may be of tactical and strategic importance to the defense.

But the press' role, of course, also includes the duty to monitor the conduct of the defense as well. Thus, a legal reporter will not serve his function if he allows himself to be manipulated by defense interests.

Sources of Defense Information

It may seem somewhat anomalous, but the accused person usually is the legal reporter's worst source. Obviously, that person is the object of the most intense human interest in the story of his case. Moreover, he may be the only one who knows what really happened in the criminal incident. But he generally will not be accessible to the press. And, when he is, the accused is not likely to be especially reliable. His capacity for candor may have been seriously compromised by the incident itself, by the way he was handled by police and prosecutor afterward, or by the way he has been counseled by a lawyer—including advice that he say nothing.

With all of those imperfections, however, the accused is still the central figure in the story of the case. A legal reporter makes a serious mistake if he allows the personality, the background, the individuality of the accused to become submerged in the issues of the proceedings. The whole theory and practice of criminal law in America emphasizes the fortunes or misfortunes of the particular individual who is accused or suspected of breaking the law.

It is true, though, that the development of news about the individual accused necessarily must come from secondary sources. His family and friends will be of value to the legal reporter. But the defense lawyer is the one absolutely indispensable source.

Within his control, in most situations, is the matter of the plea. It is also partly within his control whether "plea bargaining" with the prosecutor succeeds. He will make the critical decisions before trial about the motions to be filed and pursued (see below), and the strategy to be used. During the trial, he will control at least half of the proceeding. After trial, he will shape the decision of whether—and how—to appeal.

In the pre-trial stage, his value as a news source will depend upon whether he is willing to disclose the results of his own investigation of the case, and the strategy he intends to follow not only as to plea but as to all aspects of the initial maneuvering.

It is not uncommon for a defense lawyer to hold press conferences, or at least to be accessible for press interviews. But he is no more likely than is the prosecutor to share all of his information with reporters. There are ethical restraints—and, indeed, there may be court orders imposing limits—upon what he may say. His client's interests are paramount, and they may dictate silence or perhaps even deception toward the media.

A reporter will not be given access to defense files on a case, any more than he will be allowed to go through a prosecutor's files. But he may be able to obtain copies of formal records or documents—say, of crime laboratory results and results of psychiatric examinations—if they are entered in court. He is not likely to be given access before trial to copies of any confessions or statements the accused may have given, even though these normally could be in the defense lawyer's possession.

The reporter can expect and should insist that the court clerk provide access to formal defense papers filed in court, such as all motions and legal memoranda.

Defense Tactics and Conduct

It is a myth that the primary obligation of the defense lawyer is to win—that is, to get his client "off" either by having charges dropped or by winning the case with a not guilty verdict. In literally only a fraction of all cases is that kind of clear-cut defense victory going to emerge.

The function of the defense is much more complicated, and the results ordinarily much less discernible. Most of the time, the defense lawyer begins with a genuine handicap: his client is under a distinct legal threat, and the police or prosecutor already have accumulated evidence—perhaps a great deal of it—against him. To cope with that handicap, and yet give his client the most effective legal representation, the defense lawyer may have to settle for what will seem, at best, to be a compromise.

It is not always in his client's interest to plead not guilty, and go to trial. Indeed, it very often will be in the client's interest to plead guilty, or to hold out the offer of such a plea, in order to make it possible for his lawyer to make the best of a very bad legal situation.

Ideally, perhaps, all criminal cases would be tested by the full adversarial process of a trial before a judge and jury. But even that is not an ideal; the risk of conviction after trial may be sufficiently high, possibly even overwhelming, that the defense lawyer will want to make a "deal" with the prosecutor expressly to avoid going to trial.

The defense lawyer's obligation to his client may in fact go well beyond the legal mechanics of the case, to the protection of his client's job, family or other private interests.

If the system of justice were functioning ideally, the accused person and his lawyer could work out these considerations between them, and with the prosecutor, in calmness and deliberation, and with all the facts plainly in view. But in reality, many criminal cases—*most* criminal cases of an aggravated nature—have to be worked out amid serious tensions, for the accused, for his lawyer, and for all other principals in the case. It will be that circumstance that will most test the system's capacity for fairness and regularity, and thus those will be the kinds of cases in which the legal reporter should be most on the alert as he watches the system of justice work.

In the pre-trial period, nearly all of the maneuvers of the defense could make news. The options and procedures open to the defense are followed here step by step, to show the news potential.

(It should be kept in mind throughout the following that the accused person has a constitutional right to choose to defend himself—that is, to act as his own attorney (in legal terms, acting **pro se**). Thus, depending upon his sophistication and learning, and upon the degree to which he gets supporting help from a judge or a court-appointed assisting counsel, he may attempt each one of the following steps in his own behalf. It may be assumed that if he does not have his own lawyer but wants one and one is appointed by the court, the same steps in the defense will be taken.)

Activity after arrest. After a suspect has been taken into custody by police, he may insist upon having a lawyer at his side before he will answer any questions. In those situations, an attorney may enter a case at an early stage. How soon he is allowed to see the suspect who may be his client, however, will depend upon the circumstances at the specific police station involved. When he does get to see the suspect, he may or may not be allowed to confer with him alone. If the suspect insists, the lawyer usually will be allowed to sit in on the questioning by police, but the actual role he may play in that setting will depend upon the police. This entire process is surrounded by constitutional limitations on police conduct, such as the famous **"Miranda warning"** requirement that police tell a suspect of his rights, including the right to remain silent and the right to a lawyer.

Usually, the reporter will not be allowed to observe any of this process. Indeed, most often, the reporter will not learn of this activity until after it is past. In-custody procedures and tactics of police and of defense lawyers called in by the suspect, however, may well make basic issues that will affect the case. The reporter should make an early effort to find out what happened in these "custodial" situations.

Investigation. It may well be true that the defense begins its investigation of the case very late, possibly long after the police and prosecutor have developed the prosecution case fully. Still, there is an ethical obligation for the defense lawyer to satisfy himself that he knows as much as it is possible to determine about the case. There is no substitute for his own investigation, or one that he has authorized.

Even if the accused has given police or prosecutors a confession or other damaging statement, a defense investigation remains a necessity. Such an inquiry might produce evidence that would refute any confession, and thus provide the basis for challenging the confession.

(In some jurisdictions, the defense investigation will be aided substantially by formal "discovery" procedures, as discussed above.)

In general, a legal reporter may assume that a defense investigation could produce news, provided the defense lawyer is willing to disclose what turns up. The reporter has no enforceable right of access to the results of the investigation; again, access very likely will depend primarily on his relations with the particular defense lawyer.

Among the items of news value that may be turned up are new witnesses (those not found or not interviewed by the prosecution), new physical evidence, indications of police or prosecutorial misconduct, and new data developed from separate scientific or other investigation of evidence obtained by the prosecution.

The defense also may interview prospective prosecution witnesses as part of the defense investigation. Sometimes this effort will reveal imperfections or weaknesses in the prosecution case.

Plea bargaining. At almost any point in the pre-trial period (as at most points even after a trial has begun), the defense may decide that it is in its interest to try to make a plea bargain with the prosecutor. This bargaining may be initiated as freely by the defense as by the prosecution.

Lawyers know that they are under an ethical obligation to explore the possibility of ending a case without a trial. The calculations that will be made in determining whether to seek such a disposition will vary from attorney to attorney. But as a general rule the prospect of a conviction, revealed after the defense's own investigation, will be the controlling judgment.

A lawyer ordinarily will not undertake to bargain over a plea without first getting his client's permission to do so. He presumably will have given his client a full explanation of the options and the consequences.

Normally, plea bargaining is not subject routinely to press monitoring. It is done secretly most of the time. When a bargain is struck, however, it must be revealed in an open court proceeding, at which a judge will seek to determine whether the accused person himself has made a voluntary and knowing decision to enter the plea. Hearings at which pleas are offered ordinarily are open to the press.

Initial appearance. As indicated above, the accused person's first appearance in court may be a public event. The defense lawyer, however, may not yet have come into the case. Indeed, one of the functions of that proceeding is to determine whether the accused has an attorney and whether he can afford one.

Sometimes, a defense lawyer—perhaps a **public defender**—will be named by the court immediately at the time of the initial appearance, and that attorney may have only a few minutes at most to confer with his client before crucial court action (say, grant or denial of bail) occurs. In those circumstances, the legal reporter should be alert to the possible issue of inadequate legal representation—one that may affect the entire case thereafter.

Grand jury. In those jurisdictions where a grand jury is used, the defense lawyer's role probably will be a limited one during the grand jury phase. He will not be allowed to accompany his client into the grand jury room, and thus *his* information, too, will be second-hand. Even so, a legal reporter should seek what he can from the defense lawyer who is willing to share what he does know about what went on before the grand jurors.

Preliminary hearing or arraignment. The role of the defense counsel at the hearing at which a plea is entered will be to insure that his client's legal rights are observed—including examination by the court to insure that the plea is truly voluntary. Again, the legal reporter will have an occasion to assess the quality of defense representation.

Pre-trial motions. Perhaps the most newsworthy part of the pre-trial preparations (other than entry of a plea) will be the handling of motions. These will suggest strongly the trial strategy that the defense lawyer is preparing to use, and they may well disclose much about the prosecution's case. In addition, they are likely to have a major influence on where and how the trial is conducted.

One type of motion may make a major difference to the legal reporter's capacity to cover the case. That is a motion to control publicity, by direct or indirect means. It may be a request (sometimes by the prosecution, sometimes by the defense) that lawyers, witnesses and court officers be forbidden to discuss the case in public and with the news media. It may be a plea for an order to close a proceeding, such as a preliminary hearing. It may be a request for so-called "protective orders"—that is, orders putting under seal some evidence or holding in secret some pre-trial proceedings. It may be a request for a *direct* order against the news media, seeking to control what they may publish or broadcast about the case. The judge himself may decide, even in the absence of a request from one side or the other, to issue some of these types of orders. These orders are discussed more fully in Chapter 6.

Other motions that may be offered in the pre-trial stage include these:

- To dismiss the charges or to reduce them.
- To **change venue**—that is, to transfer the case to another jurisdiction.
- To postpone or **continue** the case to a later time.
- To **sever** one accused person from the trial of others accused in the same case.
- To **suppress** evidence—that is, forbid its use at the trial.
- To reconsider the amount of bail or to reconsider denial of bail.
- To hold a hearing on an issue, such as mental competency to stand trial, or voluntariness of a confession.
- To order a psychiatric examination of the accused.
- To challenge the method of selection or the composition of the grand jury **pool** or of the trial jury **pool.**
- To **remove** a state case to federal court—that is, to transfer it to the federal tribunal for trial. (Removal is reserved for certain civil rights cases.)
- To provide public financing for defense investigation or research needs.
- To allow an accused person to represent himself.
- To require the prosecution to disclose evidence or lists of potential witnesses or informants.
- To require scientific examination of evidence.
- To **quash**—that is, wipe out—subpoenas issued to obtain witnesses or evidence.
- To replace the scheduled trial judge on grounds of bias.

Every one of those motions has at least some news potential. The most likely among them to produce significant news, however, are motions regarding the charges, suppression of evidence, jury pools, "discovery" from the prosecution and self-representation.

The legal reporter would be well advised to obtain copies of the motions in written form if possible, and to do so in advance of any hearing on them. (Not all these motions will be dealt with in a hearing; some will be disposed of by the judge acting summarily.) Not all courts will require the other side to respond to motions. Where a response is made, however, the legal reporter should try to obtain those, too, in written form.

Hearings on motions, where held, may be in open court. That is not universally true, however. The public and the press may be excluded from some motions hearings, particularly a hearing on a motion to suppress evidence. The Supreme Court, in fact, has given constitutional sanction for closing pre-trial hearings to prevent "prejudicial publicity" about a case.

Legal reformers have been attempting to promote one "**omnibus hearing**" at which all pre-trial motions, by prosecution as well as defense, may be heard.

In acting on a motion, a judge need not wait beyond the point at which the motion is offered. Much of the time he will rule immediately and orally. Ultimately, however, he will have his ruling set out in written form (perhaps in the exact form proposed by lawyers from either side or jointly.) A reporter covering a case meriting his close attention should obtain copies of all orders issued by the judge when they become available. Many of these rulings will provide the basis for challenges on appeal.

Research on jurors. In many jurisdictions, the defense is entitled to receive, before trial, a list of all potential jurors and their addresses. In addition, the defense is sometimes allowed to review questionnaires sent out to potential jurors to get information about their financial and occupational backgrounds.

When this material is available, the defense may make significant use of it in planning for challenges when jury selection begins at the trial. In some cases, extensive sociological research has been done on potential jurors to enable defense lawyers to use the juror-examination process more effectively.

It is doubtful that a reporter will be given access to this information about jurors until it comes out during defense or prosecution questioning at the trial. A reporter, however, may learn about and be able to monitor to some degree juror research that is done by the defense.

6

Covering Criminal Cases:
The Trial

A CRIMINAL TRIAL IS ONE OF THE great American folk rituals, a form of high theatre even in the most tragic cases. The beginning of a "big" trial is always an event in any town or city, and trials are the stuff of melodrama on the stage, the movie screen and television. The air of expectation about them is as Gilbert described it for Sullivan's music a century ago in "Trial by Jury":

> Hark, the hour of ten is sounding:
> Hearts with anxious fears are bounding,
> Hall of Justice crowds surrounding,
>   Breathing hope and fear—
> For to-day in this arena,
> Summoned by a stern subpoena,
> Edwin, sued by Angelina,
>   Shortly will appear.

A trial in America calls up images of Clarence Darrow and Daniel Webster, of Edward Bennett Williams and F. Lee Bailey, and each trial seems sure to become a part of the folklore of cases like John Peter Zenger on trial along with freedom of the press, Thomas Scopes at the "monkey" trial, Bruno Hauptmann and the Lindbergh kidnap, the Rosenbergs and atomic conspiracy, Lizzie Borden and the "forty whacks" axe murder, the Chicago Seven, Lt. William Calley of the Mylai massacre, Charlie Manson and his cultists, newspaper heiress Patty Hearst as a ragtag bank robber, the Watergate "cover-up" plot.

To Damon Runyon, and obviously to many other observers, "a big murder trial possesses some of the elements of a sporting event. I find the same popular interest in a murder trial that I find on the eve of a big football game, or a pugilistic encounter, or a baseball series."

Partly, the fascination is with the substance of the case: the crime, the evidence. But part of it has to do with the method. No matter how hard reformers try to rid trials of the image, they still seem to be like gaming, in which—as Lord Wigmore observed—the lawyers use evidence "as one plays a trump card, or draws to three aces, or holds back a good horse till the home-stretch."

A trial is a fascinating event to watch, as much for the legal reporter as for the jurors themselves. Sybille Bedford described it well:

> A trial is supposed to start from scratch, *ab ovo*. A tale is unfolded, step by step, link by link. Nothing is left unturned and nothing is taken for granted. The members of the jury listen. They hear the tale corroborated and they hear it denied; they hear it pulled to pieces and they hear it put together again; they hear it puffed into thin air and they hear it back as good as new. They hear it from the middle, they hear it sideways and they hear it straight; they all hear it backward and through a fine-tooth comb.

This process, obviously, produces news. The reporter on the court beat seldom will have better or more challenging news to cover than the trial of a criminal case. Since only a fraction of all cases ever goes to trial, the chances are that nearly every trial will be novel or significant enough to justify some coverage. Of course, not every step of the trial will produce a story. But each major segment of a trial doubtless will be newsworthy.

The reporter would be well advised, however, to try to keep a fairly broad perspective of the case even as he covers its step-by-step progress. He should try to relate specific developments to the general trial strategy of each side, so that his readers will be able to sense the significance of even minor details. He should keep in mind that both the prosecution and the defense will have worked out "game plans" for the case and will try to adapt the case as it goes along to their chosen strategies.

There is another general consideration: The reporter should not become so fascinated with the legal issues and developments in the case that he overlooks the human drama of it. Indeed, he may take it as a general rule that the story will be better told if the legalities and the technicalities are woven around the story of the persons involved: the accused, the judge and the jurors, the lawyers on each side, the witnesses—even the spectators. The drama that is unfolding before him is not a sterile exercise in legal mechanics, and it should not be treated that way journalistically. The reader or listener who is unable to attend the trial personally can get some sense of its true drama only through the published or broadcast accounts in the news media.

Before getting to the trial process itself, it will be useful to deal with the special conditions that may face the press as it covers a criminal trial.

The "Free Press-Fair Trial" Issue

It is almost an axiom that the press is most interested in those trials that are likely to be "notorious" in a community: those in which the crime is a serious or even a heinous one; or those in which one or more of the principal figures is prominent or well-known. But those are the very cases that may cause judges, prosecutors and defense lawyers to be concerned about "prejudicial publicity."

The routine criminal case, having a low level of fascination to the reading or listening public, is unlikely to produce any sustained or even momentarily fascinating news. Thus, it will be of little or no interest to the media and will provoke no concern within the legal profession.

The "big" cases, then, have a potential for bringing a legal, even constitutional, confrontation between the courts and the press. That potential has become a reality increasingly in recent years.

The problem is easily stated. News of crime is sometimes believed to create an impression in the mind of a community that an accused person is "guilty" even before he goes to trial. If that impression exists in the minds of persons who may be called to serve as jurors in a given criminal case, the right of the accused to a fair trial before an impartial jury may be violated or compromised.

The American Bar Association Advisory Committee on Fair Trial and Free Press drew this conclusion about the problem:

> The law requires, in order to protect the innocent, that the state establish guilt beyond a reasonable doubt on the basis of competent, admissible evidence. The likelihood that this burden may be substantially lessened—or in some cases increased—because of the conscious or unconscious effort of extra-judicial reports seems far too great to be ignored.

The U.S. Supreme Court has treated "prejudicial publicity" as a problem of constitutional scope and has said that the legal profession—judges and lawyers alike—has a duty to deal with the problem.

Within the profession, it is an ethical obligation to avoid contributing to "prejudicial publicity." That is an obligation, of course, that is fully enforceable under the rules of discipline for attorneys.

Whether or not a true conflict actually develops over the issue—and the press and the legal profession have shown increasing interest in negotiating in advance of conflict—it is clear that there is a basic difference in views about it.

The press believes in the fullest exploration of news of crime, to provide the public with the means by which it may judge how well the criminal justice process is working.

Lawyers and judges believe in the need to confine the judgment about guilt or innocence to the controlled, disciplined atmosphere of the judicial process.

As these differing perceptions come into contact, issues will develop over the manner in which the press covers a case—including the trial phase—and over the degree to which possibly prejudicial information will reach potential jurors without being tested by the limiting processes of the law.

Sometimes these issues will arise during the pre-trial period, before a pool of jurors is ever assembled at the courthouse. Some judges feel a stronger need to impose controls on publicity at this stage than during the trial. Throughout Chapter 5 there are indications of the practical results of this apprehension, in the discussion of the closing of pre-trial proceedings.

But the question of "prejudicial publicity" may also continue to arise as a trial approaches and after it is in progress. Court orders to deal with this question will be treated here in three categories: controls on access to the courtroom, controls on access to information and controls on publication.

Controls on the press within the courtroom. Very often, a trial in which the press is likely to be interested will draw a crowd—a crowd of reporters and a crowd of spectators. Judges, concerned either about the kind of courtroom atmosphere that is to prevail during the trial, or about security, may decide to allocate space and location within the courtroom.

In addition, judges—as an added measure of control—may decide to issue special credentials to reporters, governing their right even to admission to the courtroom.

Orders directed expressly to reporters' conduct may limit their freedom to move about while court is in session, limit their contact with principals in the case in the courtroom (even when the trial is in recess), and control the seating arrangement of the press. There also may be orders controlling what the press may do in the corridors of the courthouse, outside the courtroom and in immediately adjacent areas. These orders might include regulation of press access to work areas, such as a "press room."

Of course, there may be some parts of the trial from which reporters might be excluded entirely: for example, during questioning of prospective jurors, during conferences between attorneys in the judge's chambers or at the bench, during presentation of evidence outside the presence of the jury, or during presentation of evidence that, because of its nature, the judge believes must be received without any spectators in the courtroom.

Each order by the judge on these matters is likely to have three facets to it for the press: a possible news story about press access, a possible legal contest as the press attempts to overturn or limit such orders and direct or indirect limitation upon the press' opportunity to cover possibly crucial phases of a criminal case.

Press representatives should try to anticipate a judge's actions controlling access and should seek to negotiate with him about that. A reporter would be well advised to have his lawyer participating in any such conversations or negotiations.

In many states (though the number is declining) and in the federal courts, recording, broadcasting and photography may be forbidden in the courtroom during trials. This could result in orders directly barring cameras and recording devices from the courtroom or even the courthouse, forbidding reproduction—visually or in sound—of exhibits or other evidence, or barring cameras and recording devices from the courthouse. Controls or outright bans on cameras and recording devices in the courtroom existed without serious challenge for nearly 40 years. More recently, a growing number of states have begun experimenting with televised trials as a probable prelude to relaxing the controls.

In some courts, controls meant to bar cameras have been extended to forbid sketching by artists. The tendency more recently, however, has been to relax the ban on sketching.

Controls on access to information. The most common type of judicial limitation on access to news sources will forbid officers and employes of the court, lawyers on both sides, policemen and witnesses to talk to the press about a case.

Sometimes this type of order will be absolute and sometimes it will be restricted to certain kinds of information, such as an accused person's prior record, confessions or damaging statements, results of tests, identity of witnesses, and personal opinions regarding guilt or innocence. (The American Bar Association's 1978 revision of its standards on fair trial and free press recommended a general relaxation of such controls, so that police, lawyers and others would be freer to talk to the press about pending cases.)

Enforcement of such orders may lead to trouble of a special kind for the press: the risk of contempt if a reporter publishes information covered by the order, and the judge seeks to discover from the reporter himself the source of such information.

Other types of judicial controls on access may include the sealing of evidence, even though it has been formally introduced into a case, and the barring of interviews with jurors even after the trial is over and the jury has been dismissed. The press is free, of course, to go to court to challenge each of these types of restrictive orders.

Controls on publication. In some cases—considered to be extreme—a judge may decide to control what the press may publish or broadcast about a criminal case. This is the most drastic kind of control, and almost invariably will lead to a legal contest. (The Supreme Court has restricted severely the authority of judges to assert this control, particularly in the "Nebraska Press" case.)

Such direct controls may go so far as to describe words and phrases, as well as categories of information, which the press is forbidden to publish or broadcast.

Where such orders are issued, they may be enforced under threat of exclusion from the courtroom or, perhaps, contempt of court for violation of such an order.

A legal reporter should be especially careful to avoid personal and direct negotiations with the judge over such orders. These are grave legal matters, and they should be left to attorneys. A reporter may wish to have a lawyer with him before even discussing any such restraint with a judge or other court officer.

A. THE TRIAL IN GENERAL

The steps in a trial are treated hereafter as they normally would occur, chronologically. Each is analyzed for its news potential, with specific suggestions regarding the reporter's handling of the developments. Initially, however, there are some basic considerations to keep in mind.

Scheduling

The fixing of a date to begin a criminal trial is ordinarily the responsibility of the court. This will be done either by the judge himself or, more often, by the clerk of the court after consulting with the prosecutor and with defense lawyers. The prosecutor has a major role in this process, informing the court when a case is ready for trial. If necessary, the scheduling will be made a formal order of court, and if either side seeks a postponement (technically, a **continuance**), that will be done by formal motion, to be dealt with in the court's discretion.

Trial by Jury

Generally speaking, a jury is required by law only in cases where the offense is serious—that is, where the prison or jail term may exceed a specified period, such as six months. An accused person may waive—in other words, forgo—his right to be tried by a jury. When he does, he is tried before a judge alone.

The jury's function is primarily to decide the facts in the case. It is up to the jury to decide whether to believe any witness, whether to accept any evidence as valid or credible, how much weight to give to evidence, and whether the facts demonstrate guilt or innocence. Where a judge alone tries a case, he becomes the fact-finder, deciding issues otherwise left to a jury.

A jury verdict may not have to be unanimous; that depends upon state law governing jury procedure. A jury may not necessarily consist of 12 persons; the number ranges, under state law, to as low as six persons. (In federal court, jury verdicts must be unaninous, but the jury may number fewer than 12 persons if the accused agrees.)

Burden of Proof

In every criminal case, the prosecution must prove its case. It must prove every element of the crime **beyond a reasonable doubt.** There is no burden of proof on the defense, because of the **presumption of innocence.** The prosecution must overcome that presumption, or it has not met its burden.

The jury has discretion to decide whether it has been persuaded beyond a reasonable doubt. That means it will determine whether it is convinced to the point of moral certainty. Any residual doubt of any significant dimension about any one element of the crime should be enough to persuade the jurors to vote for acquittal.

One of the most significant elements of any crime is **criminal intent;** the accused person must have intended to commit the act which has been outlawed as a crime. Even where the accused actually intended to commit the act, it may be excused—as a matter of law—if the act was justified (for example, by "**self-defense**"). A judge will give the jury instructions about the rules of law that will limit or control the jurors' discretion in weighing elements of the offense, such as intent.

"Compromise" Verdicts

For most crimes that are serious (**felonies,** generally), there will be less severe crimes that are considered to be included within that same category of crime. This provides the jury with a measure of discretion which it may exercise almost as if it were reaching a compromise in a given case. A jury often will have discretion to decide that, if not satisfied that the accused person is guilty of the principal crime, it may nevertheless convict a person of a "**lesser-included offense.**" For example, the crime of murder in the first degree may have, as lesser-included offenses, second-degree murder, voluntary manslaughter and involuntary manslaughter.

Each one of these crimes, however, has its own elements, and the jury must be convinced that each of those elements have been proven beyond a reasonable doubt in order to convict of the crime.

"Felony Crimes"

There are some crimes that include, as one of their elements, the fact that they were committed during the course of committing another crime. In other words, a person in the act of one crime may be guilty of a separate, perhaps more severe, offense if it occurs while he was in the act of the other crime. For example, a person who commits a robbery may be guilty of "felony murder" if a victim is killed during the course of the robbery, even though the accused had no intention of committing murder and even if another person taking part in the criminal act actually committed the killing.

Rules of Evidence

There are quite strict controls on the kinds of evidence that may be admitted in a case—technically, evidence that will be "**admissible.**" This is governed by state or local law, regulation or rule, or by federal law or rule. (There may be exceptions to rules of inadmissibility.)

Evidence usually is *not* admissible:

- If it is **irrelevant**—that is, it does not relate to the specific crime and does not support the point for which it was offered.
- If it is **immaterial**—that is, it is not essential to the case.
- If it is **incompetent**—that is, it is not valid in a legal sense because it was not properly introduced or was not legally or properly obtained.
- If it is **hearsay**—that is, something which a witness says he has heard from or about another person, rather than something he observed directly.
- If it is only an opinion or conclusion of the witness—that is, something other than a matter of one's own factual knowledge or observation.
- If it is **privileged**—that is, it is a confidential communication that is protected by law from disclosure, such as communications between a husband and wife, attorney and client, doctor and patient, religious counselor and believer.
- If it is not the "**best evidence**"—that is, it is not the original document or material, or is not the best available, to make the point for which it is offered.

B. OPENING MOTIONS

Despite all the motions that may be dealt with during the pre-trial phase of a case, a good many motions may be left for possible use when the trial itself opens. Indeed, motions of a wide variety may be offered at crucial points throughout the trial and afterward.

Among those that may be made at the start of a trial are motions:

- to dismiss the charges
- to postpone the trial (a **continuance**)
- to remove a judge
- to control the manner of questioning potential jurors
- to "**quash**" the jury pool because it is not representative
- to hold a separate hearing on a legal issue at stake
- to require a judge to make conclusions of law governing an issue at stake
- to "**sequester**"—that is, keep secluded—those chosen for service on the jury

Obviously, the offering of these motions and the judge's rulings on them could make news. Among other things, some of these motions may begin to reflect the trial strategy, particularly of the defense. A legal reporter should be alert throughout the trial for indications of strategy of both sides.

In some jurisdictions, the opening of the trial may include an arraignment at which the accused person is asked to enter a formal plea. This may be no more than a *pro forma* reiteration of a plea already made, and thus it may not make news. It does provide, however, an opportunity for the accused person to change his mind and plead guilty, making it unnecessary to go forward with the trial.

Some trials may include, as part of the opening preliminaries, the entry of memoranda containing **stipulations**—that is, statements of agreement between prosecution and defense regarding facts or legal questions, removing those from contest during the trial. These may include newsworthy material.

C. SELECTION OF A JURY

The process of picking a jury may be the most laborious, perhaps the most uninteresting, part of a trial. But it will provide the first reliable indication, in court, of the strategy that each side in the case intends to pursue. Each may be expected to use the occasion not only to try to shape the jury to its advantage, but also to try to "make points" with the persons who may wind up serving as members of the jury.

In some jurisdictions, the process may be closed to the press. The fact of closing may produce a news story, of course, and it may provoke a legal dispute between the press and the court.

In its simplest form, the jury-selection process works this way:

1. Assembly of a **venire,** a set number of jurors drawn from all jurors available for service during a given period. If possible, the jury will be chosen from the initial venire. But if that is exhausted, another will be assembled until a full jury plus alternate jurors, if necessary, is chosen.

2. Each venire, or part of a venire, will be brought into the courtroom, so that the judge may describe the case in general terms, introduce the lawyers, read a witness list and make general inquiries as to the availability of individuals on that venire to serve in that case. At this time, the judge may excuse jurors who have valid reasons for not serving, such as sickness, hardship or binding commitments. This is a matter of discretion with the judge.

3. Then, the **voir dire** begins. That is the process of questioning jurors— individually or in groups—so that each side may decide whether to accept or oppose individuals for jury service. The questioning may be done by the judge alone, by lawyers on each side or by the judge as well as the lawyers.

Challenges

Each side has a specified number of **peremptory challenges**—that is, opportunities to exclude individuals from service without any stated reason for doing so. Each side will also have **challenges for cause**—that is, opportunities to try to have individuals excluded from service for specific stated reasons. The number of challenges for cause may be unlimited. It is up to the judge to decide whether to allow or deny each challenge for cause. If one side challenges a potential juror for cause, the other may try to "rehabilitate" that juror—that is, ask him questions that will persuade the judge that the juror is acceptable despite the challenge for cause. Because one side loses in its first effort at challenging for cause does not mean it may not try again and again—within limits that a judge may set.

If the lawyers are allowed to participate directly in the voir dire, the prosecution usually will start the questioning, followed by the defense.

Questioning of Potential Jurors

The kinds of questions that may be asked of potential jurors vary widely. Some customary questions, however, involve the juror's awareness of the case and possible preconceptions or predilections about it, the juror's response to publicity about the case, the juror's background and philosophy, the juror's willingness to convict even if in so doing he knows a severe penalty will or may be imposed, the juror's reaction to specific categories or kinds of evidence (without mentioning the actual evidence that would be offered later), the juror's understanding of such rudimentary legal issues as the presumption of innocence and the prosecution's burden of proof, the juror's reaction to some types of witnesses that may be called to testify.

This process continues until a full jury is seated. If the case is one in which alternate jurors are chosen (something that is often done if the case seems likely to run for several weeks, with the risk of losing jurors along the way because of personal complications), each side will have a similar opportunity to question and to challenge individuals on the venire.

The Process as News

To a legal reporter, the jury-selection process poses a considerable professional challenge. It is, or can be, quite a sophisticated exercise. Superficially, however, it may appear to be quite boring and repetitive, and thus not a fit subject for news stories.

In fact, it can provide not only good feature stories—on the way in which lawyers and the judge handle themselves, on the character of the jurors and the chosen jury—but also good news or interpretive stories. There will be various attempts by each side to try to create a favorable reaction among potential jurors, there may be considerable testing of points of strategy and kinds of evidence, there can be some fascinating maneuvers showing each side's attempt to frustrate the assumed or known "game plan" of the other side, there may even be evident conflicts between members of the legal team on one side.

Much of the atmosphere of the trial can be set by the way in which the jury-selection process is managed. The lawyers, for example, may use that time for testing the mood and tolerance of the trial judge. They also may use it for examining the reaction of jurors and of spectators to key points in the case. These may be endeavors of refined subtlety; they may be blunt and coarse or something in-between.

The reporter would be well advised, at all times, to watch for the "human dimension" in this process. Most readers or listeners, potential jurors themselves sooner or later, may be quite fascinated with the accounts of what this process truly is like.

Formalities and Motions

After a full jury is chosen, there will be a few formalities that may produce some moments of drama, or at least human interest, such as the swearing-in of the jury, formal confrontation of the jury with the accused person, or reading of the indictment.

When each day of trial opens, or during the jury-selection process, or at times of recess or other interruptions, lawyers in the case may continue the process of filing motions. These may include periodic motions by the defense for mistrial, for dismissal of charges, for production of evidence, to suppress evidence, for service of subpoenas on witnesses, for provision of daily transcripts for the lawyers, for the accused to be allowed to join as "co-counsel" in defending himself.

Some of these motions may be handled simply by filing documents to which a judge may respond immediately, orally or in writing. But some may be argued at hearings, usually with the jurors or potential jurors out of the room. Many of them may produce legal issues that could figure in any appeals after the trial.

Along the way, perhaps during the trial, the prosecution may decide to reduce the charge. In some circumstances, it may even decide to dismiss or **nolle pros** the charge, thus ending the case at that point.

D. OPENING STATEMENTS

The first time that the lawyers in a case have "the stage" to themselves will be in their **opening statements.** These are not always allowed. In some jurisdictions it is a matter of the judge's discretion whether to permit any such statement.

Basically, an opening statement is a summary of that side's case: some idea of its fundamental strategy will be offered, the legal points it hopes to make may be outlined, and the evidence it expects to offer may be discussed in fairly general terms.

In its potential impact on the jury, however, such a statement may be much more than a case summary. It may be a dramatic, perhaps even emotional, pitch for the jury's sympathy or allegiance. It may fix in jurors' minds impressions or arguments that may govern their reaction throughout the case, perhaps qualifying the way in which they will hear the evidence.

Clearly then, this may be the first highlight of the trial. The legal reporter not only will get, much of the time, a good story out of this step in the case, but also may be able to check and alter his earlier findings on the likely strategy to be pursued by each side. The occasion also will show him, for the first time, some indication of the jury's responses.

Sometimes a lawyer will have prepared his opening statement, and a reporter should seek access to such a statement, in advance if possible. In most instances, the statement will be wholly or largely extemporaneous.

E. THE EVIDENCE

The heart of the case—and the part that has the most continuing news potential—is the presentation of the evidence. Here, basically, is where each side has to make its case. A great deal of the procedural maneuvering, before and during the trial, will be aimed solely at influencing the body of evidence that will develop in the case.

Types of Evidence

There are two types of evidence—**direct** and **circumstantial**—and they are offered in two forms—oral testimony of witnesses, or physical **exhibits,** including documents. **Direct evidence** usually is that which speaks for itself: eyewitness accounts, a confession, a weapon or "instrumentality" of crime. **Circumstantial evidence** usually is that which merely suggests something by implication: the appearance of the scene of a crime, testimony that suggests a connection or link with a crime, physical evidence that suggests criminal activity.

Strict rules govern the kinds of evidence that may be admitted into a trial (see earlier in this chapter), and the progress of introduction or presentation of evidence is governed by quite formal rules.

The Evidentiary Process

This, briefly, is the way the process works:

1. The prosecution opens by presenting its witnesses and other evidence.

Evidence in the form of exhibits will be offered to accompany the oral testimony of witnesses.

Witnesses for the prosecution are first subject to **direct** questioning by prosecutors. Then, they are subject to **cross-examination** by the defense lawyer. The prosecutor may then conduct a **re-direct examination** to deal with points raised during defense questioning. Finally, the defense may try to deal with points raised during "re-direct" by a final cross-examination.

One of the main tactics in cross-examination is to **impeach** the witness or the evidence. (In this sense, impeach means to reduce or destroy its credibility.) Evidence used to impeach a witness—such as evidence of prior criminal convictions—usually is admitted into a case under more relaxed standards than is evidence used to prove guilt. By taking the witness stand himself, the accused person opens himself to possible "impeachment" by the use of such evidence.

At some points along the way, the jury may be sent out of the courtroom while disputed evidence is presented, giving the judge an opportunity to decide whether the evidence is to be admitted and thus to be heard or seen by the jury.

At many points along the way, **objections** may be raised by one side or the other to specific questions asked by the other side, on the ground that some **rule of evidence** is being violated. The judge ordinarily will decide those immediately, **sustaining** or **overruling** the objection. The objecting side may then note an **exception** so that there is a record of its opposition to the question, for purposes of maintaining an issue for appeal.

2. When the prosecution has finished offering its **case-in-chief,** it is then the defense's turn to offer its case, by presenting witnesses and evidence. Remember that the defense is not obliged to present any defense. If it does so, then, it takes the risk that its defense may in fact not help its side, and might even hurt it. One of the most difficult decisions for the defense is whether to put the accused person on the stand, thus subjecting him to possibly damaging questioning (including **impeachment** of his credibility) by the prosecution.

The process of presenting the defense's case is the same as for the prosecution.

3. The prosecution then gets an opportunity to try to strengthen any points in its case that might have been weakened or undermined by the defense's case. This is called the **rebuttal.**

4. Finally, the defense gets an opportunity for rebuttal, too.

Mid-Trial Motions

Between steps 1 and 2—that is, after the state has **rested** (concluded) its case-in-chief—the defense customarily will be entitled to make a series of basic motions.

Probably the most significant one is a motion for **"non-suit"** (in some jurisdictions, a **motion to acquit**). This is a defense plea to end the case at that point by withholding it from the jury, on the ground that the prosecution's evidence is insufficient to convict. In ruling on such a motion, the judge ordinarily must consider all of the prosecution evidence as if it were true, and must draw all **inferences** from the evidence in "the light most favorable to the prosecution." If, after such a review, the judge believes that there is a reasonable doubt on any element of the crime, he will grant the motion for non-suit or acquittal, and the case will be over. If the motion is granted, the accused person may not be tried again, since a jury has already been selected to try him—in technical terms, "jeopardy has attached" to the accused, and the Constitution forbids "**double jeopardy**" (being tried twice on the same charge).

If the case involves an offense for which there are "**lesser-included offenses**," then a motion for non-suit or acquittal may be made on each of the offenses, one at a time.

Other motions that might be made at this point include **motions to strike** evidence (remove it from the case, with the jury instructed to disregard it), to dismiss the charges on grounds of misuse of prosecutorial discretion in even bringing the case, to call expert witnesses, and to perform various laboratory tests on prosecution evidence.

Post-Evidence Motions

After all the evidence is in—that is, after the defense has rested, and all rebuttal testimony, if any, has been given—the defense again may make a series of motions, including renewal of the motion for non-suit (acquittal) and the motion to dismiss, as well as offering a motion for a **directed verdict** of not guilty. A directed verdict, if granted, is by the judge, and it takes the case away from the jury before any deliberation.

The defense may also make further motions to strike or exclude evidence that has been offered.

Evidence as News

The entire evidence phase of a trial customarily is open to the public and press. There may be an exception when a judge, on his own or in reaction to the pleas of one side or the other, decides that some evidence should not be disclosed to the public. He may order an item of evidence sealed, or he may order the courtroom closed to spectators and the press during presentation of the evidence. This is less likely when a jury has been **sequestered** than when the jurors are allowed to come and go for each day's session. Obviously, any such order by a judge might be challenged by the press through its attorneys.

As a matter of law, there is no constitutional guarantee that every criminal trial will be open to the public and to press coverage in all of its phases. The guarantee of a "public trial" often has meant, in practice, less than *full* public or press access throughout.

The right to a "public trial," the Supreme Court has ruled, is a right that belongs to the accused person, not to the public. Even so, the nation has a long history of open trials, and the public and the press should expect to have access except in the rarest of cases. This monitoring role of the press may be as important to the accused person as it is to the public at large, because it opens up his prosecution to wider scrutiny.

The evidence phase of the trial is unquestionably the most crucial legally and often journalistically. Not all of the evidence, however, will be newsworthy. Much of it may be simply the legal "building blocks" necessary to support other evidence. (For example, witnesses may give extensive testimony to show who had custody over a body in a murder case, or who had custody over evidence.) Such testimony will affect the admissibility of the evidence it is meant to support.

This kind of testimony illustrates a key point that the legal reporter must always keep in mind: the importance of evidence in a legal sense and its importance as news may be quite different. A piece of very newsworthy evidence may never become a part of a trial because it is ruled inadmissible or because its introduction is dependent upon some other evidence, and that other evidence does not get into the case.

Problems of admissibility. In law, the test of evidence is its admissibility and that, as has been said, is controlled by quite rigid rules. Because it is inadmissible does not mean that it is *not* newsworthy.

The reporter, while knowing the difference for purposes of deciding *what* to report, obviously cannot ignore writing about the judge's determination about admissibility. Such rulings may themselves make news because they may affect significantly the course of the trial.

The reporter also needs to keep his readers or listeners informed when there is evidence that has been offered but not admitted. It might be advisable for the reporter, when discussing this occurrence in his story, to include some discussion of the legal reasons for this seeming anomaly.

One way to stress such a development is to note that the offered evidence was presented while the jury was out of the courtroom—to enable the judge to rule upon whether the jury may come back in to hear or see it.

The reporter also needs to know the significance, in law and in news, of the limitations which may be imposed upon the jury in considering evidence that *has* been admitted. For example, in some jurisdictions, photographs may not be offered as evidence in and of themselves—that is, they may not be shown to the jury as proof of what they show. Rather, they may be offered only to illustrate the testimony of the witness the photographs are supposed to support. The jurors may have trouble keeping the distinction in mind, and it is fair and proper for the reporter to point that out in his story.

The fact that a given item of evidence has been offered to support one side's witness, or entire case, does not mean that the other side may not make use of it to try to help its own witnesses or case. Once evidence has been admitted, it is open for use by both prosecution and defense, and the ways in which this is done may make interesting news.

Keys to strategy. As the reporter watches the evidence unfold, he will want to remain on the alert to see how it fits the basic strategy of the side that is offering it. He should assist the reader's appreciation of this less obvious dimension by pointing out—when he can determine it—the rationale behind the offer of a given item or phase of evidence.

Each witness, and each item of physical evidence, will have been chosen by the side offering it because it was considered necessary or favorable to its side. Each side is not obliged to offer all of the evidence that it gathers during its investigation and preparation of the case (although the prosecution is obliged to share with the defense anything discovered that might help the *defense's* case.) Full disclosure of each side's evidence is encouraged, but not demanded by compelling rules of law. If a reporter is aware of evidence that one side holds but does not use, he should write about that without being concerned that it will not be formally "in" the case. He should point out, however, that the jury won't (at least probably won't) learn about such evidence, and thus its verdict won't be based upon that.

Besides watching how each side's evidence demonstrates its strategy and shows its case unfold, the reporter should watch the evidence for obvious or apparent weaknesses in it. He should seek the assistance of the other side, as much as possible, in making such analyses. This may be somewhat inhibited either by general ethical restraints on lawyers, or by specific "gag" orders issued in a given case.

When evidence is subjected to cross-examination, the reporter should be alert to the issue of credibility of the witness and of the evidence. Attacks on credibility ("impeachment") are often the main core of cross-examination. But the reporter also should watch how the cross-examination is used to try to make "points" with the jury, or even to build the case for the side doing the cross-examination.

When re-direct examination comes, the key question—for news value as well as legal effect—is whether a witness or an item of evidence can be "rehabilitated" if it has been weakened ("impeached") by the cross-examination. The process of attempting to weaken may resume on the second cross-examination after re-direct questioning.

In covering this entire phase of the case, the reporter should be on the alert for the key or central testimony and exhibits that each side offers. Those will tell him much about strategy and may go far to demonstrate strength or weakness in the offering side's case. The reporter should seek to learn from each side how it evaluates its witnesses and exhibits.

Sometimes, "expert" witnesses may be most important to a side's case. More often, however, the "best" witnesses newswise are likely to be those who are not expert in anything, but merely tell the part of the story that they personally know.

Undoubtedly, the most significant witness for the defense will be the accused person (the **defendant**), if he does testify. The defense, of course, is not obliged to put the accused on the stand, because the Fifth Amendment protects him from that if he wishes. The reporter should be prepared to evaluate the meaning either of putting the accused on as a witness or declining to do so. When the defendant does testify, the reporter should seek to determine, as fully as he can, the strategy behind this.

The courtroom scene. Throughout, the reporter should remember to tell his readers about the courtroom scene—the demeanor of witnesses, lawyers, judge, jurors and the defendant, the atmosphere in the room, including the behavior of spectators, and the "color" of the testimony and exhibits.

When motions are offered during the evidence phase, these should be covered fully. The reporter should tell his readers or listeners the legal reasons for such maneuvering, and should seek—where it seems important—to discuss the legal precedents or doctrines which govern specific kinds of motions and the judge's rulings upon them. Wherever possible, the reporter should rely upon motions in written form. The same is true, generally, of the judge's rulings upon them.

The reporter also should cover fully the maneuvers or gestures that each side's lawyers use when the other side's case is being presented; many of these may be designed to divert the jury's attention from the opposition's evidence. The offering of objections is a tactic often used for this purpose. Another is for a lawyer to approach the bench for a conference while the other side is questioning a witness.

F. CLOSING ARGUMENTS

When all the evidence in a case is "in"—that is, put before the jury—each side has one last chance to try to persuade the jury to decide its way. This comes in closing arguments or, as these are sometimes called, "jury speeches," "summing-up" or "**summations.**" The defense has a constitutional right to offer a closing argument. As a matter of fairness, the prosecution also is entitled to make a closing argument.

It usually is within the trial judge's discretion how long the final speeches may be. If there is more than one lawyer on a side, the judge may require that they divide the time, and he may establish the order in which they speak.

In general, the only restraints upon the content of closing arguments are legal ethics and propriety. There is a possibility, however, that a prosecutor may bring about a legal issue, to be tested on appeal, if he makes an improper remark or argument which prejudices the jury.

Neither side, however, is free to use any argument it wishes. Both are bound to limit their speeches to the evidence that has been admitted into the case. They may suggest all reasonable inferences which a jury might draw from that evidence, but they may not go beyond it. Neither side is free to misrepresent the evidence.

Normally, the prosecutor will make the first argument followed by the defense lawyer. In most jurisdictions, the prosecution may give a final rebuttal argument. Each side is free to cast its own argument without regard to what the other says; technically, they are not answering each other, but making independent appeals to the jury.

The News Potential

It is obvious that closing arguments may make news. Aside from the rhetoric used—and that, in itself, may make interesting or significant reading—the content of the argument will tell much about the strength or weakness of each side's case and will reveal the strategy as it has evolved during the course of the trial.

Sometimes the strategy at the end will vary considerably from that which one side had hoped to follow at the beginning. This might be the case, for example, when important witnesses or items of evidence have been ruled inadmissible and thus kept out of the case, or when some part of the original charges was dropped along the way.

The reporter should compare the strategies reflected in the final speeches with those known to have existed at the outset, and offer reasons for the differences, if any.

In actually covering the jury speeches, the reporter should remain aware of the atmosphere and the personalities, and should pay the closest attention to the reaction of the jurors.

He must be careful not to suggest in his story that the inferences suggested by one side or the other necessarily are the ones the jury will itself draw.

G. JURY INSTRUCTIONS

Before a judge will permit a case to go to a jury for deliberations and a verdict, he will instruct it in the law. That is, he will tell the jury how legal rules and principles govern the scope of their discretion. This is sometimes described as "**charging**" the jury.

A judge is responsible himself for making the instructions or "charge," but each side—in many jurisdictions—may have a right to propose instructions to him, usually in writing. If he chooses not to include a proposed instruction, that may pose a legal issue to be raised on appeal. The way he phrases an instruction may also raise an issue for appeal. After a judge has finished his instructions and the jury has left the courtroom, one side or the other may then raise objections to instructions and seek to have the judge call the jury back in for a change in or addition to instructions.

In his instructions, the judge may summarize the evidence (though this is not allowed in all jurisdictions); he will state the charge and outline the elements of the offense; he will advise the jury that it is the sole judge of the facts, of the credibility of witnesses and of the weight to be given any evidence; he will specify the legal limits on the jury's discretion; and he will spell out the possible verdicts that may be reached.

Many of the judge's instructions are likely to be statements of highly technical legal principles, phrased—as much as possible—in layman's language. Still, it is the reporter's duty to distill the instructions even further if he can. The instructions are crucial to the case, and perhaps to an appeal, and they should be shared with the reading or listening public. It is not very often true, however, that a judge will use quotable rhetoric during his instructions.

H. JURY DELIBERATIONS

Juries deliberate in secret. Each jury probably will develop its own "dynamics"—that is, its own process for discussion and voting. It probably will pick a foreman after leaving the courtroom to begin deliberations.

From time to time, the jury may seek further or clarifying instructions from the judge and may ask to have testimony or evidence reviewed or read again. Usually, the judge will respond to such requests only in open court, with both sides present.

The reporter generally will be able, after the trial is over, to interview at least some of the jurors in an attempt to reconstruct the deliberation process. Some juries, however, agree among themselves not to discuss the case after trial, and sometimes juries are put under restrictions by trial judges not to discuss the case even after it is over.

In some jurisdictions, the names of jurors have been withheld from public disclosure on the theory that they otherwise may be subjected to press or other public harassment over their verdict.

The judge's handling of the jury on such matters, of course, may pose legal obstacles to press coverage, and thus a reporter's organization may seek to challenge some of the judicial controls or limitations.

I. THE VERDICT

The end of the case, the result toward which the entire trial aims, comes with the jury's decision to convict, acquit, or to remain irreconcilably in disagreement.

This is, clearly, the dramatic high point of the case, for both sides and for the public in general. Its drama is heightened by the very simplicity of the result. A jury's discretion as to verdict usually is limited to findings of guilty or not-guilty, in toto or in varying combinations. Even when a **jury** is **"hung"**—that is, it is incapable of agreeing upon a verdict—the result is simple and plain.

By the time the verdict is announced—and this will be done in open court—the reporter covering the trial should be fully aware of the exact range of the jury's discretion about verdict. He needs to know what the jury declined to do as much as what it agreed to do in its verdict.

The "Hung" Jury

The fact that a jury reports to a judge that it is **"hung"** in disagreement may not mean the end of the matter. In some jurisdictions, judges give what is sometimes called the **"dynamite charge"** or the **"Allen charge"** (the name comes from a Supreme Court decision allowing the practice constitutionally). This is a little speech to the jury by the judge, stressing the jury's duty to agree if possible, the individual juror's duty to listen to the others with sympathy and generosity, and the interest of the state—and the accused—in having the matter settled. The judge may not, however, use such a charge to coerce the jury into agreement, and the way in which he delivers a "dynamite charge" may raise a legal issue for the appeal.

If the jury ultimately cannot agree on a verdict, it so notifies the judge, and he declares a **mistrial.** Under those circumstances, the prosecution is free to put the accused person on trial again, perhaps on the same charges and using the same evidence. A mistrial may in fact result in a dismissal or a recasting of the charges.

J. POST-VERDICT MOTIONS

If the jury finds the accused person guilty of one or more charges, the defense may offer a series of motions to overturn the verdict. It may seek a **directed judgment of acquittal "notwithstanding the verdict"** (sometimes called a **"judgment n.o.v.,"** referring to the Latin phrase, **non obstante veredicto**). That is simply a request that the judge ignore the jury's result and declare the accused person not guilty. The defense also may make a motion for a new trial.

Such motions are rarely granted, and thus the reporter normally will treat them as routine. They will make news only if granted.

After a guilty verdict has been reached, and post-verdict motions have failed, the defense lawyer may be required to file a formal notice of appeal if he intends to appeal. That may not necessarily come on the same day as the verdict. Obviously, it could be a newsworthy development when it occurs. (Appeals are discussed in the next chapter.)

K. THE SENTENCE

The process of imposing sentence may be brief and simplistic, or it may be lengthy and complex. Whatever form it takes, however, it involves a many-faceted decision—even for a judge who believes it is simple and straight-forward.

There really is no sure way for the reporter—or anyone else, for that matter—to determine precisely which factors were decisive for the judge in selecting a sentence.

Of course, he will be controlled, to a greater or lesser extent, by laws governing sentences for specific crimes. But there is a wide element of discretion most of the time, and the judge may use it in ways that are hard even for him to define. His use of that discretion is not completely beyond review by a higher court, but it nevertheless is a wide discretion. (In some jurisdictions, sentences may *not* be reviewed at all on appeal, except when the sentence is death.)

Forms of Sentences

Sentences may take these forms:

- Death (only for murder).
- Definite terms in jail or prison, with or without possibility of parole.
- Indefinite or indeterminate sentences, meaning a sentence of "not less than" or "not more than" a set term.
- Multiple sentences for multiple offenses, with the judge determining whether the sentences are to be served simultaneously (**concurrent sentences**) or in succession (**consecutive sentences**).
- Limited forms of confinement in correctional or treatment facilities other than jails or prisons.
- **Suspended sentences**—that is, those for which some or all of the period of confinement does *not* have to be served.

- Probation—that is, no confinement, but close supervision by an officer of the court. (Most judges impose probation when they give a suspended sentence.)
- Fines of varying amounts—alone or in combination with jail terms.

More often that not, it is the judge alone who decides on the sentence. In some jurisdictions, however, the jury is given a role—at least an advisory one—in the sentencing process (for example, in death penalty cases).

The prosecutor and the defense lawyer may also be allowed an advisory role. Both are obliged to assist the judge if he requests. The defense lawyer has a duty to his client to be sure that the sentencing procedure is fair, and that all facts bearing on the sentencing decision are put before the judge.

In some jurisdictions, a sentencing hearing is held at which the judge hears each side discuss the factors that each believes should be taken into account. (This is required when the sentence could be death.)

Often, a judge will ask for a formal **sentencing report** before he decides what sentence to impose. Such a report, often prepared by a **probation officer,** will contain background material on the convicted person. Unlike formal evidence at a trial, the contents of this report are not tested by strict rules of admissibility. Usually—but not universally—the defense will have an opportunity to comment upon and perhaps to challenge derogatory information in such a report.

The process of actually imposing sentence is done in open court. The defendant must be present except in rare circumstances and often will be given an opportunity to make a statement on his own behalf—perhaps a plea for mercy, perhaps an admission of his error (formally, a plea of **allocution**)—and the prosecutor and defense lawyer may be allowed to make statements seeking to advise the judge. The degree of the prosecutor's discretion to recommend a sentence varies from jurisdiction to jurisdiction.

Sentencing as News

The entire sentencing process clearly is newsworthy. The reporter may not necessarily have access to all of it. For example, the pre-sentence report customarily is not a public document.

The reporter should be fully advised, even before a verdict is in, on the range of possible sentences in the case he is covering. At various points throughout a case, he will want to refer in his stories to the possible sentences. In reporting the actual sentence, he also will want to indicate what discretion the judge had and how he used it.

The entire process of sentencing in death penalty ("**capital punishment**") cases is controlled by quite strict and rigid constitutional limitations, and the reporter should be fully familiar with the process in his state. A death sentence is always news.

L. POST-TRIAL COVERAGE

When everything is finished in a trial, the reporter will still have obligations to provide continuing coverage of a newsworthy case.

Sometimes, there are press conferences—perhaps even by the judge. But even when there are no formal, scheduled press events, the reporter may want to pursue stories on the jury's deliberations, on the preparations for appeal, on preparations for serving the sentence and on the human consequences of the case—for all who were involved.

Just as importantly, the reporter should consider one or more interpretive stories attempting to "wrap-up" or to analyze the case. He may want to do stories, for example, on the performance of the prosecutor, the defense or the judge; on the strategies used and how they fared; on the meaning of the case in the development of new legal theories or the changing of old legal precepts; on the impact of the case on a community; and so on.

There is a continuing need for popular explanation of the legal process, and sometimes that need has to be postponed until after the "breaking news" of the trial itself has been covered. Very often a reporter will find that persons who can help him to understand what went on, and why, will not be available for interviews until the case has been tried. Access may indeed be quite free when the trial is over, and the reporter should seek to exploit that.

Special Problems in "Trial de Novo"

There is one form of criminal trial that is something of a hybrid, a cross between a trial and an appeal. For the legal reporter, however, it is more like a trial in its news dimensions, and thus it is discussed here rather than in the next chapter.

Ordinarily, **trial de novo** is a process used for the trial of cases that involve petty or minor criminal offenses. Those offenses will be tried in the first instance before a judge or magistrate, customarily without a jury. Such proceedings are quite simple and very often they will not even be recorded, except for the bench notes made by the judge or magistrate.

If the accused person is found guilty in that "first-tier" proceeding, he may then seek a **trial de novo** in another court, ranking somewhat higher in the hierarchy but still qualifying as a first-tier or trial court.

In that court, the case will be tried all over again, as if there had been no prior proceeding at all. Often, the right to a jury will exist at this second stage, but the accused person may waive it if he wishes.

The new trial will be conducted as any other criminal trial. The rules of evidence will be the same; the procedures will be the same. The trial is not to be influenced at all by the outcome of the first proceeding before a judge or magistrate.

The reporter will cover it as he does any criminal trial. There is, however, the special problem that it is, in fact, a "second chance" proceeding, a kind of appeal. The reporter thus will want to point out this facet in his stories. But he should be careful to stress that the verdict in the first proceeding is not in any way binding, or even relevant, to the new proceeding. It would be desirable, perhaps, to leave out any mention of the prior proceeding if the reporter is unable—for space or other reasons—to offer some explanation of the process.

7

Covering Criminal Cases:
The Appeal

A REPORTER FOLLOWING A CRIMINAL CASE ON APPEAL may find himself in the midst of the true development of law, where law grows beyond the particular to the general. It is a process that can be most satisfying to the journalist who is a serious student of the legal process.

But, as a newsman with a predominantly lay appetite in his work, he may also find that it is a rather sterile process. Law in the appeals court is not usually a continuation of the dramatic human contest of the trial courtroom. It is, much of the time, an inquiry into legal error in the atmosphere of a seminar.

A reporter who has experienced the battle of the courtroom and then pursues a case to the appeal is, perhaps like Ezekiel, coming upon a field of very dry bones. After being asked whether "these bones can live again," Ezekiel began to prophesy:

> As I prophesied there was a rustling sound and the bones fitted themselves together. As I looked, sinews appeared upon them, flesh covered them, and they were overlaid with skin.

But, the prophet then discovered that "there was no breath in them," and without breath, they could not come to life and rise to their feet as a "mighty host."

It is not stretching the analogy too far to suggest that the remnants of a criminal trial, seen from the vantage of an appeal, are a scattering of dry bones, much in need of being brought to life as news. The reporter's task, for his readers or listeners, is to put the wind of breath back into them. Some of the popular fascination with the human dimensions of the case may have to be recreated by the newsman.

The risk that always exists in legal reporting—that is, that the reporter will emphasize the legal issues on his beat beyond any likely interest of his readers or listeners—is the greatest in covering the appeals process. If the audience were made up solely or even largely of legal professionals, heavy emphasis on the legal questions at stake would be appropriate. But the audience probably will be largely illiterate in law. Its interest will be more mundane.

Some cleverness and ingenuity is required for the reporter to hold that interest at the same time that he conveys the real news of a criminal appeal: the determination of the purely legal questions raised. As in trial coverage, reporting and writing on the appeals process is best done by telling the law through the medium of the facts and personalities in a given case.

In a criminal appeal, the dominant personality still will be the defendant—now a convicted person. But the facts will become somewhat submerged, because they probably will not be in contest in the appeal. The reviewing court will take them largely as they came from the trial, and proceed from there.

There will be a shift of some emphasis to the institution of the appeals court and its personalities. There is a dynamic at work in these courts and among the judges who sit on them, and the reporter should turn a good deal of his attention to that. That should be, it bears repeating, against the background of one specific case, the one that produced the issues and the verdict that are at issue on appeal. A theory of law, the turn of mind of a judge, the direction of a court's rulings can best be described within the particular dimensions of that case.

The law that emerges from the appeals courts is not an abstraction, any more than is the verdict that emerges from the trial court. It affects real people in real ways, it settles an actual case or controversy.

But the judgment of the court settling a case or controversy, not its real-life result, is the legal news in a decision by an appeals case, and the reporter covering the courts must also convey that. Moreover, he should feel an obligation to deal as expansively as he can with the development of the law as such—in other words, the refinement of legal principle that will govern like cases when, in the future, they come to trial.

This chapter, like the others on criminal law, discusses the process step by step, showing first how an appeal moves forward and then how it creates news along the way.

A. APPEALS IN GENERAL

It is an American tradition, with very deep roots, that every person convicted of a crime should have a chance to appeal his case if he wishes. Interestingly, there is no such thing as a constitutional right to appeal a conviction. But, as Professor Delmar Karlen has commented:

> The right is so firmly established in practice that it has come to be regarded by the profession and the public as virtually inalienable.

What this means in a practical sense is that a person found guilty may file an appeal without asking a court's permission in advance. At the same time, however, it is a general rule that an appeal does not occur automatically; the convicted person must take the initiative with his lawyer; and he usually must do so within a specified period of time after the trial verdict is in (in technical terms, the appeal must be "timely"). There is one notable exception to this general rule: cases in which death sentences are imposed. Review of the death sentence (but not the guilty verdict) by the state supreme court must be automatic in every case.

General Characteristics

In most appeals courts in America, the initiative throughout the appeal process remains largely with the appealing party. Generally speaking, courts are not free to reach out beyond the questions and issues put to them by a party to consider other matters. The U.S. Supreme Court is free to do so, but it uses that authority most sparingly. Some other appeals courts have a similar authority under state law or state constitutional provisions.

Another general consideration in appeals is that they may be pursued most of the time only after a final **judgment** or decision has been issued by the court below. Ordinarily, even a controlling issue of law may not be appealed until after a decision has been reached on the case itself in a trial court. So-called **interlocutory appeals**—appeals to test an issue raised during the course of a trial, while the trial is still going on—are usually discouraged in most jurisdictions. The exceptions are just that: exceptional.

A further rule-of-thumb about appeals is that they are confined to the facts and the issues as they were put into contest in the trial court. Neither side in an appealed case is free, ordinarily, to go "outside the record" to bring up a question that was not presented when the case was on trial.

Even among the issues that may be raised on appeal, some selection may be made by the convicted person's lawyer as he prepares an appeal. Not every potential appealable issue necessarily will be raised. Again, it should be stressed that it is within the party's discretion to cite the issue or issues upon which he seeks to win a reversal of a conviction resulting in either a dismissal of charges or a new trial.

In criminal law, with only a few exceptions in a handful of states, only the convicted person has the right to appeal. The prosecutor is ordinarily forbidden to appeal if the person has been found not guilty, because of the constitutional rule against more than one trial for the same crime—that is, **"double jeop-**

ardy." Where prosecution appeals are allowed, only issues of law may be appealed, not the judgment of acquittal. The idea behind such appeals is to obtain clarification on a crucial law question.

Usually, the first appeal will bring a case to an end, even though by law a person may have a right to pursue his case even beyond the initial appeal level. (See discussion of supreme court cases, below.)

Categories of Appeals

The discussion that follows deals with the two general types of appeals and then with appeals to the supreme courts. The supreme courts are another tier in the appeals process, but they are special and thus are treated separately.

There are two broad categories of proceedings in which a convicted person may attempt to overturn the verdict against him: the **"direct" appeal,** which is the challenge pursued right after the trial is over, and the **"collateral attack"** or **"post-conviction remedy,"** which is the challenge that may be pursued (depending upon state and federal laws) after the original conviction has become final.

A conviction is said to have become final:

- if the verdict is left unchallenged because no direct appeal is filed;
- if an appeal was filed, but not within the specified time limit (it was not **timely**);
- if a verdict has been appealed, but was upheld on review at the highest level to which the **direct appeal** has been pursued.

There are variations from the norm, but direct appeals in most jurisdictions are pursued in the "second tier" of courts, the intermediate courts of appeals above the trial court, and post-conviction remedies start out in the court where the trial was held, and move upward to the "second tier" if frustrated in the trial court.

Direct appeal customarily is allowed as a matter of right—in other words, the convicted person need not obtain an appeals court's advance permission to file. There are some tiers in the state and federal system, however, where appeal is allowed only as a matter of discretion with the court to which an appeal is sought. That is true of some state supreme courts, and it is true of the U.S. Supreme Court (see below). Many of the forms of post-conviction remedies are discretionary, but federal **habeas corpus** (see below) may be pursued as a matter of right.

"Quasi-Appeals"

There are two other kinds of criminal proceeding that, outwardly at least, seem to have some of the attributes of an appeal because they do involve action by a court other than the original or "first tier" trial court. One is **trial de novo,** which is discussed at the close of Chapter 6. The other is a trial that is **removed** (transferred) from state court to federal court.

The **removal** procedure is not an appeal as such, because there has been no trial in the state court before removal. The procedure, restricted in its use in criminal cases to those involving claimed violations of federal constitutional rights, provides that a case where such violations are a strong likelihood may be transferred before trial to the federal court, and then trial goes forward in the federal tribunal. The federal court will apply state, not federal law, however.

B. DIRECT APPEALS

In every jurisdiction, it is the practice to allow direct appeals. This is the tradition of a "right of appeal—once." Between states, the actual process of direct appeal varies.

It is more common for states to have only trial-level courts and then, above them, a state supreme court to which appeals from guilty verdicts in criminal cases are taken. But in a minority of the states, there is a middle tier or intermediate court to which appeals from guilty verdicts first go. When such "second tier" courts exist, it is often the rule that any appeal from them to the state supreme court is discretionary with that court, not mandatory.

The Beginning Stages

The appeal process begins with the filing of a **notice of appeal,** which is simply a brief notation of the convicted person's intention to appeal the verdict. Sometimes it will specify the trial errors which the appeal will seek to correct.

The next step is for the appealing party to designate the parts of the trial record that are to be prepared for the **record** in the appeal. The parts to be designated will depend upon the errors cited in the appeal. These excerpts from the trial record will accompany transcripts of a stenographic report of the oral proceedings in the trial court, and together they constitute the **record** on appeal. The other side may also be allowed to designate parts of the record.

Next, there may be filing of **briefs**—that is, written arguments of the legal issues being tested on appeal. Some appeals courts dispense with formal briefs and rely only on the record of the trial proceedings.

Hearings and Deliberation

A **hearing on the merits** or **oral argument** may be held in the appeals court, and this may be brief or it may consume several days, depending upon the complexity of the case and the issues, and local court rules.

In some appeals courts, a memorandum on the case, for the private guidance of the judges, may be prepared by law clerks before or after the hearing. After argument, the case probably will be assigned to a judge to prepare a proposed opinion. (In some appeals courts, written opinions are the exception rather than the rule, and decisions are issued in order form only.)

The News Potential

The reporter may want to cover the briefs as they are filed, the hearing or argument, and the opinion or decision when issued. Normally, each of those steps in the appeal is public, and the press is allowed full access.

Seldom will a reporter write about the preparation or designation of the record.

As a case begins its movement through the appeal process, the reporter will be monitoring the development of the issues—and the omission of issues that might have been raised but were not. He may compare those with the strategies and results at the trial, watching to see how and where the emphasis changes, if it does.

The briefs. Where they are required, briefs may be of substantial practical help to the reporter. Normally, he will rely upon the research that the lawyers put into them, rather than doing his own independent search for precedents and authorities.

In fact, a reporter should report the case as the parties see it, not as he might have viewed it were he in their position. Obviously, he may consult legal experts, including practicing attorneys and law professors, for their commentary or analysis of the case as it develops.

The facts. Again, it is important to stress that, in monitoring the development of the legal issues, the reporter should do it in the factual context of the case he is covering. He should seek to determine how the outcome of the legal questions will affect the convicted person directly or indirectly.

The argument. In covering the oral argument, the reporter will encounter for the first time in the case the phenomenon of the multiple-judge court. He will want to pay the closest attention to the interaction of the judges on the court, because that may bear importantly upon how the tribunal does its work and upon the kinds of decisions it is likely to reach.

An argument in an appeals court may have some drama in it, but nothing to compare with the drama of the jury speeches in the trial. The argument probably will be more refined and often will be more expansive philosophically and legally than were any of the oral presentations at the trial. The stress will be on the law, not on the facts, because the law is the field of combat on appeal.

The decision. When an appeals court issues its decisions through oral or written opinions, spelling out the rationale for the court's judgment or ruling, the reporter often will find these documents quite quotable. Indeed, they may be eloquent essays on the law. However artfully they are composed, they will reveal much about the judges on the court—their philosophy, their scholarship, their literary style, their attitude about the use of judicial authority and discretion.

Fairly typically, an appeals court's opinion will open with a brief statement of the issues to be decided, a recitation—usually quite brief and often incomplete for the reporter's purposes—of the facts in the case, a discussion of the rulings upon the issues and why they were reached, and, finally, a judgment or concluding order. The opinion may be signed by a judge or issued by the court in its own name (**per curiam**).

The reporter would be well advised to be prepared, in advance, on the facts of the case because of the propensity of many appeals courts to omit facts that may be essential, in a news sense, to a full exposition of the case in the media.

In writing about opinions resulting from appeals, the reporter will want to relate the legal results as much as possible to the convicted person involved. But he also will want to give his readers a full account of the legal rationale for the ruling, particularly pointing out where, if at all, the court set new precedents or established new legal doctrine.

The news in such rulings is twofold: the result in the case itself and the development of the law. It is impossible to generalize about which is likely to make the "lead" of a story. Sometimes, the novelty of the development in the law will justify leading with that, with the story thus emerging as somewhat more general in application. At other times, the factual result itself plainly will claim the "lead."

Rehearings. In some appeals courts, the first ruling that emerges may not be the court's final one. That will be true where the court sits in **panels** of fewer than the whole number of judges on the court and decisions of the panel are subject to review by the full court (sitting **en banc**). Review **en banc**, typically, is a matter of discretion, reserved for issues of novelty or great moment.

Another quite common characteristic of appeals courts is that they may allow a case to be **reheard** even after they have given their decision on it. Sometimes, this is a matter of rehearing **en banc** the decision of a panel, and sometimes the full court, having heard a case once **en banc,** may rehear it.

Rehearings, however, are sufficiently uncommon that they almost always will produce a news story of some significance.

Other stories. Most of a legal reporter's stories on criminal appeals will be based on decisions in specific cases. But the reporter should also try to report and write analytical stories on the appellate process in general and the trends that he will discover in a given appeals court.

(Where a state has no intermediate appeals court, the process described above will exist in much that same form in the state supreme court. The final section of this chapter deals separately, however, with supreme courts, state and federal.)

C. POST-CONVICTION REMEDIES (COLLATERAL ATTACKS)

Once a conviction has become final, because it was not appealed or because a direct appeal failed, a variety of alternative remedies may be potentially available to the convicted person. These are the post-conviction or collateral remedies.

They are not, in a strict sense, "appeals." They are, rather, attempts to start over, usually in the trial court, to undo the consequences of the conviction. They will have some of the attributes of appeals, though, because they are based upon errors either in the original trial or in the sentence. But they are not restricted to cases that have gone to trial, because among the remedies are a motion to withdraw a guilty plea entered before a trial could begin or a motion to correct or reduce a sentence imposed following a guilty plea.

Types of Remedies

Varying widely from state to state, and between the states and the federal judicial system, the most common post-conviction remedies are:

- **petition for writ of habeas corpus**—a plea to release a person held in custody on the ground that he is wrongly confined because his rights have been violated in the prosecution or appeal
- **petition for writ of error coram nobis**—a plea to overturn a conviction because of error in the trial or sentencing process
- motion for new trial based on newly discovered evidence
- motion to reduce or set aside a sentence
- motion to correct a sentence illegally imposed
- motion to withdraw a plea of guilty
- motion for leave to file a **nunc pro tunc** appeal—an appeal that would not be allowed if the normal rules governing appeal were observed.

The most significant of these is **habeas corpus.** Every convicted person may, if he wishes, pursue this form of collateral attack through the federal courts under federal law and constitutional rulings. If the continued detention of the person cannot be justified, he is to be released.

Under controlling decisions of the Supreme Court, there is no binding limit on the number of times that a convicted person may seek such a writ. (The court has, however, put some limits on the use of habeas corpus to raise some specified constitutional questions in state cases.) The convicted person may not file his first petition for a writ of habeas corpus until after he had used up all of his opportunities of direct appeal (in legal terms, exhausted his remedies).

More importantly, there is a practical limitation: few habeas corpus cases succeed in reality. Many are filed by prisoners themselves and are without real substance. Hundreds are disposed of by the federal courts in summary fashion. Out of the vast numbers attempted, only a minute percentage result in the release of the convicted person. The federal courts are particularly reluctant to overturn most state convictions.

In those states that allow post-conviction remedies, the form varies widely. It may be somewhat akin to the federal writ of habeas corpus, with the challenge based upon a claimed violation of a right guaranteed by state law or constitution or by the U.S. Constitution.

It also may take the form of some other ancient writ, such as the **writ of error coram nobis.** That means, literally, error "before us." This is a request to the trial court to release the convicted person because of an error committed in the trial stage.

There may also be a **nunc pro tunc appeal.** That means, literally, a "now for then" appeal. It is a form of appeal pursued after a convicted person has failed to file an appeal when he should have. If such an appeal is allowed, it means that the appeal may be pursued as it normally would have been if properly filed, thus overlooking the failure to appeal in a **"timely"** fashion.

Characteristics of the Remedies

These remedies exist to alleviate the consequences of criminal conviction through a "second chance" proceeding. They provide means to ease the rigid time limits and procedural restrictions of the regular appeals process, and are a means to insure that a convicted person's constitutional rights be husbanded as carefully as possible.

Among the grounds upon which a convicted person may pursue one or more of these remedies are: that rights guaranteed by federal or state laws or constitutions were violated; that the law under which the person was convicted is invalid; that the court which tried him had no jurisdiction to do so; that there is evidence, previously not offered or considered, to justify overturning the conviction; that the law has changed sufficiently in procedure or substance to justify overturning the conviction; or that the sentence was invalid because it was excessive or was not legally imposed.

The procedure for handling these remedies is basically simple: a petition or motion is filed, a hearing may be held on it in the trial court (before a single judge without a jury), a decision is reached granting or denying the petition or motion, and an appeal is pursued through the regular route to higher courts.

The News Potential

Coverage of collateral attacks by the reporter will be much the same as in covering regular criminal trials and appeals. The filing of a petition or motion, however, is considered quite routine, and thus seldom will make a news story—except, of course, where the case is particularly celebrated because of the nature of the crime or the identity of the convicted person or the victim.

Hearings on these matters often are quite brief, and they may be perfunctory in scope. If the basis for seeking the remedy is the discovery of new evidence, however, the chances are that that will provide a basis for covering the proceeding.

Except in the most routine cases, a reporter should expect to write a story about decisions reached on collateral attacks. If the case was worth covering in the first instance, it at least is worth reporting when a post-conviction attack fails.

Over the years, decisions in post-conviction cases have often resulted in major breakthroughs in criminal law precedents. In making news, they may be just as important in the contribution they make to the development of law as they are in reaching a factual result applying to a specific individual. Many of the U.S. Supreme Court's far-reaching decisions on the rights of criminal subjects have come in **habeas corpus** cases. The fact that a convicted person rarely wins a post-conviction case thus does not mean that there is not significant news potential in this branch of the criminal law.

D. SUPREME COURT CASES

The supreme courts in America, state and federal, do not stand out in the system because their approach to the law is novel in procedure and substance. Indeed, they operate very much as other appeals courts do. But they are conspicuous because they are ultimate in their respective judicial systems and because they are highly selective, most of the time, in the use of their reviewing authority.

As a simple statistical matter, little of America's business in the criminal law field is done in the supreme courts. In addition, little of the day-to-day development of the law in that field is done there. The intermediate appeals courts and the trial courts "make" more law, so to speak, than do the final tribunals.

Much of the time, in fact, appeals in criminal cases simply never reach the supreme courts. They are decided at the intermediate level, and the supreme courts do not grant permission to appeal them further.

The very idea of having intermediate courts was to give the supreme courts the time and opportunity to deal only with the more significant issues of law that arise in the state or federal systems. It is part of a theory that the best way to add to appellate capacity is to provide more intermediate courts rather than adding to the supreme courts' workload. As that theory becomes reality in more jurisdictions, the supreme courts are able to focus their own energies more and more.

The courts at the pinnacles of the state and federal systems are important news-makers for some of the same reasons that make them important in the law. Their power attracts attention, the comparative selectivity of their work tends to enhance the significance of each action, and their leadership role in developing law makes them important instruments of government that bear watching.

Special Status

There is another, somewhat subtler distinction shared only by the supreme courts. They tend to generate political and popular issues that will draw them into the realms of political discourse elsewhere in government and may, in fact, pull them into the policy considerations and actions of the other branches. Some politicians, indeed, have found a success formula in "running against" the U.S. Supreme Court, or a state supreme court, precisely because of the high level of visibility and the strong potential for popular controversy in the work of those courts.

Not surprisingly, much of the visibility and the controversy comes from supreme court rulings in the field of criminal law. Although there may be many judicial acts that will attract popular interest, none is so sure to do that as is a precedent-setting ruling on the rights of persons accused of crime or the powers of police to deal with crime.

Here again, however, there arises a risk for the reporter covering the law: the issues with which a supreme court deals in a criminal case may be so fascinating, so significant in themselves, that they may tend to overwhelm the human dimensions of the case, with the possible result of losing the popular audience.

That risk is often enhanced by the fact that most state supreme courts are *not* covered by reporters who have followed criminal cases through the lower courts and, because of that, may be more sensitive to the need to deal with the specifics of a given case. Rather, the state supreme courts most often are covered by "statehouse" reporters, those assigned to cover perhaps a wide array of state government activity, possibly including the governor's office and the legislature as well as the court. It is an occupational hazard that such a reporter will view the supreme court in his state as another source of politics-related issues, rather than as a specialized tribunal dealing with real-life cases.

But it would be naive for the reporter to assume that the judges on a supreme court do not themselves see the political dimension to their work, or that they do not ever let that influence the way they decide cases.

Covering the supreme courts, then, will pose a special challenge to the reporter, to treat stories always in their two-dimensional frame of mixed law and politics, mixed human interest and politico-legal issues.

Each of these characteristics is likely to show itself at each step in the supreme courts' review of criminal cases. They will show in the selection of cases to be reviewed (where review is discretionary, as it usually is); they will show in the manner in which judges on the court pose the issues as they see them, particularly in oral argument; they will show in the judges' varying reactions to the points made by lawyers in their briefs; and they will show in the results reached by the judges. The reporter's task is to try, continuously and conscientiously, to determine how a supreme court's members are reacting to the law and to the politics (within the court and without), and how they are treating the practical realities as well as the legal ingredients in the cases before them.

It should be stressed at this point, however, that the reporter necessarily will be making his journalistic judgments about a supreme court and its work largely on the basis of only a segment of the court's overall workload. As is true at every other tier of the judicial system, the supreme courts will deal with much that simply is not newsworthy by any definition of that term. What draws the reporter's professional attention may be the most fascinating to the widest audience, but it still will be much, much less than the whole of what a court encounters on its docket.

Criminal cases, it may be said generally, will make up a great portion of that part of the docket that a reporter will want to monitor. That will be true particularly of the state supreme courts.

The News Potential

The reporter covering a supreme court, state or federal, will encounter little if any difficulty that he has not experienced in dealing with criminal cases at lower levels in the court hierarchy. As has been indicated, their procedures are much the same as those used in the intermediate appellate courts. Appeals will be filed, followed by answers from the opposition, followed by the court's grant or denial of review (where that is discretionary), followed—if review is granted—by written briefs, then oral argument, then the decision of the court.

There may be some complexities in the court's jurisdiction to review matters offered to it. For example, there may be some classes of cases which involve a right to appeal, and thus the court has less authority (or none at all) to decline review, and there may be other classes of cases in which the supreme court has full discretion to grant or deny review.

It may make a difference, too, whether a criminal case has come up to the court on direct appeal or in a post-conviction proceeding. There is no way to generalize for all the supreme courts about the scope of their variable powers in those circumstances.

Grant or denial of review. It is quite common in the supreme courts, including the U.S. Supreme Court, for their discretionary power over cases to be exercised through **writs of certiorari.** Technically, that means a grant of judicial permission to "certify" the case to the supreme court from the last court below to review or decide it. If "cert" is granted, the case comes up to the supreme court for review. If the writ is denied, that is the end of the matter. Normally, a supreme court will not explain its reasons for denying such a writ. In some supreme courts (including the U.S. Supreme Court) it may require the votes of fewer than a majority to grant discretionary review of a case. (The U.S. Supreme Court requires, for this purpose, the votes of only four of the nine justices.)

There is potential difficulty for the reporter in reading too much into a denial of a **writ of certiorari.** It is not a ruling on the issues at stake; it is not a ruling even on the judgment at stake. All that it means, usually, is that the case is over as it was decided in the last court which reviewed it. But the exercise of certiorari discretion may, in fact, tell a good deal about the supreme court's attitude on case selection.

Non-discretionary review. When a supreme court is faced with a case in which there is a *right* to appeal, supposedly it has no discretion but to do so. But there still may linger a jurisdictional question—that is, the basic issue of whether the right of appeal does, in fact, exist. Often, a supreme court (and it is very often with the U.S. Supreme Court) will find it has no jurisdiction to review a case that has come up on supposedly mandatory review. There also may be times when, although jurisdiction to review does exist without doubt, the supreme court will announce a decision on it summarily: affirming the decision of the lower court without allowing full-dress review through briefing, argument and a written opinion. When it does so, however, it still is acting on the merits of the case that is before it, at least for purposes of settling that case finally. Its decision functions as a binding precedent at least until the court addresses the same issues anew.

Once a case is granted review, either by grant of a writ of certiorari or a **notation of jurisdiction,** the question of authority to review is put to rest. From then on, the powers of the court to proceed are usually quite straightforward and simple, and the reporter will be able to follow the exercise of those powers with ease.

Briefs. Aside from the stories that may be done when a case is initially appealed to a supreme court, there may be stories in the written briefs. Their contents, however, are likely to be only a considerable enlargement of the issues already posed at the point of initial appeal.

But if the court allows "friends of the court" **(amici curiae)**—that is, interested outside persons or organizations—to join in the case, the briefs filed by their lawyers may be of considerable news interest. These briefs may enlarge the scope of the issues at stake, showing how those issues may have an impact beyond the parties and specific facts involved directly in the case. A reporter should pay attention to the filing of these documents, even if he then decides not to write about them.

Argument. In covering oral argument, the reporter would do well to focus much of his attention on the reaction of the members of the court.

There will be few surprises in the points made by the lawyers; what is crucial at that juncture, in a news sense at least, is the way that those points seem to go over—or fail—with the judges. It is not always clear what their reactions mean in fact, and it is never a certainty that those reactions show how the judge ultimately will vote. But they do have a way of exhibiting a judge's turn of mind.

Deliberation. After a case has been heard, the reporter very likely will learn no more about it until it is decided. The work of most supreme courts as they proceed to decide is kept secret. Judges are not free, ethically, to discuss such matters with a member of the press. "Leaks" do occur, but they are uncommon.

The decision. The real news, of course, will come with the final decision of the court, provided that the ruling is on the merits and is not a dismissal or rejection of the case for lately discovered procedural or jurisdictional reasons.

Supreme court opinions will vary in content, but their basic format will be much like that of other appeals court opinions: a brief statement of the issues; some recitation of the facts; and then an analysis of varying length of the arguments, concluding with a fairly concise statement or order spelling out the exact holding of the court on the case.

A reporter covering a supreme court (as, indeed, one covering *any* appeals court) should pay quite close attention to dissenting opinions. They often are a strong practical aid in discovering, when it is not abundantly clear, what the majority has decided. More significantly, perhaps, they often provide strong indications of the difficulty in deciding a case and perhaps of a tension that may exist among the judges over a case or issue. And frequently, they are quite quotable.

Other stories. Beyond the judicial work of the courts, there will be much about them institutionally that may make news or feature stories. Their interaction with other branches of government may be newsworthy. The personalities and activities of the judges—on or off the court—may be of news interest.

The reporter assigned to cover a supreme court, state or federal, also will be in a good position to do analytical stories about the development of the law. They can be expected to have a high readership because of the peculiar place, in popular fascination, that is held by the supreme courts.

8

Covering Juvenile Cases

CRIMES BY YOUTH ARE HANDLED BY A PROCESS that is special and un-usual, as much for the legal reporter as for the legal profession. It has its own theories, its own procedures, its own system of "correction," and little of it resembles the regular system of criminal justice.

The juvenile justice system is an amalgam of law and sociology, a system that is managed according to the "rule of law" and yet conducted with a special sense of mercy and understanding.

Its basic character shows in the fact that it is a branch of "family law." The parents or guardian may be, and usually are, quite heavily involved and their "delinquency" as much as that of the child sometimes controls what juvenile courts do. If a child errs seriously and breaks the law, this special system of jus-tice treats that as a breakdown in family life. More, then, is involved than sim-ply finding a way to punish the child.

In theory, this is a system of adjustment rather than adjudication. Its ul-timate goal is to give the juvenile in trouble a "second chance," and any "cor-rection" that is ordered is supposed to serve that goal.

The reporter covering the law may find juvenile crime the most difficult part of his beat to cover. The legal restraints that will affect his work directly are different from those in any other part of the law, and there are special ethical restraints, too.

The juvenile justice system is the only branch of the law that, almost com-pletely from start to finish, goes forward under a regime of secrecy. That is en-forced both by law and by a journalist's ethical sensitivity. Both seek to protect the privacy of the child because his error may be due to his age and he needs to be protected from the perhaps lasting consequences of having his error exposed publicly.

That, of course, does not mean that the juvenile who violates the law is not held to account. He must answer for his actions, and often he will be punished—sometimes severely—for them. The community in which he lives will expect that, and it has a right to expect that the press will monitor how the youth is held accountable.

There can be no formula to guide the legal journalist in fulfilling that expectation. At times he should feel compelled to provide the fullest possible exposure of a criminal incident involving a child—even, perhaps, including the identity of the youth. At other times, he should feel obliged to provide no coverage at all. And, on still other occasions, he will feel compelled to provide only part of the story.

There may be situations in which the legal mandate for secrecy will run counter to the felt duty to publish a story or stories about juvenile crime. The reporter will find it not only difficult, but perhaps legally hazardous, to try to breach the curtain of secrecy surrounding "juvenile justice."

This chapter seeks to acquaint the reporter fully with the way the system is supposed to work and how it often works in practice. It will show where the system might produce news, if the reporter is able to cover it.

A. THE SYSTEM IN THEORY AND PRACTICE

Since 1870, the criminal law has treated juveniles uniquely. The first innovation, in Massachusetts, provided that juveniles be tried separately from adults.

But the true innovation began in 1899, when the first juvenile court, set up solely to deal with children in trouble, was established in Cook County, Illinois. It was created in an attempt to implement the then-new theory that a child who broke the law should not be treated as if he were a criminal: he should be treated, rather, as if he were "misguided and errant," and he needed "treatment" and "protection" rather than "punishment."

The goal of the juvenile justice system became rehabilitation, to protect the child from himself, his environment, perhaps even his parents and friends, so that he might be restored to normal life.

This approach spread quite rapidly, so that by 1925 only two states did not have a separate court system for juveniles. Now all states do.

Most jurisdictions have long treated anyone under the age of 18 as a juvenile for purposes of prosecution. The age level sometimes varies, however; in some jurisdictions it may be different for boys than for girls, and in some, the age maximum for all juveniles is 16 years.

Basically, the juvenile justice process is a civil rather than a criminal proceeding. A review of the terms used indicates the sharply different approach that prevails. A youth who gets into trouble is not arrested; he is "taken into custody." A youth who is found to have committed an offense is not convicted; he or she is said to be "**delinquent**" or "in need of treatment." The kind of "treatment" received usually is not set in fixed terms in the law; it is left largely to a judge's discretion, acting in "the best interests of the child." And, of course, there is the requirement that the proceedings and the records involved be kept secret.

Procedures in juvenile court (which may operate as one branch of what is called "family court") are informal. There are no strict rules of evidence or formal legal pleading. The child is entitled to have a lawyer, but the lawyer's role may be considerably different than in the formal, structured setting of a criminal trial. Parents or guardians may sit in on the proceeding, and the judge's ultimate orders may impose obligations on them, too.

Types of Cases

There are two kinds of proceedings in juvenile courts: one is used when the child has committed an offense which, if he were an adult, would be a crime; the other is used when the child has committed an act which is said to be "uniquely juvenile"—that is, an act that shows he is "beyond control" or "ungovernable," the kind of conduct that would not bring any legal action against an adult.

In the first of these, the purpose of the proceeding is to determine whether there is a sufficient basis for "an adjudication of delinquency." This is like a guilty verdict for an adult. Before such a finding may be made, the judge must be satisfied that the proof establishes delinquency "beyond a reasonable doubt"—the adult standard of guilt.

In the second kind of proceeding, the purpose is to determine whether the child is a "**person in need of supervision**" ("**PINS,**" in lawyers' shorthand). Such findings, in some jurisdictions, may be based on less than a "**beyond a reasonable doubt**" standard; instead, a "**preponderance of the evidence**" standard is used. This kind of case is considered to be less serious than a "**delinquency**" case and the accused child may be subjected to different, perhaps more lenient, "treatment" than would a child ruled delinquent. The theory behind PINS cases is that the children involved have not broken the law, but rather are beyond control by parents or guardians. Such cases often begin with a complaint by a parent. In some jurisdictions, a child who has been found more than once to be a PINS may be treated as a delinquent, in the legal sense of that word.

In most of the nation, jurisdiction over "delinquency" and "PINS" is joined in one juvenile court system. In a minority of the jurisdictions, however, there are separate sections of the juvenile court for the two approaches.

Consequences

It is not clear that the "treatment" that emerges from a "delinquency" proceeding will differ in any significant way from that in a PINS case. Both may lead to confinement in a detention facility of some kind, to some sort of modified confinement system such as a "halfway" house, or to some form of supervised freedom—a kind of probation. Supposedly, the treatment is to be fashioned according to the individual child's needs or "best interests."

The average sentence for juveniles who are sent to institutions is six to nine months. Some may be detained, however, for much longer periods, including many years.

In several states, youths are committed by juvenile judges to a separate "Youth Authority" which determines how the youths are to serve their confinement, and sometimes how long. In most states, however, youths are committed to the state prison or corrections department which decides the kind of institution to which the youths will be sent. Institutions range from regular prisons to reform or "training" schools, halfway houses and various types of work camps.

By and large, administration of the juvenile justice system is left largely to the states. The U.S. Supreme Court decided its first case on juvenile justice in 1966. In a series of decisions since then, the court has imposed some of the procedural requirements of adult criminal cases upon the juvenile system.

Problems With the System

In recent years, the system has come under increasing criticism. As Chief Justice Warren E. Burger remarked in a 1975 opinion for the Supreme Court in a juvenile case:

> Although the juvenile court system had its genesis in the desire to provide a distinct procedure and setting to deal with the problems of youth, including those manifested by anti-social conduct, our decisions in recent years have recognized that there is a gap between the originally benign conception of the system and its realities.

Rather than conferring special advantages on children, the system was found often to have subjected them to special disadvantages. As the Supreme Court remarked in its first decision in this field:

> There is evidence, in fact, that there may be grounds for concern that the child receives the worst of both worlds: that he gets neither the protections accorded to adults nor the solicitous care and regenerative treatment postulated for children.

The problems that came to be recognized included arbitrary use of discretion by juvenile court judges, failure to respect a child's most fundamental rights to fairness, excessive confinement—sometimes longer than an adult could have received for a like offense, and failure to receive training or any form of "treatment" in detention facilities.

Many of the problems have been traced to the lack of standards—or, at least, the failure to follow standards—and the general lack of any form of true accountability outside the system (see the next section of this chapter).

One area where standards had been lacking was in the basic decision whether to treat a juvenile offender as a juvenile or to transfer him to adult court to be treated as if he were an adult defendant in a criminal action, with the normal criminal procedure being used. More recently, however, the Supreme Court has required that this decision be made at an early point, preferably with a hearing, and that the decision be based upon some objective evidence supporting a conclusion that the child is one who could not benefit from the juvenile court approach.

B. MONITORING THE SYSTEM

The juvenile justice system, like every other part of the law enforcement mechanism in America, is a governmental function that bears watching by the public. But in reality, the system has been left largely to govern itself. Two scholars who made a study in 1974 of the absence of monitoring concluded that there "is an almost complete loss of accountability on the part of juvenile organizations." The two, Paul Nejelski and Judith LaPook, commented:

> Individual components of the juvenile justice system have not been required either to give reasons for their decision making or to give accounts of their performance. Consequently, their activities often are not observed and the impact of their programs is rarely measurable.

Part of the difficulty, as those scholars saw it, is that the juvenile justice system is not an integrated system within the judiciary, but rather is a collection of agencies—most public, some private—that seeks in one way or another to deal with the errant, neglected or abused child. The police are involved and so are the courts. But in addition, there are various "social service" agencies which may make use of the juvenile court system, or may be used by it. As a result, there is fragmentation. The Nejelski-LaPook study found that

> each system—law enforcement, education, social service and mental health— has the power to reject cases, divert them to nonjudicial process or arrange for court hearings and judicially mandated treatment. As a result, large numbers of children may be dealt with by the various systems with little external control.

Within the juvenile court system itself, there has been little monitoring by the usual technique of appellate court review. One study showed that, from the beginning of the juvenile court in California in 1906 until 1960, an average of only two juvenile cases a year were appealed. That is not atypical, apparently. Studies have shown that appellate courts generally have followed a "hands-off" approach on the theory that the juvenile court judges know best how to run their system. The Supreme Court itself has been reluctant to tamper extensively with the juvenile justice system on the ground that the system should be left with a good deal of flexibility to experiment.

The Issue of Secrecy

But there is another issue involving the monitoring of the juvenile court system arising out of the secrecy surrounding the process. As a result, there can be little or no public monitoring of the system.

The Supreme Court has made clear that confidentiality of juvenile proceedings is a choice the states will remain free to make. In 1967, the court commented that "there is no reason why, consistently with due process, a state cannot continue, if it deems it appropriate, to provide and to improve provisions for the confidentiality of records of police contacts and court action relating to juveniles."

A fairly typical state law on the secrecy of juvenile cases states:

> The records of any proceeding in the Family Court shall not be open to indiscriminate inspection. However, the court in its discretion in any case may permit the inspection of any papers or records . . .
> All police records relating to the arrest and disposition of any person under this article shall be kept in files separate and apart from the arrests of adults and shall be withheld from public inspection.

A New York court has said that the policy behind such restrictions is "to avoid the perpetual stigma of conviction as to persons who in early life have run afoul of the law. In cases of offenses by juveniles, there was to be a type of amnesty by oblivion."

Some states provide not only for secrecy of juvenile records; they go further and provide for destruction or **"expungement"** of those records at some point after the juvenile has been released from custody. In fact, legal reformers have suggested that there have been so many breaches of confidentiality of juvenile records that the only way to maintain secrecy in practice is to provide either for their destruction or their permanent sealing.

Breaches of Secrecy

A study of the New York City Children's Court in 1953 showed that supposedly confidential juvenile records had been examined by the Federal Bureau of Investigation, the state Civil Service system, the Army and various social agencies—including private agencies such as the Red Cross. Alan Sussman of the Legal Aid Society in Brooklyn, N.Y., concluded after a 1971 study of confidentiality of juvenile records that the secrecy provisions are "often ignored or even actively flouted."

But the secrecy itself may be a factor in preventing any form of public monitoring of the whole issue of access to these records and proceedings.

C. NEWS ABOUT THE SYSTEM

Most cases involving juvenile crime come to an end before a court gets to them. Like adult crimes, juvenile offenses often do not lead to a formal proceeding in court, for some of the same reasons: police make arrests that do not lead to prosecutions, prosecutors decide against going forward with cases or cases are settled by arrangements that do not involve the judicial process. Thus, the legal reporter is not likely to encounter most juvenile crime if he is assigned to the courthouse and does not have professional duties related to covering the police.

In fact, most of the problems of children who get into trouble very likely will be covered by reporters assigned to "social service" beats. The variety of agencies that deal with problem children is large, and many of them—most, apparently—are not arms of the police department or of the juvenile court system.

If the courthouse reporter is responsible for all of the agencies in the courthouse and not only the law enforcement offices and the courts, he may encounter a good deal of juvenile delinquency activity in agencies like "children's bureaus" or welfare agencies.

It would appear, however, that when the child in trouble is one who has committed an offense that would be criminal if he were an adult, his case might be encountered most of the time by a police beat reporter. It has been estimated that perhaps three-fourths of all juvenile delinquency petitions have been filed by police officers.

Coverage of crimes by youths on the police beat will be hampered, of course, by secrecy provisions. Most jurisdictions, as has been indicated, seek to protect juvenile offenders at every stage of the justice process, not just at the judicial stage. Records of juveniles who have been "taken into custody" ordinarily will be kept confidential, under state or local law.

Discovery of Juvenile Cases

The reporter from time to time will learn about juvenile crime through the normal process of monitoring the police or sheriff's department. He will know of many crimes soon after they have occurred without knowing immediately whether they have been committed by juveniles or by adults. If the suspect in the case is a juvenile, the reporter may well become aware of that, perhaps even by disclosures made by the police.

It is obvious, then, that the reporter may know something about a juvenile case despite the mode of secrecy that is supposed to exist in this branch of law enforcement. Thus, the ethical problems in determining whether and how much to report will arise whether or not the legal problems of breaching required secrecy do arise.

The real difficulty in covering the juvenile justice process exists when it does become a matter for the courts.

Petitions for **"adjudication of delinquency"** or complaints about a juvenile who is **"in need of supervision"** (the "PINS" situation) very often will be sealed as a matter of law, or an attorney or someone else involved in the case will obtain a court order sealing such documents.

Obviously, some of those documents would produce news, if they were available. But the courthouse reporter may have no other way of knowing about them than the reliance upon his sources' willingness to tell him. If those source relations are sufficiently sound, a reporter may be told about a juvenile case as it arises. Sometimes he will have to pledge secrecy before any such disclosure will be made to him. This kind of "silent monitoring," however, has its own evident shortcomings.

If a reporter does become aware of the filing of a juvenile case, and does so in circumstances leaving to him the discretion whether to print or broadcast, his problem at that point may be only an ethical one. But it also might be a legal one, if there is a state or local law regarding confidentiality. Some of these laws treat breaches of confidentiality as a criminal offense, punishable by fines or jail terms. The Supreme Court has ruled, however, that such laws may not be used to punish the press for identifying a juvenile offender—if the press obtained that information legally.

The chances are that, if a crime is particularly notorious in a community—either because of its nature or because of the persons involved—the press will learn about it. If, however, a case does not have those qualities, the chances of becoming aware of it are or may be remote.

Following a Case

A reporter's opportunity to follow a case all the way through the juvenile justice system may depend upon the same considerations of notoriety.

If he has learned about a case, the reporter may continue to press for information about it as it moves from step to step through the juvenile court. There will be limitations on what his sources can or will tell him about it, but they may reveal enough to allow him to monitor at least the key steps.

The most significant development, legally and journalistically, after a case has been taken to juvenile court will be the decision on whether to try the involved youth as a juvenile or as an adult. The judge has a constitutional duty to settle that issue before the juvenile is subjected to any of the proceedings of juvenile court.

If a youth is to be transferred to the regular court for trial as an adult, the reporter probably will have an opportunity to see documents and perhaps to conduct interviews that will show why the judge considered the juvenile to be unsuited for the juvenile justice system.

Conversely, however, he probably will not be able to learn a great deal about a judge's decision to keep the youth's case in juvenile court. The reporter may be able to get limited information about that from the youth's lawyer or family, but the lawyer obviously is under ethical restraints.

As the case goes forward in juvenile court, the reporter will have to rely more or less continuously on those secondary sources. The judge and other court personnel probably would not share with the reporter what has been done in the informal, closed sessions with the juvenile, his parents and (if he has one) his lawyer.

Even when a decision has been made on the kind of "treatment" the youth is to receive, the reporter cannot count upon the judge or his aides to provide information. At this point the family is likely to be the best source on what is to happen to the youth.

Post-Adjudication Coverage

If the youth has been sent to a "reform school" or other youth detention facility, there will be little opportunity to follow the individual's experience there—except through contact with the family. The reporter, however, may be able to monitor the operation of the facility in general. Strong investigative news stories have been done about such institutions, revealing in some cases instances of brutality or lesser mistreatment of the youths there.

Monitoring Challenges to the System

Overall, it is clear that the legal reporter will have major difficulty obtaining even the basic facts about the juvenile justice system. He will have even greater difficulty obtaining reliable information on the justification for what is done at each step of those proceedings. The absence of accountability, through appeals or other external means of monitoring, tends to cut off the journalist as well as others who would inquire into the functioning of the system.

Much of the reporter's opportunity to get news about the juvenile courts, or indeed about the handling of juvenile crime from start to finish, will be after the fact. Increasingly, youths who believe they have been wronged by the system have been filing test cases, and the process of deciding and reviewing those will reveal much about the way given cases have been handled.

"Right to treatment" cases. One of the legal means that may be chosen to make such a test is the "right to treatment" lawsuit. This would be a normal civil suit, filed by the youth directly or perhaps by his parents or guardian, complaining about mistreatment or lack of any treatment while he is confined in a youth correction facility.

"Right to treatment" suits may be brought either in federal or state court. The state cases probably will proceed on a theory that the state's own laws governing juvenile justice mandate treatment, and will contend that that treatment has not been forthcoming. The federal cases will proceed on a theory of violation of federally guaranteed civil rights. It normally would not be necessary for a juvenile filing such a federal case to "exhaust" any legal remedies he might have under state law.

Cases alleging a violation of a "right to treatment" have increased in number since the first federal appeals court decision (in 1974) recognized that a youth committed to a facility after being found to be delinquent had a "right" to be treated.

That first decision declared that the "right to treatment" included "the right to minimum acceptable standards of care and treatment for juveniles and the right to individualized care and treatment."

A legal reporter probably will be able to cover such cases, both in state and in federal court. Some parts of the record in the case—perhaps including the identity of the youth involved and some of the identifying facts of his case—may be ordered sealed by the court in order to protect the youth's continuing privacy. Even if the records are not sealed by court order, the reporter should consider whether, as a matter of journalistic ethics or taste, some steps should be taken to guard the youth's privacy.

(Coverage of "right to treatment" suits will involve the steps outlined in Chapters 10–12 on civil cases in general.)

9

Covering "Prison Law"

IT IS NO LONGER TRUE THAT PRISONS MAKE NEWS only when a celebrity convict checks in, the prisoners riot or there is an escape. The nation's prisons and the local jails are burgeoning sources of news for the legal reporter.

Two developments have contributed to that:

- The civil rights "revolution" reached the prisons, and courts came to recognize that at least some constitutional rights are not totally lost or set aside when a person becomes an inmate. Many more prisoners began to challenge conditions of prison life.
- The discontent over rising rates of crime, and especially of the number of repeat offenders, gave new impetus to the long-frustrated effort to reform prison conditions. The theory was that prisons had themselves become "schools of crime."

As the processes of law seemed more open for review of complaints about life in prison, the number of prisoner cases filed in the courts began to rise rapidly. That, in turn, caused judges and others to begin looking for alternative procedures for processing inmate grievances.

Of course, the courts had long been open to prison inmates as they appealed the convictions that had led to their imprisonment. (These appeals are discussed in Chapter 7.) But the courts until quite recently had been most reluctant to hear cases in which inmates were challenging the conditions of their confinement. Many of those cases were routinely dismissed, usually on the finding that judges had little or no authority to interfere with the internal management of correctional institutions by prison officials and supervisors.

When the courts began to recognize that inmates had a right to legal assistance—including a right to a lawyer as and when available—it was quite predictable that the legal testing of corrections procedures would increase. Exactly that occurred.

Decisions in many of those cases required prison administrators to respect some of the inmates' rights. In general, rights were recognized in a somewhat qualified or diluted form, so that an inmate was found to have retained rights if they were "not inconsistent with his status as a prisoner or with the legitimate penological objectives of the corrections system," as the U.S. Supreme Court remarked in a 1974 decision.

But it was not left to courts alone to interpret and apply those rights. New procedures were adopted within many prisons to deal with inmate discipline and grievances. In addition, some states began to experiment with new agencies somewhat removed from the prison system to handle inmate complaints. A fairly typical approach was the creation of "grievance commissions" to investigate complaints and make recommendations to state prison administrators, with the possibility of court review of the results.

For the legal reporter, then, there exist perhaps three layers of judicial or quasi-judicial review of the conditions in prison. The press is as much obliged to monitor those aspects of the corrections process as it always has been to monitor prison management. Supreme Court Justice William O. Douglas once stated a basic justification for such monitoring:

> Prisons, like all other public institutions, are ultimately the responsibility of the populace. Crime . . . is a matter of grave concern in our society and people have the right and the necessity to know not only of the incidence of crime but of the effectiveness of the system designed to control it. On any given day, approximately 1.5 million people are under the authority of federal, state and local prison systems. The cost to taxpayers is over $1 billion annually. Of those individuals sentenced to prison, 98 percent will return to society. The public's interest in being informed about prisons is thus paramount.

A. THE PRISON SYSTEM

Prisons and jails exist at all levels of the government: city, county, state and federal.

Usually the local jails will be used only for temporary holding of persons prior to trial, temporary holding of convicted persons awaiting transfer to prison, and detention of persons convicted of minor offenses serving short jail terms. There may be perhaps 90,000 persons in such jails at any given time. These jails are managed by local law enforcement officials: police and sheriff's departments.

There is a state prison or a prison system in every state. These institutions hold persons convicted of more serious crimes; the usual rule is that a person who has been convicted of a **felony** is sent to prison, rather than to a local jail. The terms for such convictions are generally a year or longer.

The state system may include only a single, perhaps ancient "fortress-type" prison or it may consist of a wide variety of institutions performing differing correctional functions: work farms or camps, halfway houses, clinics, work-release facilities and so on.

In about a fourth of the states, the prison system is managed by a separate department of correction which is responsible to the governor. Another fourth of the states manage prisons through a larger "catch-all" department, such as public welfare. But in nearly half the states there is no full-time agency with responsibility for prisons: there, they are supervised by part-time boards, many of which have unpaid members.

The federal prison system, managed by the Bureau of Prisons in the Justice Department, has more than three-dozen institutions, varying in character and holding perhaps 20,000 inmates/residents at any given time.

Within each of these systems, the methods of inmate discipline and the machinery for processing inmate grievances vary widely.

At the local level, disciplinary and grievance procedures will be highly informal, left dominantly to the discretion of the ranking law enforcement officer but implemented day-to-day in the discretion of individual jailers.

In the state systems, there may be either informal or highly structured disciplinary and grievance processes. Some exist within individual prison facilities, while others exist somewhat outside them—as in the case of state inmate grievance commissions. "Release proceedings"—that is, the parole machinery—may be operated by the prison administration itself or by a state board of parole.

At the federal level, the Bureau of Prisons has a full-scale inmate discipline program, with "institution discipline committees" set up in each facility to hold hearings and decide upon punishment for inmate misconduct. Appeals from its rulings may be made to the chief executive officer of the institution. Specific controls are set on the kinds of special detention facilities used for inmates being punished. There is also a Board of Parole with a staff of its own, following regularized procedures for hearings and decisions on release of inmates before their full terms have been served.

B. PRESS ACCESS TO PRISONS

The press will be able to monitor the prison system some of the time from the outside. Law enforcement authorities at the local level and corrections officials in state and federal governments will be more or less accountable because they are elected or appointed officials subject at least to indirect scrutiny.

Not uncommonly, prisons are covered by reporters who specialize in state government in general or in the "social services beat" for their station or publication. At the local level, the courthouse reporter probably will be responsible for covering the local jail.

The legal reporter, however, will have responsibility for covering inmate cases that go to the courts. There ordinarily will be no difficulty in monitoring those. They will be filed, much of the time, as civil rights complaints and their progress through the courts will be open to the public and the press. (A prisoner case of this kind will follow the steps outlined for civil cases in general in Chapters 10–12.)

Lack of Access

Within the prison community itself, however, there is no similar guarantee of access to the legal proceedings. The variety of disciplinary and grievance-processing methods inside prisons and the parole proceedings within or outside the system generally are not public.

The legal reporter has no exclusive or special opportunity to cover any of the internal workings of the prison legal structure. The Supreme Court has recently said that

> Newsmen have no constitutional right of access to prisons or their inmates beyond that afforded the general public. . . . The Constitution does not require government to accord the press special access to information not shared by members of the public generally.

Thus, it will be up to the individual reporter to develop relationships with prison or jail administrators or their supervisors in corrections departments that will enable him to have some access to prisons and to the results of disciplinary, grievance and release cases.

Generally speaking, the press can expect to gain little access by going to court seeking orders allowing entry into prisons for professional purposes. Some lawsuits of that kind have been pursued, but the record of success is negligible.

Help From the Lawyer

Some help in gaining access may be obtained from lawyers who have clients in prison. Those attorneys may be able to assist the reporter in getting permission to conduct an interview with a specific prisoner. Even if an attorney has not been instrumental in getting a reporter in for an interview, the reporter would be well advised—in almost all cases—to have the attorney's permission before he talks to the client. An inmate's attorney is often his most trusted confidant outside the prison, and the inmate may be more willing to talk freely with the reporter if he knows he is doing so with the knowledge and approval of his lawyer.

A legal reporter often will want to try to do some investigating of his own, inside the prison, to obtain background or support material as he seeks to cover cases of inmate grievances or operation of the disciplinary system. That kind of activity, obviously, will be subject almost entirely to the discretion of the chief prison administrator, the warden. There may be, however, some opportunity for court review of his decisions.

C. SPECIFIC ISSUES IN PRISON COVERAGE

Whether the reporter is allowed to cover prison activity, including its legal and quasi-legal procedures, directly and on the spot or only indirectly through coverage of prisoner cases in court, he will encounter three categories of issues. The news potential in each is discussed in this section.

Conditions of Prison Life

Many prisoner grievances and the disciplinary problems that sometimes result involve the basic conditions of life behind penitentiary or jail walls. Issues about access to medical care, proper food, sanitary conditions, recreational and training facilities and legal aid have arisen with increasing frequency in inmates' civil rights cases.

A legal reporter will need to watch the development of the law in (1) defining the minimum enforceable standards on living in the prison environment, (2) defining means or processes by which those standards may be monitored judicially, and (3) defining the remedies or relief to be provided to individual inmates who have been denied what is minimally required.

Not every unappealing condition in prison life will be controlled by courts in reviewing prisoner complaints. A very large measure of discretion will still remain with prison administrators, and even more discretion will be left with state legislatures and local legislative bodies. But in some jurisdictions at least, there has been a widening scope of judicial review of the conditions of confinement, and this obviously will make news.

Some of these issues may be worked out in the grievance commissions, or other quasi-judicial agencies being created as alternatives to the regular judicial process.

Discipline and Punishment

The area of prison activity that is most likely to produce issues for the courts or alternative reviewing agencies is the handling of inmates accused of misconduct.

A reporter, in monitoring the law bearing on that phenomenon, will need to watch (1) the degree to which prisoners are assured of some procedural protection before they may be punished for misconduct, including possible notification of the specific complaints against an inmate, the opportunity to reply in some way to the complaints, the possibility of a hearing before a more or less impartial panel, and the possible need for written decisions on discipline so that judicial review may be possible; (2) the degree to which courts will limit the scope of punishment, including segregation in "**solitary confinement**" or other restricted quarters and loss of "**good time**" **credits**; and (3) the degree to which courts or other external agencies will be permitted or required to review disciplinary action.

Not every procedural right that exists in normal criminal trials will exist in the prison disciplinary process. But some of these rights will be recognized in at least a modified or diluted form. It is obvious that any judicial rulings establishing or significantly expanding prisoner rights will be newsworthy.

Parole of Prisoners

Release on **parole**—that is, allowing an inmate to leave prison prior to the expiration of his sentence—is permitted in every state and at the federal level. Usually, such release is accompanied by conditions, including the duty to report regularly to some supervising officer. Other conditions may include an obligation to find steady employment. Increasingly, the terms upon which parole is made available have been contested in prisoner cases.

The legal reporter will be watching for the development and application (1) of procedural safeguards for the inmate; (2) of standards that will guide the decision for or against parole; (3) of standards that will guide the kinds of post-release conditions that must be observed; (4) of procedures for revoking parole where conditions have been violated; and (5) of judicial or other external review of the entire parole process.

News about the parole process is of major significance, because it deals with an issue of doubtlessly wide popular interest: when to allow a convicted offender to return to society without serving his full sentence. In many ways, the parole system provides a continuing test of the success or failure of prisons in preparing or assisting offenders to become rehabilitated so that they may function again on the "outside."

The reporter should expect to provide full coverage to grant of paroles. He will be handicapped in trying to provide equally full coverage of parole denials, because that is not as visible a result.

Similarly, the reporter should attempt to provide full coverage of parole revocation proceedings. These are another test of the success or failure of the corrections process, and the public will be much interested in the results.

Mandatory parole. A developing issue which the legal reporter will want to monitor is the degree to which parole in his state or area becomes a mandatory matter. Mandatory parole in this sense means a requirement that every prisoner who is released from custody, even after he has finished his term, is subject to some supervision for at least a transitional period prior to regaining full freedom in society.

D. THE SPECIAL ISSUE OF PROBATION

"**Probation**"—an alternative to confinement in prison or jail—is not a part of the law of prisons but it is a part of the law of corrections. It is discussed here because it similarly involves the handling by the courts of persons after they have been found guilty of a crime.

Although the word is popularly understood to mean the absence of a sentence, probation is in fact a sentence. A judge imposes probation as a form of post-conviction sanction. Almost always, a probation sentence will include a specified term during which the convicted person is obliged to remain under supervision outside a prison or jail, and, perhaps, to satisfy other conditions.

Probation is routinely imposed when a prison or jail sentence has been given and then suspended at the discretion of the judge. In some jurisdictions, some crimes do carry fixed sentences. But in nearly all jurisdictions, the judge retains the discretionary authority to impose probation as an alternative to actual confinement in prison.

If probation is given along with a suspended prison term, it often is true that a violation of the conditions or terms of probation will result in a commitment to prison for the term specified in the sentence. It also may be true, however, that the penalty for probation violation could be an entirely different sentence. Legal reformers are promoting the notion that a judge's sentencing discretion should be as wide in the face of a probation violation as it is at the point of initial sentencing after conviction.

Although the reasons for putting an offender on probation as an alternative to confinement vary widely, the generally accepted reasoning is that this is all that is necessary to deal with a given offender. Thus, probation will *not* be given if a judge believes that the person needs to be confined to protect the public from him, or that the person actually needs confinement for his own rehabilitation, or that the person's crime was so serious that it would be unacceptable to allow him his freedom, even under conditions.

The News Potential

The legal reporter will encounter the probation process at two stages:

First, he will usually be able to cover the sentencing proceeding at the close of the criminal trial, and it will be at that proceeding that the judge's decision to impose probation as a sentence will be disclosed or discussed. The reporter should seek to learn all that he can about the reasons for the use of probation as an alternative to confinement. Most judges will feel obliged to say, at least in a summary fashion, why they believe probation is the proper sentence in a given case.

Second, the reporter often will be able to cover probation revocation proceedings, since they commonly are held in open court. At such a proceeding, the charges of violation of probation will be explored much as evidence of crime was explored at the criminal trial. (The formal **rules of evidence,** however, do not apply at this stage.) If the judge is persuaded that there has been a violation, he will then determine what sentence to give. As has been said, this may be only the reimposition of an earlier prison term that was suspended, or it may be an entirely new sentence, calculated by the judge to fit the circumstances of the probation violation. Either way, the reporter should seek to learn the specific reasons for the judge's decision. He should also pay close attention to the procedural safeguards or the absence of them in this whole process.

Many jurisdictions have separate probation offices or services, and they customarily exist as a part of the court system. The reporter on the courthouse beat may have probation activity within the normal range of his responsibilities.

E. THE SPECIAL ISSUE OF PARDONS

Normally the use of pardoning power will not be a facet of the legal reporter's beat. That authority is exercised either by state governors or by the President, and it is rarely reviewed in court.

The legal reporter needs only to be generally acquainted with the pardoning process should one of those rare court cases arise.

At the state level, the process sometimes features a board or commission acting as an advisor to the governor. Ultimately, however, the decision to pardon is one dominantly or solely within the governor's discretion. There is no such thing as a "right" to a pardon because the grant of clemency is, in law, a matter of executive grace. The only time that it is likely to become a legal issue is when the recipient of a pardon seeks to challenge conditions that might be attached to it. Even in reviewing that kind of issue, however, the courts will seldom second-guess the governor's decision.

At the federal level, applications for pardons are first reviewed by the pardon attorney, who is an official in the Justice Department. He will make recommendations to the attorney general, who in turn will advise the President. Pardons are seldom granted by the President. They are even more rarely challenged in court.

A pardon at either level may be granted even before a criminal case comes to trial, or it may be granted after the criminal justice process has run its complete course. One form of pardon—reduction of sentence or, as it is technically named, "**commutation**"—comes only after conviction and sentencing.

Obviously, pardons will make news because of their limited numbers and because they are commonly used only in quite exceptional cases. But they will be news to be covered mostly by the reporter assigned to the statehouse or the White House, not the reporter on the court beat.

Covering an Extradition

Another legal issue affecting custody and detention of an accused person, not necessarily related directly to the prison system, may arise on the courthouse beat. It is **extradition**—the detention of a person, followed by his transfer from one state to be tried for a crime in another state.

Ordinarily extradition involves only the office of a state governor, and thus it will be covered by the statehouse reporter. At times, however, there will be an attempt to challenge the process judicially. That may make it a matter for the legal reporter to cover.

It is appropriate to discuss the issue at this point because, in many cases of extradition, the person will already be in custody, serving a prison or jail term, and another state will seek his return for trial for a crime committed before he was confined by the state which has present custody.

The Constitution provides that a person may be extradited from one state to another, if a demand is made for his transfer or return to that state on the ground that he has committed a crime there and is fleeing from prosecution for it.

Congress has passed a law to implement this provision by providing that a person may be handed over to the accusing state if that state sends a copy of the actual criminal charge to the governor in the so-called "asylum" state—that is, where the accused person is located.

Extradition is largely within the control of a governor, who may decide— on whatever evidence is satisfactory to him—that a person should be extradited. No hearing is required and no formal **rules of evidence** control the governor's use of his discretion.

The person involved, however, may seek to block his transfer by filing a **habeas corpus** petition in state or federal court. The only issues in the court review are whether a crime has been charged, whether the particular person is the one who actually has been charged in the other state, and whether he is a "fugitive"—that is, whether he is intentionally remaining away from the charging state in order to avoid prosecution on the charge.

The reviewing court is not likely to inquire deeply into the basis of the charge—in other words, whether it was ill-founded or arbitrary. Rather it probably will want to satisfy itself only that a charge was, in fact, issued by an authority competent to make such a charge. The charge itself is subject to challenge only in the state where it has been made, and this, of course, is done by defending the accused when the case is being prepared for trial or is tried.

A legal reporter will cover an extradition case in the "asylum" state as he does any other **habeas corpus** case (see Chapter 7).

10

Covering Civil Cases:
The Beginning

CIVIL LAW IS THE GROWING SIDE of the legal reporter's beat. The new and novel controversies that a complex society has produced have not been left routinely to be settled by other branches of government, but rather have gone to court. Many of a community's most newsworthy disputes are now worked out in the processes of civil law ahead of any action elsewhere in government, or at least simultaneously with it.

As the civil docket grows, so does the courthouse reporter's duty to keep up with it. He still will find that he must cover fewer civil than criminal cases. For every newsworthy civil case, there will be perhaps scores that simply will make no news at all. But some of the biggest stories on the beat will be coming from this other side.

Civil rights cases, for example, are handled as civil lawsuits, and those can take in significant local disputes ranging from race relations to the rights of women and youth and the poor, to the structure and methods of government itself. Even the more traditional forms of civil lawsuit—contract cases and damage claims—may produce news because the widening scale of legally protected private rights brings more of a community's fascinating controversies into court.

The reporter who is in the habit of covering criminal law will discover quickly two things about the civil law:

First, it is very much different, in form and procedure, from criminal law. It is basically much more complex. Its language and methods often are highly technical, even obscure.

Second, for all the complexity, it is "easier," in a manner of speaking, to cover civil cases. Fewer of the steps that a civil case goes through will produce news, and thus the job of actually covering it is considerably less time-consuming.

Both of those considerations require the reporter to become familiar with **civil procedure.** Its very complexity makes it potentially troublesome to the reporter, because of the high risk that ignorance may cause him to mislead his readers or listeners. In addition, he must know what it is all about in order to form journalistic judgments about the parts he need *not* cover.

Covering a civil case is, in at least some respects, no different for the legal reporter who is used to covering criminal cases. He must be just as aware of the specific facts of the case, and he must try as often as he can to tell about the legal issues in a case by showing their relationship to the facts. This is important for his journalistic purposes. But it also is important because of the role of facts in civil cases. As Judge Lee Loevinger has observed:

> It is the observation of most experienced lawyers that at least 9 out of 10 cases are determined in their result by the opinion of the court or jury as to the 'facts' of the case. . . . A very slight difference in the 'facts' found by the tribunal may make a vast difference in the result of a case.

That is true, in part at least, because legal principles now exist in almost incredible variety and complexity. The result is, as Loevinger suggests, that "legal rules, refinements of rules, distinctions in the refinements, exceptions to the distinctions in the refinements, refinements and distinctions in the exceptions" can only be made meaningful in a given case by letting the specific facts control. That is as true for reporters as for lawyers and judges.

William Farnum White, a practicing lawyer who has written a book devoted solely to handling facts in civil cases (*Winning in Court on the Law of Facts*), published by Prentice Hall, makes the point with this advice to other lawyers as they decide how to press their clients' cases:

> It is much better to fit the remedy to your client's facts at the very beginning than to select the remedy and hope, as more facts become known, your client can prove the action you have chosen for him to secure his needed relief.

The legal reporter will become aware promptly of the central role that facts play in a given case. Indeed, much of the pre-trial activity in civil proceedings is devoted to **discovery,** in the legal sense, of the facts (see below). At the trial, many of the main contests will be over the meaning and import of the facts.

This will become evident in this and the following two chapters as civil cases are followed chronologically, showing the points at which they are likely to produce news and the significance of those news developments.

Before proceeding with the pre-trial phase, it is important to stress again that many civil law disputes will end before they ever reach the court. Just as the prosecutor in criminal law chooses to bring many criminal matters to a close without prosecuting, lawyers involved with civil matters will negotiate them into settlement or simply drop them without formally proceeding in court. In addition, of course, many civil cases that have been filed in court will be settled along the way—sometimes before trial, sometimes during trial.

In this chapter and the next two, however, the discussion proceeds as if the case a reporter is covering is destined to go all the way through trial and on to appeal.

A. SOURCES OF INFORMATION

Civil law, much more than criminal law, is a private activity. The triggering incidents that set off civil law disputes often will be private matters. The parties involved and the events which lay the foundation for legal controversy between them may have no visible public character (though the government *is* frequently a party). Thus, there may be little occasion for such disputes to come to the attention of the press. Even when a governmental agency is a party, the dispute may not surface early.

A criminal case, by contrast, always begins with an event that immediately involves conspicuous public business: a breach of a community's peace and order. Right away, the government becomes involved, through the police. As Chapter 5 shows, the reporter will be aware of a developing criminal case from a very early point.

But in civil matters there is also a public interest at stake. The community needs to be able to rely upon a dispute-settling process that will get results likely to be accepted as satisfactory. But that is a much more generalized public interest, one that does not *always* or necessarily involve direct acts of agencies or officers of the government. A civil case may proceed for a very long way, after a triggering incident, without ever becoming a matter of public knowledge or concern.

The reporter, then, has no assured way of monitoring the disputes that may become civil lawsuits in the courts he is covering. He will have to depend upon his acquaintance with lawyers for much of his early information about a developing civil dispute. His awareness of such a dispute may come in the first instance from non-lawyer sources—the people or organizations involved in a budding controversy, for example—but his opportunity to keep track of the dispute along its way toward a formal lawsuit may depend quite heavily upon the value of his lawyer sources.

Since almost any controversy between two sides has within it the potential of producing a legal "**cause of action**"—that is, a basis for a lawsuit—a reporter simply has no way of following all such controversies in their earliest stages.

Most of the time, the reporter will learn about a civil case only when it has come to court in some fashion, either as a formal filing of a **complaint** or **petition,** or as a request for some temporary judicial order. At that point, the private dispute has taken on a public character, and it is the reporter's business to begin to monitor it. Although some parts of the proceeding thereafter may be sealed and thus kept beyond his reach, the case will go through a series of formal steps that, in considerable part, will be open to the public and the press.

B. CIVIL LAW AS NEWS

The news interest in civil lawsuits exists primarily because there is conflict or controversy, and the settlement that ultimately may emerge has the potential of creating "new" law or establishing new duties or rights.

A civil case involves either a breach of an agreement that has been entered voluntarily (this may produce a **contract** case, for example) or a breach of a duty that has been imposed by law (this may produce a **tort** case, for example). In either kind of case, the controversy will require a court to determine legal rights, to decide how those rights have been violated if at all and to provide a remedy for any wrongs done. Obviously, there is news potential in each of these aspects of a civil case.

Even when a civil lawsuit is fairly routine, in the sense that it involves no novel law questions or principles, it may produce news simply because of the identity of the parties involved or the factual nature of the controversy. Any kind of lawsuit involving a person or institution well known in a community is likely to be at least minimally newsworthy. When one of the parties is a governmental official or agency, the case may well be quite newsworthy because of its potential impact on public policy, affecting a community in general.

In a more general sense, civil law makes news because its progress tells much about a community's sense and style of justice. As Justice Benjamin Cardozo observed:

> Life casts the moulds of conduct, which will some day become fixed as law. Law preserves the moulds, which have taken form and shape from life.

The reporter covering civil law will find, perhaps between the lines of complex legal procedure, much of the stuff of life as it is lived in his community. That is where the focus of his work should be.

C. HOW THE CIVIL LAW DIFFERS

It would be well, before proceeding to the initial steps in a civil case, to note briefly some of the basic ways in which civil law differs from criminal law. Other differences will become evident as each of the steps is followed. Some of the most fundamental differences (*not* allowing for the inevitable exceptions) are:

- A civil case need not be confined solely to the parties directly involved in the immediate controversy. The lawsuit may be filed—in some jurisdictions at least—on behalf of a whole class of persons who share a common interest or identity. Moreover, as a civil case proceeds, new parties may be added to the case, either as **plaintiffs (complainants)** or **respondents (defendants),** or as **intervenors.**
- A court may not hear a civil case unless it definitely has jurisdiction over the persons involved or property that is involved and over the "subject matter" at stake. A key question in every civil case may be whether the parties had a legal right to be before that court, whether the case is one over which the court has authority to act and whether the dispute is one involving a remedy within the capacity of the court to grant.
- A party sued in a civil case is not necessarily confined to defending himself from the claims of the other party. He may pursue his own claims ("**counterclaims**") just as vigorously as the original suing party pursued his.
- A party sued in a civil case may lose it simply by failing to answer in court. So long as he is made aware by formal **notice** that he has been sued, he risks losing by **default** if he does not go to court to defend himself.
- The variety of results that may emerge from a civil case is much broader than in a criminal case. Many civil courts have broad discretion about the kinds of orders they may issue to require a party to do something or to refrain from doing something. In addition, money damages may be awarded.
- A civil court may have broad authority to issue temporary orders to control a controversy well in advance of any decision on the merits of the dispute. In fact, the whole process of preliminary or temporary judicial action may settle a controversy for all practical purposes thus avoiding further process in court.

D. FIRST STEPS IN A CIVIL CASE

If a civil controversy has gone through a period of lawyer negotiations or exploratory conversations and still persists, the stage is set for it to become a matter for the courts.

This may happen in one of two ways; in some cases, both will occur at the same time. They are the filing of a complaint or petition, and filing of motions for **temporary "relief"** from a court.

Filing of Complaint

A case actually begins, in a formal sense, when a **complaint** (sometimes it will be called a **petition** or **declaration**) is filed in court. This is a statement by the suing party which identifies the parties involved on both sides, recites some of the facts of the relationship which gave rise to the controversy, lists the specific legal grounds for the claims or grievances and specifies the relief or remedies being sought. The claims or grievances will be called **"causes of action"** and often they contain **"counts"** to the cause of action.

The filing of a case, obviously, will produce news if there is anything about the parties, the facts or the relief sought that fits the usual definition of newsworthiness. The legal reporter in examining the complaint or petition will be able to determine swiftly whether there is a story in it. In addition, he will begin forming at that point his assessments of the likely strategy that will be pursued and the possible outcome of the case as it proceeds through the court.

Sometimes, if a case is of major significance, parties or attorneys involved may hold a press conference to discuss the case and the legal purposes behind it. At that point, the reporter should press for a broad understanding of the strategy that is to be pursued and the ends being sought. He also should attempt to learn the potential for settling the case without a trial. It is not unusual for attorneys to use the filing of a case to bring pressure upon a stubborn adversary to begin negotiating toward a settlement. The reporter may also seek to get this information even if no press conference is held. Interviews with parties and attorneys may also yield the answers.

At the point of the filing of a case, the reporter may also learn the reasons why a particular court has been chosen as the forum for a lawsuit. There often will be a **choice of forums** available to hear a case, because more than one may actually have jurisdiction to hear it. The **choice of forum** may reveal a good deal about the attorney's own expectations about his chances of winning.

At this early point, it also may be clear that the lawsuit is being filed on behalf of an entire related **class** of persons or institutions. In jurisdictions where **"class actions"** are allowed, as in federal courts generally, the filing of a case on behalf of a class does not necessarily mean that it will proceed on that basis. This is often a matter of discretion with the court. The court must be satisfied that, in fact, the class does have common interests, that the other members of that class not directly involved in bringing the suit will, in fact, have their interests represented adequately in that case, and that there is a way to notify the other members of the suit. It is quite common, in federal courts, for civil rights cases to be pursued as class actions.

Temporary Relief

Before a complaint is filed, or simultaneously with its filing, the suing party may ask the court to issue special orders preserving the status quo in a legal dispute.

Quite commonly, this will come in the form of a motion for a **temporary restraining order, "TRO,"** for short, or a **temporary injunction.** The idea behind such an order is to keep matters unchanged for the time being, to allow a brief interval for the court to decide whether a more lasting order maintaining the status quo is required.

A TRO does not settle anything, in a legal sense. It simply keeps a relationship as it is, to avoid "injury" to the complaining entity, pending a court hearing to determine whether in fact injury will result if the status quo is not kept. Sometimes, a court will hold a hearing before issuing a TRO, to satisfy itself that "injury" will result if some temporary action is not taken.

The function of a TRO is to protect the court's jurisdiction over a legal dispute until a court can take a more considered look at the dispute. Thus, a TRO often will remain in effect only until after a court has had an opportunity to decide whether to issue a **preliminary injunction.** Before such an injunction is issued, the court probably will want to be satisfied that the suing party has a chance to win the case on the merits.

The filing of a motion for a TRO often will produce news because it may be the first signal of a developing legal controversy. Moreover, the nature of the potential "injury" that may result if the status quo is not maintained may make news.

A reporter covering a TRO proceeding or a hearing on a preliminary injunction must be careful not to indicate that a legal controversy is actually settled by such temporary exercise of judicial authority. He must be sure to acquaint his readers or listeners with the meaning—including the limitations—of temporary court orders.

The Summons

A civil lawsuit is not considered begun, in a technical sense, until after the other side (the party being sued) has had formal notification that it is being sued. In fact, a court has no jurisdiction to proceed in any way on a civil complaint or petition until after it has been assured that a **summons** has been served on the party being sued. A summons is simply a notification that a suit has been filed: It notifies the defendant or respondent to appear in court and defend himself or else lose by **default.** Sometimes a deadline is set for an appearance.

If the sued party does not concede that it is being sued properly or legally or that the court has jurisdiction over the case, that party may enter a **special appearance** in court. This means that, through an attorney, the sued party makes the court aware that the sued party knows he has been sued, but is contesting the court's power to act in the case. This avoids a **default judgment** while preserving the argument that the case should *not* go forward.

If the sued party concedes the court's jurisdiction, that party then enters a **general appearance** if he wishes to defend himself. That provides the court with notice that the sued party knows he has been sued and is ready to let the case proceed.

The serving of a summons and the entering of appearances by the sued party seldom produce significant news stories. Of course, if the sued party decides to ignore the case, thus forfeiting it by default, that may make news. Otherwise, the summons and the appearance procedures are routine formalities.

It should be noted that the sued party need not necessarily reside in the same state as the suing party in order to be within the court's jurisdiction. So-called "**long-arm statutes**" provide that a defendant or respondent may be sued in another state, through the cooperation of authorities in that state.

E. ANSWER AND REPLY

The Pleadings

After a civil case has begun, it still may not proceed until after the party being sued has had a chance to answer in writing, and then the suing party has a chance to reply. These various written documents—**complaint, answer,** and **reply**—constitute the formal **pleadings** in a case, informing the court of the basic claims at stake. (The pleadings also include various written motions that are made in the case.)

The purpose of the pleadings is to spell out quite clearly the issues that the parties want to be tried in the case. For many years, civil pleadings were highly ritualistic, technical narrations, often resulting in the smothering of the case in formalisms. But beginning in 1848 with a reformed civil procedure in New York state, civil pleading has become much simpler. It is now common to have the pleadings in a form that is readily and easily understood.

The legal reporter will have little trouble, in fact, understanding nearly any complaint that he will encounter in a civil case, any answer to it and any reply.

The answer and the reply contribute significantly to illuminating the content of a civil case. The reporter should pay as much attention to them as he does to the complaint. It is not unusual for a civil case to be settled on the basis of these pleadings, without any further documentary offerings and without any hearing.

Preliminary Motions

Before a case gets to the point where a formal answer is filed to a complaint, however, there may be a series of motions, many of which may be very significant to the case and some of which may produce news.

Dismiss, demurrer. Perhaps the most important of these, at least in legal if not journalistic terms, will be the various motions to dismiss. Sometimes, this will take the form of a **demurrer,** which is a formal request to bring the case to an end at that point because it may be legally insufficient. (Technically, a judge grants or denies a motion to dismiss, but he sustains or overrules a **demurrer.**)

Among the reasons upon which a motion to dismiss, or a **demurrer,** might be filed are:

—that the parties filing the suit did not have legal **"standing"** to sue—in other words, they had no direct right to raise the legal issues they are seeking to press or no present interest in those issues;

—that the court does not have jurisdiction over either the subject matter of the case or the person or property involved, or any or all of these;

—that the case more properly should have been brought in a different court: a state court rather than a federal court or vice versa, or in a court more conveniently located because of the residences or places of business of some of the parties involved;

—that the complaint does not raise a **justiciable** claim—that is, a claim subject to resolution in the courts, rather than some other arm of government;

—that the complaint does not state a genuine **cause of action**—that is, a real legal issue;

—that the complaint raises an issue or issues that have been previously settled in a prior case (technically, the issues are **res judicata,** meaning settled before);

—that the parties bringing the case are not the proper ones, or that the claim that a lawsuit should proceed as a **class action** is not valid, or that the parties who should be sued have been left out of the case;

—that the parties being sued are not subject to being sued, at least in the given case, because of some form of legal immunity, such as governmental (**"sovereign"**) **immunity,** official immunity of a government officer, immunity for a charitable institution, immunity of family members.

It is obvious that many of these motions are quite technical, and thus are not likely to provide a basis for a news story. The reporter, however, should monitor the filing of such motions to dismiss in order to prepare himself in the event that one is granted and, at times, to obtain clues to the legal strategy that the sued party may pursue.

It may be stated as a general rule that if a complaint is sufficiently newsworthy to be covered, dismissal of it for any reason is equally worthy of being reported. The reporter, in doing so, should attempt to provide his readers or listeners with an understanding of the legal basis for granting a motion to dismiss. This should be done in the simplest possible terms. Most importantly, in reporting a dismissal of a civil case, the reporter should cover the practical consequences, in terms of the actual parties and circumstances involved.

Other motions. Among some of the other motions that may be made after a complaint has been filed are motions of other parties to join in the case, as **intervenors** (usually worth covering) or as friends of the court—that is, **amici curiae** (often worth covering). There also may be a series of routine motions, including such things as requests for extensions of time for the filing of the answer or reply.

Memoranda of law. Filing of motions may bring with it, or be followed by, filing of **memoranda of law**—that is, formal, written arguments in support of the motions on legal grounds. Some of those will make illuminating reading for the legal reporter, adding to his awareness of the scope of the case. More often, however, they will *not* produce significant news stories.

Motion to amend. Another early motion that may come into a civil case is a motion by the suing party to amend the complaint. That would be quite common if the court had granted a motion to dismiss or had sustained a demurrer. The amendment would be an attempt to rescue the case before it is ended entirely. Some amended complaints, of course, will make news.

The Answer

When the case reaches the point at which the sued party is prepared to react directly to the complaint, the **answer** is filed. This probably will be an item-by-item, paragraph-by-paragraph response to the points made in the complaint. The answer may deny or challenge some of those points, and it may concede some of them. It may contain a different, or at least partially differing, recital of the facts at issue. It also may include a series of points that are called, technically, **affirmative defenses.** Those are assertions that the actions taken by the sued party were justified, in a legal sense, and therefore may not be the basis upon which the suing party could win.

The reporter should pay close attention to the responses made in the answer. They will help refine the issues in the case and they will provide hints—perhaps more than that—of the strategy of the defense. It is generally true, however, in a practical sense, that the answer will make news less often than the complaint does. It is in the nature of lawsuits, as news, that the claims of the suing party commonly will be more newsworthy than will the formal response to the complaint.

An exception to this generalization, however, might be present if the answer contains not only answers to the complaint, but actually states a claim of its own against the suing party. So-called **counterclaims** may make quite significant news because they are like a new complaint, the only difference being that it is originated by the other side, the sued party.

The Reply

The suing party gets another chance during the pleading stage to refine its claims. This comes in the **reply,** filed after the sued party's answer.

In form, this will be much like the answer: an item-by-item response to the statements or assertions made in the answer. If the answer has included a counterclaim, the reply will serve as the formal, written answer to that.

Again, the reporter will find that the reply illuminates the case but usually does not produce news. At this stage, the issues in the case are being shaken down, and this process—while crucial to the law of the case—is not likely to attract lay attention.

Motions After Pleading

After the reply has been filed—or, in some cases, while the various pleadings are in the process of being filed—either side may file other motions. These may be inconsequential **motions to "strike"**—that is, expunge—some parts of the other side's pleadings or motions to make claims more definite.

There also may be other motions that are quite significant, including:

- motion for **discovery** (see the next section for a fuller discussion of the discovery process);
- motion for a jury trial (see Chapter 11);
- motion for **summary judgment.** This is a motion by one side or the other seeking to have the judge rule upon the case solely on the basis of the written pleadings. At this point, the judge may grant a motion for summary judgment only if there is *no* genuine issue of fact still open, and the moving party is entitled to prevail as a matter of law. The judge must be able to conclude, in other words, that that side has already made its case. In ruling on such a motion, the judge will assume that all the factual allegations made are true and beyond dispute, leaving him with the decision only on whether the case has succeeded on strictly legal grounds.

The reporter may want to cover some of these more significant pre-trial motions. Motions for discovery and for a jury trial may be disposed of quite briefly, journalistically speaking. A motion for summary judgment, however, should be treated at length—but only if granted. Such motions are made quite routinely, and the mere filing of them is not newsworthy. Whether he reports them or not, however, the reporter should acquaint himself with such motions when they are filed, because they could bear importantly on issues and strategies in the case.

F. THE DISCOVERY PROCESS

In civil lawsuits, as in criminal cases, there is a method by which each side may seek to learn as much as possible about the evidence in the other side's possession. The aim is the same: to reduce the possibility of surprise later in the case and to increase the prospect that a case will be decided on its full merits rather than on the ingenuity of lawyers in managing the scope of the case.

The discovery process does not necessarily produce evidence for use in court. Merely because some information has turned up in the discovery stage does not mean that it will be admissible at the trial (admissibility is discussed in Chapter 11). The data that do turn up in discovery may, however, be extremely valuable to the preparation of a case and, of course, it frequently does include usable or admissible evidence.

In seeking material in discovery, the requesting party must be able to show that the data would be **relevant,** that is, the information would bear on issues and facts at stake in the case, and that it is not protected by some form of **privilege** preventing disclosure.

Methods of Discovery

The methods by which discovery proceeds may include these:

- **Depositions,** oral or written. These are questions put, under oath, to persons who are likely to be or will be witnesses in the case or to others possibly having information bearing on the claims. The questioning for a deposition is done much as the questioning during trial, with the opportunity for cross-examination after direct questioning. Depositions may be substitutes for testimony at the trial.
- **Interrogatories.** These are written questions put, under oath, to parties in the case (and *not* to witnesses).
- Requests to produce documents.
- Requests for admission of facts or allegations, or for denials. Some of these may be entered in the case as **stipulations**—that is, matters upon which the two sides agree.
- Requests for mental or physical examinations, where mental or physical health is or may be an issue in the case. "**Good cause**" must be shown in order to obtain permission for such tests.

It is quite common for the discovery process to be done in private, with exclusion of the press. The results may, however, become available for public inspection at a later point in the case—perhaps before trial, or at the trial itself, when material obtained by discovery is offered as evidence.

Obviously, the information turned up during the discovery process may be quite newsworthy. Moreover, the pursuit of this information will reveal the strategies—or at least part of them—of the opposing sides in the case. The reporter, however, should also be prepared to find that there is a great mass of minutiae—in a news sense—that emerges in the discovery stage.

G. PRE-TRIAL CONFERENCES

In order to reduce conflict at the trial, and to narrow and sharpen the issues to be tried and the evidence to be offered, it is quite common for pre-trial conferences to be held in civil cases. These will be meetings attended by the lawyers and usually the trial judge at which the entire scope of the case is examined.

In addition, the conference may be used to promote a settlement without a trial.

The press normally will be excluded from such conferences. It often is quite easy, however, to learn, after the fact, whether major decisions have been reached at the conference to narrow the case. Of course, if such a conference does produce a settlement, that customarily will become a matter of public record, and the reporter will learn about it.

H. "CALENDARING" OF CASES

The only remaining step before a civil case is pronounced ready for trial is the scheduling of a trial date. This will be arranged at the convenience of the court and also, usually, at the convenience of the attorneys involved. The setting of a trial date may produce a brief item of news.

I. DECISIONS WITHOUT TRIAL

Special mention should be made of the means by which a case is ended by a decision in the pleading stage or at any point in the pre-trial period. A great many civil cases will come to an end without a trial. Of course, the results in those instances might be quite newsworthy.

A case may be decided solely on the basis of the pleadings, as in the granting of a motion for **summary judgment.** It also may be decided on the basis of **proposed findings of fact** and **conclusions of law** submitted by each side after the pleadings; this is not a motion for summary judgment, but rather it is a proposed decision prior to trial. A hearing may or may not be held on proposed decisions in civil cases.

These approaches to decision without trial may provoke a series of legal memoranda, many of which could be quite newsworthy.

When the judge is satisfied that he has before him the materials necessary to aid his decision, he will announce an entry of a **judgment**—in other words, he will decide the case. He may award money damages, he may issue permanent injunctions, he may issue **declaratory judgments** that simply state whose rights or obligations have or have not been violated without necessarily issuing any binding orders or granting damages, or he may issue quite explicit orders requiring one side to do or to refrain from doing something.

After a judgment has been entered, one side or the other may file motions asking that the judgment be postponed temporarily (technically, "**stayed**"), pending the filing of further memoranda or pending an appeal. There may also be a motion for **judgment n.o.v.** or a motion for a new trial.

In addition, there may be notices of appeal, which will set the beginning of the time allowed for pursuing an appeal.

A decision prior to trial will be no different, in a news sense, than a decision after trial. If the case is one that justifies coverage, the decision will justify stories about it. The reporter will want to explain, as fully as he can, the basis upon which the decision was reached, and the practical consequences of at least the main parts of the decision.

11

Covering Civil Cases: The Trial

A CIVIL TRIAL IS MUCH LIKE A CRIMINAL TRIAL—but without the drama and mostly without the tension. It has many of the same ingredients, but it is, at least as a source of news, noticeably different. The legal issues are more central in a civil case, journalistically speaking, even though the human dimension obviously is still there.

Those are reasonably valid generalizations the legal reporter should consider as he approaches the coverage of a civil trial. Some civil cases may be said to be dull because of the fact that a great many are tried without juries. That, alone, reduces considerably their potential for high drama. But some of them are considered to be dull because the kind of contest that goes on in civil cases often simply does not have the potential for attracting a wide popular interest.

The news interest in a civil trial, as has been suggested, is in the controversy that is being tried. Even though there are people and institutions involved in the controversy, and even though the interests at stake may be serious and even gravely so, the dispute may not bring the reporter to the raw edges of conflict that he routinely faces in criminal trials. In a word, a civil trial is likely to be more sterile as news.

It is for these reasons that the reporter will discover a peculiar challenge in covering a civil trial. While actually reporting less of it than he would a criminal trial, he nonetheless will discover that it may be considerably harder to make it interesting to a lay audience. The mix of facts and law is so close that the very process of translating it into news of general interest is exacting and difficult.

The reporter will be aided if he maintains a keen and attentive eye on the facts, as was suggested at the beginning of Chapter 10. But he must never get very far from a tight focus upon the law.

The process of translation will be hopeless, of course, if the reporter is unfamiliar in the comparative maze of the law that governs civil trials. This chapter will guide him through that maze; again, in chronological fashion. First, however, it is fundamentally important to deal with the issue of jury and non-jury civil trials.

A. THE JURY ISSUE

It is true, everywhere in the nation, that there is a "right" to a jury trial in civil cases. But that is only the broadest of generalizations. This is a far less pervasive "right" than is the right to a jury trial in criminal cases.

There is a federal constitutional right to a jury in civil cases, but that applies only in the federal courts and it does not apply to all forms of civil trial. A similarly limited guarantee of a jury trial in civil cases exists in state courts under state constitutions.

Basically, the question of whether the right exists is a two-part question: does it exist at all, and if so, may it be waived and does the jury, where used, decide all possible issues?

Background of Civil Juries

Traditionally, the right to have a case tried before a jury was limited to **common law actions** and did not exist for **suits in equity.** A common law case is one in which the parties' legal rights are determined; the remedy for violations of those rights is the award of money damages. A suit in equity is one in which the judge concludes that a party's right to be treated equitably (under general principles of proper or "right" conduct) has been violated; the remedy is to order someone to take some action or refrain from taking an action.

As the civil law developed in America, however, issues of "law" and questions of "equity" became mixed in some lawsuits. Some claimed wrongs were based upon legal error, others on breaches of equity. In such a mixed case, the jury's role became a confused one. In some jurisdictions, a jury now is confined to deciding issues controlled by principles of law, and the judge decides issues controlled by principles of equity. In other areas, no jury is permitted at all unless the issues in the case are predominantly issues controlled by law.

It should be stressed that when the jury decides common law questions, it is not ruling upon points of law as such. Rather it is deciding the facts under rules or principles of law spelled out for it in the judge's instructions.

Even where it is clear that there is a right to a jury, it usually may be waived. In federal courts and some state systems, the right to a jury is assumed to be waived unless it is demanded in writing within a specified period of time. Other states assume the jury is to be used unless expressly waived.

The News Potential

It may be said generally that the presence or absence of a jury itself seldom makes news. In other words, a reporter is not likely to write a story simply because a jury is demanded or is waived. However, when writing about a civil trial, the reporter might note in passing that there is or is not a jury, and what difference this makes, if any. The presence of a jury may influence significantly the kind of strategy used and the evidence offered by either side—particularly where the controversy or the persons involved generate emotion.

B. JURY SELECTION

When a civil case comes to trial—that is, when both sides have completed their filing of the **pleadings** as outlined in Chapter 10—the most significant first step will be the selection of a jury when one is used.

Preliminary Motions

The case actually may open with the filing or pursuit of other motions, procedural or substantive. This may include, for example, renewed motions to dismiss, motions to transfer the case to another court, motions to **remove**—that is, transfer—a state case to the federal court on grounds that a fair trial could not be obtained in the state case on the "federal questions" involved or the parties were from different states, or motions to ask the judge to send the case to a higher court for a prompt decision on unsettled questions of law that may control the outcome of the trial.

Some of these motions clearly will produce news; that is particularly true of motions to dismiss, if granted, and of motions to **certify** controlling questions of law to a higher court for decision. (See Chapter 12 for a discussion of these **interlocutory appeals.**)

If a jury is waived, or no right to a jury exists in a given case, the case begins with the presentation of the case by the lawyers, after motions have been decided.

Picking a Jury

If a jury is to be used, selection of the jurors will proceed in a civil case much as it does in a criminal case. A **pool** of potential jurors will exist, from which a **venire** will be chosen as the source of potential jurors to try a given case.

Jurors will be questioned singly or in groups, by the judge and lawyers separately or together, about their qualifications to serve on the case. Lawyers for each side will be able to exclude some jurors by exercising a set number of **peremptory challenges**—that is, rejections of jurors without specifying a reason—and a usually unlimited number of **challenges for cause**—that is, requests to the judge to dismiss a juror for a specified reason, as outlined by the lawyer making the challenge.

The News Potential

The selection process is less likely to produce news in a civil case than in a criminal case, generally speaking. It is just as important to the lawyers, but the makeup and character of the jury is not as important to lay readers or listeners. A reporter, however, may be able to learn much about the strategies of each side by the manner in which a jury is chosen, and he may also learn something of the scope of the evidence. Such indications could produce stories, immediately or at a later time.

C. TRIAL MEMORANDA OR BRIEFS

In some jurisdictions, it is quite common for attorneys to file **trial memoranda** (sometimes, as in federal courts, called **briefs**) as part of the process of refining the issues to be tried. These may include discussions of the evidence or of the legal questions to be tried and may be, in some cases, quite extensive legal arguments. They may be filed before trial opens or at an early stage of trial.

When these are filed, the reporter will find them of major assistance in settling in his own mind the scope of the case, and suggesting to him the key points that are to arise during the trial. They may also produce stories when filed. The reporter should be alert during a trial to see whether the actual strategies follow or vary from the memoranda or briefs.

The reporter should also watch for the filing of **stipulations**—that is, statements of the facts that are not in dispute between the attorneys for the two sides. These will be facts that are or may be **material** to the case—that is, facts which are essential to the case.

D. OPENING STATEMENTS

To acquaint the jurors with each side's case, opening statements are often allowed (but not always made) in civil cases. The "right" to make such a statement may depend upon permission from the judge. In cases where a jury is *not* used, it is customary not to make an opening statement.

The statement will be a recitation of the main points the lawyer for that side expects to make during his presentation of evidence. He may outline his legal theories, and may cover—but usually not in detail—some of the evidence that is to follow. Clearly these may produce news as well as significant guidance to the reporter on the case.

The Burden of Proof

In a civil case, the first side to make an opening statement, where allowed, will be the side that has the **burden of proof.** While in a criminal case, one side—the prosecutor—always has the burden of proof, in a civil case, the burden may shift. The burden of proving the case rests upon the side that is making the claim or asserting the legal cause. Usually, this will be the party that filed the case in the first place. Where, however, there are counter-claims filed by the party that has been sued, that party bears the burden of proof on those claims. Depending upon preliminary rulings by the court on legal points, the burden may shift from one side to the other.

It should be stressed again here that the scope of the burden of proof is different in a civil case. The usual standard is that a point must be proved by the **preponderance of the evidence**—that is, considering all of the evidence, whether the point has been proved by the greater weight of the evidence. In some jurisdictions, the standard that is used is that a point must be proved by **clear and convincing evidence.** The difference between that and a "preponderance standard" may be quite subtle.

After opening statements, if any, the case proceeds with the presentation of the evidence—again, with the side bearing the burden of proof offering its case first.

E. RULES OF EVIDENCE

It is just as true in a civil case as in a criminal case that the evidence that may be put before the jury or judge is limited quite strictly by **rules of evidence.** These are rules, enforced by the judge who tries the case, that govern whether a given item of evidence (a witness, his testimony, exhibits, documents, and so on) may be offered formally as part of the case—in other words, whether it is **admissible.**

In some jurisdictions and before some judges, the rules may not be enforced as strictly when there is no jury in the case. The judge himself may decide, as a matter of discretion, to listen to evidence of doubtful admissibility and then decide whether he will consider it to be a part of the case. When a jury *is* being used, the judge may decide to hear such evidence with the jury out of the room and then rule upon whether it may be presented to the jury as admissible evidence.

Admissible Evidence

The rules of evidence most commonly used provide that evidence *may* be offered if it is:

- **relevant**—that is, it relates to the controversy on trial, and it tends to prove the point for which it was offered;
- **material**—that is, it is essential to the case;
- testimony by a witness relating what he has heard or seen but not what others have said *they* heard or saw, which is barred as "**hearsay**";
- testimony by an expert witness, qualified in his field to make expert analysis, regarding his opinion or conclusion about something in his field.

In addition, it is commonly required that the evidence offered to make a point be the **best possible evidence** available to make that point. For example, original documents are better evidence than copies.

Finally, some evidence is *barred* because it is protected by a legal **privilege,** assuring its non-disclosure against the wishes of the person or persons protected. Depending upon the jurisdiction, this may include communications between husband and wife, doctor and patient, religious leader and believer, lawyer and client, and perhaps others, including journalists and sources. The privilege may be waived.

As each side's case unfolds, the judge's rulings on admissibility may produce news. Indeed, a case may be won or lost on the basis of such rulings. The reporter should cover the more significant rulings on evidence, pointing out as best he can the basis upon which the judge did or did not allow an item of evidence or testimony into the case. He also should try to explain how that bears upon the strategy of that side's case and on the other side's case, and he should try to explain how it might affect the case if there is an appeal after the trial is over. Perhaps the reporter might use such rulings as a basis for a feature story explaining how the rules of evidence work.

The News Potential

In covering rulings on admissibility, the reporter usually should put the emphasis on the content of the evidence itself, with the judge's legal rationale for his action subordinated. This does not mean, however, that the legal rationale should be so little emphasized as to deprive the reader or listener of a basis for his own opinion on the merits of what the judge has done.

F. PRESENTATION OF EVIDENCE

The evidence is offered by each side in its own turn. The process follows these steps:

1. direct examination—that is, introduction of the witness or exhibit by the attorney for that side, followed by direct questioning of a witness regarding his testimony or regarding the exhibit offered.
2. cross-examination—that is, questioning of the witness by the other side, to test or even to challenge his credibility ("impeachment") or to get information to aid the other side in making its case when its turn comes.
3. re-direct examination by the side offering the witness or exhibit.
4. re-cross examination by the other side.

This process will be repeated when the other side's turn comes. That is usually referred to as the **rebuttal.** After that, the side which began may offer evidence in answer to any new matters that were brought out during the rebuttal. Such **rejoinder** evidence may be strictly limited by the judge.

The News Potential

The evidence phase is the crux of the case. It will make news of an immediate "spot" nature or the basis for an analytical story. It tests the strategies of each side thoroughly and it controls how the case will come out. In covering this phase, the reporter should be especially careful to relate the evidence, as it develops, to the strategy and to the case as a whole. A given item of evidence may seem to mean nothing standing alone; it needs always to be put into context.

Moreover, the reporter must relate the evidence to the law that is governing the case. It is not enough to show how one item of evidence relates to another or to the whole; its legal context is as significant.

The reporter covering this phase of a civil trial will have many opportunities to do feature stories that will explain the processes of civil law. Having "real-life" evidence upon which to base such features clearly strengthens them.

G. MOTIONS DURING AND AFTER EVIDENCE

At the close of the case made by the side which opened, the other side may attempt by motion to have the case dismissed. This will be based on the argument that the suing side has not been able to substantiate its claims with sufficient facts or as a matter of law, and thus the matter should be dismissed. Ordinarily, such a motion will be granted only if the judge concludes that the offered evidence, considered in the way most favorable to the suing side, could not satisfy a "reasonable man" that that side's claims have been supported.

Such motions to dismiss (sometimes they are called motions for **non-suit**) are made quite routinely, and they usually would not produce news unless granted.

If such a motion is denied, then the other side presents its evidence, as outlined in the preceding section.

After the evidence is in, but before the case has been submitted to the jury—of if there is no jury, to the judge—for a judgment or verdict, either side may make a motion for a **directed judgment** or **verdict**. This is a motion made with the jury absent, if there is a jury.

Such a motion will be granted if the judge concludes that the side which offered the motion has made its case and that "reasonable men" would not disagree that it had made its case.

Again, these motions are made quite routinely and would not produce news unless granted.

H. CLOSING ARGUMENTS

When all of the evidence is in and all motions have been disposed of, the case is ready to be submitted for judgment. Before this occurs, however, it is common in most jurisdictions to allow each side to sum up its case with a **closing argument** (sometimes called a **summation**).

This will be, as its name implies, a final attempt to persuade the decision-maker (jury or judge) to find in favor of one side or the other. Such arguments sometimes produce news. A reporter should pay attention to them, among other reasons, for indications as to how the strategy may have changed or had to be changed along the way because of rulings on evidence and other matters during trial.

I. INSTRUCTIONS TO JURY

If there is a jury in a civil case, the judge will give it final **instructions** before it begins its **deliberations.** Instructions are legal advisories to the jury on the scope of its function, the manner in which its discretion is limited by the principles of law that control the case, and the kinds of verdicts that it may return.

Obviously, instructions are not given when there is no jury. In some jurisdictions, however, the judge may summarize the evidence.

J. JUDGMENTS OR VERDICTS

The result in a civil case is the **judgment** or **verdict.** If a jury is used, its ruling is a verdict and the order of the judge implementing that verdict is the judgment. If there is no jury, the judge's ruling is the judgment.

When a jury is used, it may be instructed either to bring in a **general verdict**—that is, a verdict "finding" the facts, and applying the law as described by the judge to those facts—or a **special verdict**—that is, answers to questions of fact put by the judge. Where special verdicts are allowed, the verdict by the jury provides the basis of fact upon which the judge makes his judgment.

It goes without saying that the result in a newsworthy civil case is very likely the most important news to emerge from it.

K. REMEDIES IN CIVIL SUITS

The judgment or verdict in a civil suit may take several forms.

Money Damages

If the case involves a judgment or verdict in an **action at law** (a "**common law action**") where one's legal rights have been violated by the other side, money damages may be awarded. The terminology used for damage awards varies widely between jurisdictions, so the reporter must acquaint himself with the terms used locally. Terms used fairly commonly describe these forms of damage awards:

- **Compensatory damages**—payment of money that will make a person "whole" for losses he has suffered or may in the future suffer because of the legal injury done to him by another. This form of damages may be **general**, if the injury was a natural and necessary consequence of the other side's wrong, or **special**, if the injury did result from the other side's wrong but was *not* a necessary consequence.
- **Punitive damages**—payments in addition to compensatory damages, or alternative to them, to punish the wrongdoer for his action and to make "an example" of him to deter others from similar action. Sometimes these are referred to as **exemplary damages.**
- **Nominal damages**—payment of an insignificant amount (perhaps $1) when there is no basis for establishing a set amount of compensatory or punitive damages for the wrongdoer's action. This form of damages usually is awarded when there is in fact no real loss to the suing party. It is a form used merely to settle a civil case where

there was a damage claim, as opposed to an equitable claim (see section A of this chapter and see below).

- **Liquidated damages**—payment of an amount specified in advance by agreement of the parties as the sum that *would* be paid if a contract or arrangement were violated ("breached"). It often is within the discretion of the court, however, to refuse to allow such damages or to modify their amount if the judge finds they are excessive or unreasonable.

Equitable Remedies

If the case involves a judgment or verdict in a **suit in equity,** the result may be a court order of one of these kinds:

- **Mandatory injunction** (usually called a **permanent injunction**) ordering one party to do something, technically speaking, to give **"specific performance"** of a duty undertaken by agreement or imposed by law.
- **Prohibitory injunction** (it, too, may be called a **permanent injunction**) ordering one party to refrain from doing something because that has been found to violate a duty imposed by law or by agreement.

(Temporary or preliminary injunctions are discussed in Chapter 10. Those are issued at earlier stages of civil cases.)

L. MOTIONS AFTER VERDICT

When a result has been reached in a civil case, there still remains an opportunity for the losing side to try to salvage a victory, or at least to succeed in starting the case over afresh.

This is the point for offering a motion to set aside a verdict, a motion to rule in favor of the losing party despite the verdict (**"judgment n.o.v."**) or a motion for a new trial.

These are fairly routine motions and seldom produce news.

It is after such motions are finally denied by the judge that he issues the final **judgment** to implement the result of the case. If the judgment imposes damages and the losing side does not pay, then an order may be issued requiring **execution** of the judgment—that is, payment. If the judgment requires that something be done or not done, failure to obey the order may result in an action to cite the erring party for contempt of court.

M. CONCLUDING MATTERS

A case may not be all over in the strictest technical sense even when a judgment has been issued. The losing party may attempt to get the judge—or perhaps a higher court—to issue a **stay of enforcement** or **stay of execution** of the judgment. This is usually sought in an attempt to keep matters as they were until the judgment is appealed by the losing party.

Depending upon the case, such motions for stay may produce news.

If there is to be an appeal, the losing party must file a notice of appeal within a specified time after judgment in order to "preserve" his right of appeal where that right exists. (Civil appeals are discussed in the next chapter.) A notice of appeal very often will be newsworthy. In practice, however, a reporter may learn that a case is going to be appealed some time before a notice of appeal is formally filed in court. Attorneys usually will tell the reporter about that in advance of the formal act of filing the notice, perhaps immediately after announcement of the judgment or verdict.

12

Covering Civil Cases: The Appeal

MUCH THAT AMERICA READS OR HEARS about civil law deals with civil appeals. Very often, perhaps most of the time, the press gives heavier coverage to appeals than to trials in civil cases—the reverse of the norm in covering criminal cases. This is especially true in broadcast coverage of the law.

Partly, this is a function of numbers: the process of appeal in civil cases is quite rigorous in winnowing out cases, so that the ones which do survive to a decision that will make news are quite conspicuous.

Partly though, the phenomenon is due to the nature of news about civil law: the legal result that emerges may easily overshadow, in a news sense, the particulars of a given case itself, and this is almost predictably true at the appellate level.

Legal journalism about civil appeals is, in short, coverage of the law as law. The "human interest" dimension of legal controversy, focusing upon the facts of specific disputes, tends to diminish as civil cases move through the higher courts. A decision is likely to be newsworthy because it shows law developing, not because it brings a controversy to a close. To put it the other way, unless a civil appeal *does* add to the development of law, it may not produce much news.

There is a risk in all of this for the reporter. He still has his lay audience, largely unlearned in the law and often quite baffled by it, and he may write over the head of that audience. While a reporter covering civil cases at the trial level has the facts of a given case to help him make his story interesting (even though, as Chapter 11 shows, he may have to make do without drama), the reporter covering civil law at the appeals level must make the law itself interesting; that is what his story is all about.

This is true even though, as has been stressed throughout earlier chapters, the facts in a case are always important to the reporter covering the law. Facts do remain a significant part of the story about a civil case on appeal. But, as Chapter 2 and this chapter show, civil appeals are not concerned basically with the facts. Only rarely do appellate courts allow themselves to second-guess the trial judge or jury on their "findings" of fact. This chapter, in following the civil appeals process chronologically, shows how that shapes the news.

A. SCOPE OF THE RIGHT TO APPEAL

In civil cases, just as in criminal cases, there is no "right" to appeal guaranteed or required by the Constitution. This is a right that must be provided by a state or federal law, and its scope may be quite restricted by such laws. In every jurisdiction, however, the right to appeal in a civil case is codified to some extent. As a general rule, there is an assured chance—once—to file an appeal. There is no such thing as multiple appeals of the kind that may occur in criminal law through habeas corpus or post-conviction review (see Chapter 7).

To appeal in a civil case, the party must have been a loser, in a genuine way, in the trial court. If the suing party got what he sought at the trial level, he has no right to file an appeal even though he is dissatisfied with the legal rationale for his victory there: he may not test the law issues that produced his remedy. If the sued party won, he too, is barred from appealing on the law. But if either side got nothing at all, or less than they had tried to get, either may resort to the "second chance" process of appealing.

As the appeal is pursued, the challenge that the loser makes to the judgment against him turns upon legal principle. He may not base his appeal on a claim that the trial court got the facts wrong.

If it should occur, in a given case, that new facts become available after the case has moved to the appeals court, the case probably will be sent back to the trial court to deal with that situation. The case may come to an entirely different judgment as a result of the new facts, thus eliminating any basis for the appeal.

B. CHARACTERISTICS OF APPEALS

Before moving on to the steps that an appeal will take, it is worthwhile to go over again some of the basic procedural characteristics of civil appeals.

- Appeals must proceed on the initiative of one or both parties (assuming they have a right to appeal). The appeals courts do not have the authority to bring cases before them unless a party asks them to review a case, and the trial courts do not have the authority to send a case up to appeal unless asked. The special situation of **interlocutory appeals** should be kept in mind; that is discussed later in this section.
- Appeals may be filed only when the case is over in the trial court—in other words, the case has reached a final judgment of one of the kinds described in Chapter 11. A significant exception to this, however, is the **interlocutory appeal** (see below).
- Appeals must be based upon the arguments or theories pursued in the trial stage. An issue that is posed for the first time when the case is before an appeals court is considered "**untimely,**" in a technical sense, and normally it will be barred from review on appeal. If such an issue is raised, and if it is significant enough, the appeals court may send the case back to the trial court for action upon it before the appeal is allowed to proceed. An exception to this would be an attempt to raise, for the first time, a challenge to the trial court's jurisdiction.

Interlocutory Appeals

Some aspects of a case may go through an appeals process *before* the case is tried before a judge or jury in the trial court. This is what is called an "**interlocutory appeal.**"

Its purpose is to allow a court with power to do so to settle questions of law, *not* fact, that will control the way that a case would be tried. It is designed to save judicial time—and, of course, the time and money of the parties involved—by avoiding the need for a second trial because the first one proceeded on what turned out to have been a faulty legal premise.

Interlocutory appeals, however, are discouraged in most jurisdictions, partly because they usually are piecemeal in nature and partly because they may actually lengthen, not shorten, the time it takes to dispose of a case. The legal reporter probably will encounter few of them. When he does, he should cover them fully if the underlying case itself is at all newsworthy, even though they raise purely legal issues.

Usually, the right to pursue such an appeal depends upon the approval of a trial court judge or of the appeals court to which the "**controlling**" **questions** would be sent for decision. If the authority lies with the trial judge, he will grant or deny **certification**—that is, referral—of the issues to the appeals court. If the authority lies with the appeals court, it will grant or deny permission to certify.

C. APPEALS, STEP BY STEP

Opening Formalities

Once a reporter has written about the decision by an attorney and his client to pursue an appeal in a civil case, there will be no occasion for further stories about the other steps that occur at the very outset of the appeal process. A series of legal formalities occurs and, although they are necessary in a legal sense, they will generate no news interest at all.

The reporter, however, needs to know about them and perhaps sometimes to monitor them because they could have value as points of future reference as the case unfolds.

Preparation of the record. These steps involve the preparation of the documentary record that will form the basis of the appeal.

Because an appeal will be more limited in scope than the trial had been, it is unnecessary for appeals courts to have before them all the materials that were before the trial court. The **record** therefore will be limited to those documents, exhibits and testimony that bear directly upon the legal questions being raised on appeal.

The attorney for the losing party in the trial court (technically, the **appellant** in the appeals court) will notify trial court clerks of the materials to be copied and sent to the appeals court. These will be documents and exhibits used at the trial. If the attorney for the other side (technically, the **appellee**) concludes that additional materials should be included, these, too, will be made a part of the record.

Next, the attorney for the appellant will ask that a full transcript be made of the oral testimony at the trial. This is added to the record for the appeal. Technically, this is termed "designating the record on appeal."

In many jurisdictions, the record will be submitted in typewritten form. In federal courts it often is printed, though this requirement may be set aside by the appeals court. Some significant delays often have resulted in getting cases ready for appellate review because of the time consumed in getting sometimes massive records printed.

As an appeal proceeds, the reporter may have occasion to go back to parts of the record for background information on the case. Such records routinely are available for public and press inspection—unless, of course, there is only a single copy of it before the court, and the court itself is using it. Sometimes, however, parts of a record may be sealed by court order and thus will be unavailable.

As has been indicated, these materials will serve only as source documents for the reporter. He is not likely to be able to get much from them to show the appeal strategy of either side.

It should be noted that the preparation and filing of the record will not necessarily occur automatically after a notice of appeal has been filed. That *will* happen if there is no question about the party's right to appeal the case—in other words, the appeals court has no discretion to decline review of the case. But, as a later discussion in this chapter shows, there are courts to which an appeal is discretionary with the court involved. In those circumstances, the record will *not* be prepared and filed until after the appellate court has granted permission to appeal—that is, it has accepted the case. This is the norm for supreme courts, at both the state and federal level.

Appellate Briefs

The final "paper" step in preparing a case for appeals court review is the filing of written **briefs** by both sides. Normally this is governed by a time schedule provided in the rules of the court.

A brief is a statement of the case as each side sees it. The contents of the brief will be controlled by the scope of the case. No legal issues may be raised, generally speaking, unless they had been first brought up in the trial court. No new evidence may be offered. If new issues seem to have arisen since the trial court judgment or if new evidence has become available, the appeals court may insist upon being informed of that, but it is unlikely to allow them to become a part of the case; at most, the court ordinarily would send the case back to the trial court for an initial reaction.

Contents. Typically, a brief on appeal will include the following:

- Formal "**style**" of the decision or decisions in lower courts—that is, name of the case, name of the court involved, date of the decision, listing of the volume number and page (**citation**) where the case is officially recorded if that has been done.
- Brief statement of the legal issues being raised.
- Recitation of enough of the facts to illuminate the legal issues.
- Legal arguments supporting the kind of decision on appeal that the appellant (or appellee, in his brief) wants the court to make.

In some courts, it is required that briefs be printed. Others (including the federal courts) allow that to be waived, with briefs submitted in typewritten form.

Quite often a brief will produce news. The way in which the issues are stated, the legal points made on either side of those issues, and sometimes the rhetoric itself will be worth covering perhaps as "spot" news. The brief obviously can give the reporter a full indication of the theory that each side is pursuing on appeal, and the filing of the brief frequently will provide the basis for analytical stories on the scope of a case being covered.

Other briefs. If there are any **intervenors** or **friends-of-the-court** (**amici**

curiae) involved in the case, they, too, may file briefs. These may serve to expand the scope of the case, and they often will make news.

Since hearings in appeals courts are usually quite short, with each side given a specified and limited time, the written briefs in the case must carry most of the burden of making each side's case for it.

Hearings (Oral Arguments)

Not all civil appeals necessarily include oral hearings (technically, **oral arguments**). Some cases may be decided solely upon the written materials. When a hearing *is* held, its functions ordinarily are to illuminate the most significant legal points at issue and to allow the judges of the appeals court to get the attorneys to clarify or perhaps to expand upon points made in their briefs.

The hearing gives the reporter his first opportunity to gauge the potential reaction of the appeals court to the case. Reporters always are cautioned that they should not "read into" the performance of judges at appeals hearings any indications as to how the judges will decide the case. That is good advice. But the reporter also should feel obliged to report what the judges ask or say, if it is of news value, and to try to explain to the reader or listener how the question or comment *might* be significant. Speculation of that kind—and it often is no more than that—should be shown as such in the story. Otherwise, the chances of misleading the public may be considerable.

The hearing also gives the reporter another opportunity to gauge the strategy of the lawyers. Because the attorneys' hearing time is limited, they are often forced to shape their arguments to what they consider to be their strongest points. If the attorney, however, uses his time simply to reiterate well-known points already covered fully at the time of filing his brief, his courtroom appearance is not likely to add much of news value.

A reporter should try to cover fully any hearing held in a civil case he deems newsworthy. Hearings frequently make good stories simply because of the atmosphere they create and the "human interest" that may exist in seeing the court in action.

Prof. Geoffrey C. Hazard Jr. has described oral hearings in appellate courts as "something like contentious seminars." To some, that may imply that they are too technical or scholastic to be of popular interest. In fact, however, they may be of considerable fascination to a lay audience if stories about them are written so that the legal exchanges between the judges and lawyers are easy to comprehend and are understood against the factual and legal background of the given case.

Deliberation

After the hearing is over, the reporter usually will learn no more about the case until a decision is reached and announced. The court's deliberation of the case after it has been "taken under advisement," the formal phrase for the deliberation process, goes on in the privacy of the judges' chambers or their court's conference room.

That process is not particularly well understood outside the courts. Quite commonly, judges are most reluctant to discuss it with reporters and the public, and other court employes or officers—such as clerks—either do not know much about it or are very reluctant to discuss what they do know. The judges are restrained by ethics from discussing the way they reacted to a particular case, and some feel similarly restrained from discussing the process of deliberation.

In general, however, it is common for the judges to assign the case to one of themselves—the assignment function may be performed by the chief or senior judge—for the preparation of a proposed decision. This may be in the form of a proposed order or it may be a full-dress opinion giving the legal rationale for the decision that is to emerge.

One or more formal votes may be taken by the judges as the deliberation process goes forward. One or more discussion conferences of the full court or of judges meeting in smaller groups may be held.

The reporter should attempt, from time to time at least, to offer his readers or listeners a feature or analytical story on the deliberation process, so far as he can learn anything about it. It is likely to be a fascinating activity with its own institutional and personality dynamics, and thus it can make stories of quite wide popular interest.

Decisions on Appeal

When the court has made up its mind in a final way, it will announce its decision. This may come in an order, written in legal form and language, deciding some or all of the legal issues. It also may come in the form of a written opinion which will give the appeals court's reasoning for the decision it has reached. (When the court puts its ruling into effect, in a legal sense, it may issue a separate document, technically a **mandate**, which advises the court from which the appeal came what it is to do with the case as a result of the decision on appeal.)

Contents of opinions. When an opinion is issued, it may be signed by a judge or it may be unsigned ("per curiam"). It may include:

- Brief recitation of the history of the case in the court below from which it came.
- Brief recitation of the facts in the case that bear upon the legal issues at stake in the appeal.
- Discussion of the legal issues involved, with the court's explanation of why it decided as it did, and perhaps why it accepted or rejected arguments offered to it by one or the other side in the case.

The reporter should understand that there will be a legal **holding** in the case, and that this is all that the court settles in a formal sense. This will be the declaration of the rule of law that the court has determined applies to the facts of the case.

Not uncommonly, courts will issue opinions or decisions in which they make comments of a legal nature that are not, in fact, necessary to the **holding** of the case. This kind of more or less extraneous judicial commentary is called **dicta.** It has no formal bearing on the legal result in the case. It may, however, give attorneys firm indications of how the court is reacting to an issue that it sees lurking in the case or that seems likely to arise in the future.

The reporter, obviously, will want to cover decisions and opinions in full. He should be careful, in doing so, to make clear just what has been decided— in other words the formal **holding** in the case. He also should cover any **dictum** that the court utters in its opinion, but this should be done in a way that makes clear what the court was doing in making such an utterance.

Opinions by appeals courts do contribute significantly to the development of the law. Thus the reporter also will find in their decisions and opinions much material for analytical stories about the law.

His most fundamental obligation, however, is simply to tell how the case came out. He should try to relate its holding to the practical circumstances of the given case itself, as well as to the situations involving others that may be controlled or strongly affected by the holding.

When a court issues an order settling a civil appeal without an opinion, the task of the reporter is more difficult. He sometimes, however, may be able to get from the judge or judges some "guidance"—perhaps not to be attributed to the judge or court directly—about the rationale behind an order that was issued without written explanation.

D. REARGUED CASES

An appeals court at times may find itself unable or unwilling to decide a case after it has gone through all of the steps up to the point of decision. It may then order the case reargued, perhaps asking the attorneys involved to file new briefs and to argue new points that they had not covered before or had covered incompletely. Sometimes a party in the case may ask that the case be reconsidered.

If a court is sitting as a **panel** of an appeals court, cases may sometimes be ordered heard by the full court, sitting **en banc.** This may be done at the initiative of one of the parties or in some jurisdictions at the initiative of the court.

In any of these situations, the reporter probably will want to cover the reargument or reconsideration. When a case is reargued or reconsidered, it will follow the same procedure as the case when originally handled: that is, briefs (if requested or allowed) will be filed, a hearing may be held, and the court will deliberate toward reaching a decision.

E. FURTHER APPEALS

In the federal system, and in an increasing number of states, the right to appeal a civil case basically means a right to take it to an **intermediate court of appeals.** Beyond that, any appeal to the U.S. Supreme Court or to a state supreme court is—with only a few exceptions—discretionary with those courts. Those senior courts do not sit to hear all appeals, however routine; their function is to decide only those cases likely to raise novel or fundamental questions.

It is true still in some states that the right to appeal does remain a right to appeal directly to the state supreme court from a trial court. In those states, there is no middle or intermediate layer of appellate review. If there is to be further appeal from the decision of such a state supreme court, it will go only to the U.S. Supreme Court as a discretionary matter with that court.

When a state does have a two-tier appeals system in its own courts, and in the federal courts' two-tier system, the volume of civil appeals that will be accepted for review by the supreme courts is comparatively small. Many more cases are taken to those courts, seeking review, than are actually accepted for decision.

Usually, the supreme court exercises its discretion about reviewing appeals through a process of certifying (or refusing to certify) the case for appeal. In technical terms, the court issues a **writ of certiorari** to notify the lower court that the supreme court is willing to accept the case. The U.S. Supreme Court uses both a writ of certiorari and a separate method—**noting jurisdiction**—because of the differing forms of jurisdiction that it has. These are discussed more fully later in this chapter.

Petitioning for Review

Typically, when the party that lost in the intermediate court of appeals wishes to seek further review in a supreme court, it files a formal request to the supreme court. This is often called a **petition for a writ of certiorari.**

Contents. It will include:

- A citation to the decision being challenged, showing where the case is officially reported, if it has been. This will also give the date of the lower court's judgment.
- A brief statement of the issues being raised on the new appeal.
- A brief summary of the facts that lie behind those issues.
- A discussion of the legal issues, generally aimed toward convincing the supreme court to review the case and deal with those issues.

Usually, this will not be an extensive argument; it will not try to argue fully the issues themselves.

- The text of the judgment of the court below and the text of any written opinion of the court below, if there was one.

The function of such a petition is simply to persuade the court that the case is worthy of the supreme court's attention. If done well, it will be a fairly limited document that will give the supreme court an opportunity to know quickly and quite easily what is at stake.

The full details of the case history in the lower court or courts will be supplied later in the formal **record** if the supreme court does accept the case for review. The full legal arguments on the issues involved will be supplied later in formal written (usually, printed) legal **briefs.**

A reporter assigned to a supreme court, or following a case up from a lower court, often will find that requests for supreme court review do make news. Aside from the news value of the case itself, the filing of the petition may be newsworthy because of the way it poses the questions before the supreme court.

The News Potential

A more significant news story usually will result if the supreme court does agree to hear a case. Since comparatively few cases are granted review at that level, it may be assumed—as a general matter—that most of those that are accepted are sufficiently novel or significant to produce news.

The fact that a supreme court agrees to review a case does not necessarily signal that it is going to rule differently than the court below did. In most jurisdictions, less than a majority of the members of the supreme court has the authority to grant review. In the U.S. Supreme Court, for example, it takes only the votes of four of the nine justices to grant review. Moreover, the supreme court, after completing its own review, may decide that the lower court was right about the case.

Thus, in doing stories about a grant of a writ of certiorari, the reporter should stress that the supreme court has only agreed to hear or review the case, not that it has settled it nor that it has telegraphed how it will settle it. Depending upon his awareness of the particular supreme court's tendencies in given fields of the law, the reporter may have a basis for speculation about the way an appeal may be decided. If he does speculate, it should be made clear to the readers and listeners that that is all that it is.

When a case has been accepted for review, the supreme court generally will follow the steps outlined earlier in this chapter for civil appeals in general: preparation of the record, filing of written briefs, oral argument, deliberation, decision. Generally, none of those steps differs in any fundamental way in the supreme courts from the procedures in the intermediate courts of appeals.

The final decision by a supreme court, however, will be of more significance—in law and in the news—than a decision by an intermediate court of appeals. There is only one supreme court in each state (although in Texas there is one for civil and one for criminal cases), and only one in the federal system, and thus their decisions are binding on all courts below them. The rules of law that emerge are final for that system—except that a state supreme court ruling may remain subject to further appeal, in some circumstances, to the U. S. Supreme Court (see Chapter 2).

In writing about supreme court decisions, the reporter not only will want to cover the specific rulings as they come out, but also will want to analyze them for their contribution to the development of law. He also may want to do analytical stories about the meaning of decisions in institutional terms—that is, what do decisions tell about the way a supreme court is operating, what do they say about the relations between the supreme courts and lower courts, what do they tell about the relations between the judiciary and other branches of government?

U.S. Supreme Court Jurisdiction

Special mention should be made of the different modes of getting cases before the U.S. Supreme Court. As has been said, it exercises discretionary review power through the **certiorari** process, described earlier. In addition to that, however, there are specific kinds of cases in which there supposedly is—by law—a "right" to appeal to the Supreme Court. In those cases, the Supreme Court supposedly has no discretion but to review them when asked.

As a practical matter, however, it has developed over the years that the Supreme Court in fact uses a kind of discretion about reviewing those cases. It does so by the way in which it concedes, or fails to concede, that it does indeed have jurisdiction over the case as a matter of law, or by the way in which it summarily affirms or, more rarely, reverses the decision being appealed.

If the Supreme Court is willing to accept such a jurisdictional case, it either will **note probable jurisdiction** or else postpone the jurisdictional issue until it reaches a decision in the case after review.

If, however, the court is unwilling to give the case full-dress review, it may conclude that it has no jurisdiction in the case—and it will say why it does not—or it may issue a brief order summarily affirming or reversing the court below without giving any reasons or explanation.

Lawyers and judges have long debated whether a Supreme Court ruling summarily affirming or reversing in a jurisdictional case actually sets a precedent binding on lower courts. That issue is not settled in a final way, because a majority of the Supreme Court has never said precisely what such rulings mean in law.

The reporter may treat such a disposition as a decision on the merits of the case at least for the parties involved in that case. The decision will provide guidance for all others, too, at least until the Supreme Court should agree to review the merits in a future case.

In reporting on a summary decision by the Supreme Court, the reporter should point out the limited meaning of such a ruling.

Supreme Court voting. The U.S. Supreme Court decides cases, after review, by majority vote. A quorum of at least six of the nine justices must participate in a case. It is not necessary that all nine take part; a justice's disqualification of himself from participating in a decision is quite common. This is usually done without public explanation of the reasons.

If the Supreme Court casts a tie vote in any case, the result is that the decision of the court below is upheld—technically, affirmed. It is the court's practice to write no opinion in tie-vote cases. Thus, the result and the reasoning of the court below stand.

13

Covering Special Courts

A LEGAL REPORTER MAY HAVE HIS BEST CHANCE to cover "celebrity law"—lawsuits involving noted personalities or well-known figures—in one of the courts of special jurisdiction. Many cases in criminal courts do, of course, become "celebrated," but more because of the crime than the personalities involved. In the special courts, though, there is hardly any reason to cover a case unless a celebrity is a party.

These courts process tens of thousands of cases, but they are largely ignored by the press. They seldom make news in the legal precedents they set, and there are only a few of them that are ever likely to provide news on appeal.

Thus, they clearly are, from the press' point of view, sources of "human interest" news, a good story when a celebrity is involved and perhaps only then.

Occasionally, however, there may be a strong feature story about one or more of these courts. A legal reporter can, by using some ingenuity, make even the routine output of a special court into a significant analytical story on the law.

The special courts are an important part of the American judicial system, but they are not well understood by the public or the press. No doubt nearly everyone has heard of divorce courts or of military courts-martial. But that is surface awareness at most. The press could do well to add to that awareness by giving some added attention to all of these unusual tribunals. In giving more attention to these courts, however, the reporter should be aware that this type of coverage may involve significant risks of lawsuits against the press for libel or invasion of privacy.

There has been some tendency in recent years to expand the special court approach to law. Growing complexity in codes of law and in legal relationships has encouraged legislatures, particularly at the state level, to confer jurisdiction over a defined field of law to a special court.

Sometimes this expansion in special jurisdiction has been done as part of the general growth of regulatory law—that is, the "administrative" process. That field is the subject of Chapter 14. Examples of special tribunals in the regulatory field would be a housing court, created to administer codes governing landlord-tenant relationships, rents, safe and sanitary housing conditions, and so on, or a labor or arbitration court, created to administer laws governing management-worker or union-member relationships.

The growth of special jurisdiction, however, has also brought the creation of new tribunals that are true courts. In other words, it has brought the development of new arms of the judiciary, created to decide cases and controversies according to rules of law and lacking power to make policy in the first instance. These tribunals hold limited jurisdiction because the fields in which they operate exist to serve special needs that supposedly require a developing expertise.

This chapter will deal with only a few of these courts, the ones an average legal reporter is most likely to encounter sooner or later in his work. These are the divorce courts (technically, "domestic relations" courts), probate courts, military courts (technically, "courts-martial"), and two special federal tribunals: the U.S. Tax Court and the U.S. Court of Claims.

Others do exist, such as the U.S. Customs Court at the federal level or small claims courts at the local level. These, however, are likely to be so specialized in nature that they almost never produce news, or they are so localized in character that only reporters in those locales could expect to have a professional interest in them. A reporter who is specializing in legal news should become fully familiar with all of the court structure in his area.

(Another form of special court, the juvenile court or the juvenile branch of a "family court" having some other forms of jurisdiction, too, is discussed fully in Chapter 8.)

Two other kinds of special judicial proceeding—involving adoption of children and commitment of mentally defective persons to institutions for treatment—customarily are conducted in closed proceedings, and thus are not open to press coverage. They are not discussed further here.

It is generally true that most special courts a reporter will encounter are civil in nature. They will operate, therefore, under the usual rules of civil procedure, including the rules of evidence (see Chapter 11). They also will have their own rules, peculiar to each court, but those commonly will overlay the normal civil rules. Military courts are something of a combination between civil and criminal courts; they *do* have the authority to impose punitive sanctions for violations of military law and discipline.

It also is generally true that special courts operate primarily as trial courts—that is, courts of original jurisdiction in their fields of law. Quite commonly, appeals from their decisions will be permitted and, in most jurisdictions, those appeals will go to regular civil courts of appeal. Again, the military court system is an exception. Thus, this chapter deals primarily with special court operations at the trial level.

Proceedings in the special courts are discussed here step by step, to show the points at which news may be made.

A. DIVORCE ("DOMESTIC RELATIONS") COURTS

Divorce law is administered at the state level only, since the power to legislate in this field lies solely with the states. Occasionally, a federal case will arise, based on constitutional arguments, but in general, federal courts will defer to state discretion in this field.

It is not universally true that divorce law is entrusted to a court of special jurisdiction. In many areas, the regular civil courts handle "domestic relations" cases simply as another form of civil practice. In other areas, however, there *are* special "family courts" with exclusive authority in that field.

This is a highly specialized field of the law, no matter in what kind of tribunal it is practiced, so this chapter treats it as a form of special jurisdiction. It should be noted that it is quite common for domestic relations law to be practiced by attorneys who specialize exclusively or primarily in such cases.

The News Potential

The interest of the press in domestic relations law is confined almost entirely to cases where a well-known figure or personality is involved. There are two basic reasons for that: one, the obvious one perhaps, is that the personal lives of such celebrities often seem to be extensions of their public personalities, and it is assumed that there is a substantial amount of reader/listener interest in their domestic situations; second, for persons other than celebrities, a domestic dispute or breakdown is largely if not exclusively a private matter, and the press is obliged—by ethics if not by law—to acknowledge that privacy. Many domestic relations cases thus are simply none of the public's business, journalistically speaking.

The reporter who covers a domestic relations case should understand that, even when celebrities are involved, there may be risks of libel or invasion-of-privacy lawsuits. A reporter would be well advised to have a lawyer's counsel—at least in a general way—to aid him and his editors in professional planning and execution of such coverage, if there are any serious doubts about the legal risk that may arise.

Before moving to a step-by-step analysis of the news potential in divorce cases, it would be helpful to understand some basic concepts.

Forms of Action

Domestic relations law varies from state to state, but it generally exists in one or the other of two basic forms:

- a **cause of action** based upon a claim by one spouse that the other has caused fundamental change or even destruction of the marriage;
- a **"no-fault" proceeding,** testing only whether the marriage is broken down regardless of who may have caused that.

Obviously the two forms differ absolutely. The first, involving concepts of fault or blame, is a proceeding in which one side generally is accusing the other of a breach of the marriage relationship. The second is a proceeding in which the dominant issue is whether the marriage itself has any continuing validity.

The difference between the two forms exists primarily in the nature of the claim that is made by the suing party. There is basically no difference between them in terms of the burden of proof. In both, the party that comes to court seeking an end to the marriage, or a change in the relationship, has the burden of proving that its claim is justified. In the first, or fault concept case, the suing party must prove that the grounds upon which change or dissolution is sought are valid and convincing. In the no-fault case, the suing party must prove that the marriage itself is "irretrievably broken down," or some variation of that concept.

Not all domestic relations cases seek the end of a marriage—in technical terms, **divorce a vincula,** meaning complete divorce or dissolution. Some states allow for a change in the marriage relationship short of complete divorce. This is usually called a proceeding for **"separate maintenance"**—technically, **divorce a messa et thora,** meaning divorce from "bed and board." A decree granting separate maintenance usually frees each spouse in all legal respects except that they cannot re-marry.

As a general principle, there is no reason why a legal reporter should treat either proceeding differently, journalistically. If the case is newsworthy at all, it will be so because of the identity of the persons involved, not because of the legal form of their domestic relations complaint.

Filing of Complaint

A domestic relations case, like any civil case, begins with the filing of a complaint or cause of action. If the marriage is to be changed in a legal sense or dissolved, it may be done only through the action of the court. The parties may make their own legal agreement to live separately (see below), but the basic bond of marriage remains until a court has acted to change or end it.

<u>Forms.</u> A complaint may take one of these forms:

- If the end of the marriage is sought, it will be a complaint or petition for divorce or dissolution, or, in some jurisdictions, a petition for an **annulment**—a finding that the marriage never existed legally, because of some basic defect in its legal origin.
- If the end of the marriage is not sought, it will be a complaint for separate maintenance.
- If an order providing for separate maintenance has been issued previously, but its terms are not being met, a complaint may be in the form of a petition for alimony or child support "unconnected with dissolution." Such a petition also may be filed to enforce the terms of a separation agreement privately made between the spouses; such agreements are binding contracts, legally enforceable.

A separation agreement is often made between spouses having marital difficulty but who do not wish to seek complete divorce—perhaps for reasons of religious principle—or who wish ultimately to seek a divorce that is to be uncontested but which may be sought only after a waiting period established by state law. The agreement remains a private one between the spouses either until a divorce is sought or until enforcement of the agreement is sought by one of the parties.

Complaints in domestic relations matters usually are on public record and thus available to the press. In some jurisdictions, however, all or parts of domestic relations proceedings may be sealed by court order, putting the records of the cases out of the press' reach. In such circumstances, a reporter may not become aware that a case is going forward unless he learns it from one of the spouses, their friends or associates or their attorneys.

The filing of a complaint will make news, as a general matter, only if the parties involved are newsworthy. Sometimes, too, the formal filing of a complaint comes long after the news media have become aware that the marriage of a newsworthy couple is in some difficulty; then, the filing may be less than a major story.

Temporary Orders

In some jurisdictions, a domestic relations court has authority to issue temporary orders—almost of an emergency nature—to deal with serious problems that may arise immediately after a complaint is filed in court.

A **temporary restraining order** may be issued—sometimes, at the request of one spouse with no advance notice to the other and without a hearing—to protect the person suing for divorce or separation, a child or children, or assets or property of the married couple.

A judge who issues such an order is acting only on a finding that some emergency protection is needed; he is not acting on the basis of a conclusion about the merit—or lack of it—in the complaint for divorce or separation.

Such an order may be quite drastic in its terms; for example, it may order one spouse to leave the house they jointly occupy, or it may order a spouse to give up a child to the other spouse's custody.

In some jurisdictions, the spouse who is the target of a temporary restraining order may have a right to a prompt hearing on the validity of the temporary order and perhaps a right to a prompt appeal.

There is an even more extreme form of temporary order that is permitted in some jurisdictions. It is a form of an ancient **"writ of ne exeat."** If one spouse advises the court that there is a danger the other spouse will leave the state and thus be beyond reach of any orders issued dealing with children or property, the judge may issue an order requiring the arrest of that spouse and his jailing until he posts a bond assuring he will not flee and committing himself to obey any orders of the court.

Almost invariably, a spouse who is the object of such an order has a right to make an immediate plea to the issuing judge or to an appellate court for relief from the order.

Because temporary orders are issued on the request of just one side in a marital dispute (technically, an **ex parte** request), the legal reporter may not know about them until after they are issued. Because of their sometimes extreme nature, a reporter should report such orders in a newsworthy case when he does become aware of their existence.

Procedure After Filing

After a complaint has been filed, the spouse who has been sued may make a motion to dismiss the case or some procedural motion, such as the absence of jurisdiction in the court where the complaint was filed, or he may file a motion for **discovery.**

If the divorce or separation is contested, the sued party may file an answer or perhaps a cross-claim or cross-petition, seeking a remedy of his or her own. For example, if one spouse has sued for separate maintenance, the other may cross-file seeking complete divorce.

Uncontested divorces. The vast majority of divorce cases are uncontested. After the filing, a sued party may simply file no answer at all, thus conceding that the divorce may be granted by default, or may file a simple answer to lay the basis for a brief hearing on the final order to be issued. Sometimes, even though divorce or separation is not contested, the sued party may wish to have a hearing to determine issues of alimony, child support or division of property. It should be noted that some states do not allow for division of property in cases of separate maintenance.

"No-fault" cases. In some states having "no-fault" divorce laws, if there is no contest and if there are no minor children involved, the marriage may be ended almost automatically on the pleading of one side. This will not occur, however, if there are disputes over alimony, custody or property division.

Depending upon the nature of any contest in a divorce or separation case, a reporter may seek to cover the proceedings on those disputes. Again, however, there is a possibility in some jurisdictions that some or all of these proceedings will be closed to the press.

Hearings

"Evidentiary hearing." In some cases, a hearing on preliminary or temporary relief may be ordered. The purpose of such a hearing is to gather evidence so that the judge may decide whether to provide temporary alimony or child support, temporary custody, temporary rights of visitation to the home or children, and temporary possession or use of property.

These proceedings do not deal with the basic merits of the complaint, but only with the need for temporary arrangements between the spouses. They will result in a written order directing those arrangements.

It is not universally true, but these proceedings may be open to the public and press. Their news value may be comparatively low, however, because nothing final is being settled.

The judge's order specifying the temporary relief similarly may be of little news value. It usually will *not* include a legal justification or rationale for the action he has taken.

Final hearing. Before a judgment or decree is issued in a domestic relations case, the judge may hold a concluding hearing. At such a proceeding, every issue that exists in the case, from the change or dissolution that is at stake to the forms of final relief or remedy, will be open for review. Sometimes separate hearings may be held: one on the basic decree, a separate one on issues of remedy.

Such a hearing is a form of non-jury trial. Juries are seldom used in domestic relations cases, and where used at all, they may have only an advisory capacity. The normal rules of evidence will be followed, and the procedure will follow that of a normal civil trial (See Chapter 11).

Evidence in a final hearing may be offered through documents, witnesses or both. The burden of proof at the hearing is on the party seeking some action by the court; the burden of proof is the usual civil one of "preponderance of the evidence" or "greater weight of the evidence."

If the case is a newsworthy one, the chances are that the reporter will find the final hearing of considerable news value—at least it is likely to have considerable "human interest" value.

Forms of Decree

At the close of a domestic relations case, the judge will issue a judgment or final decree. Aside from settling the basic question of whether to dissolve a marriage, or to order a formal separation, the decree may include some or all of the following forms of relief or remedy:

- Awarding of custody of the child or children; this may be awarded to one spouse singly, to the spouses on a divided basis or to a third party.
- Right of visitation to the children or to have the children visit.
- Division of personal property. Sometimes the scope of a judge's power to divide property of any kind is quite limited by a specific law; his power may be limited solely to ratifying agreements of the spouses—if they are able to reach any such agreement.
- Division of real estate. Usually, a judge's power to divide such property is even more limited than is his authority to divide personal property. He may, however, have considerable discretion as to how the property is to be used or occupied, at least for a temporary period.
- Alimony. This may be awarded to either spouse. It is based upon need and upon ability to pay. It may be ordered for a temporary period—often, until the receiving spouse is "rehabilitated"—that is, able to function alone financially or permanently, at least until re-marriage of the spouse. Alimony may take the form of a lump sum award of property or assets, or of periodic, continuing payments or allowances, or a combination of lump sum and periodic forms. (In some states, alimony may not be awarded if the ground for divorce is adultery.)

Delayed decrees. In some jurisdictions, judges have authority to postpone final decrees in domestic relations cases in order to provide a "cooling-off" period that might lead the couple to be reconciled. Sometimes judges also have authority to order one or both spouses to have professional counseling—another device designed to encourage reconciliation.

As is true of most civil court orders, final decrees in domestic relations cases will be open, public records available to the press. Again, however, that is not a universal rule; in some jurisdictions a judge may have authority—on his own or at the request of the parties—to seal a decree.

Appeals

When a domestic relations case has been contested, an appeal is quite common. Appeals will be processed in the same way that normal civil appeals are (see Chapter 12), and the appellate court probably will treat the trial court decision with great respect unless there is a clear showing that the judge has abused his discretion. Appeals will be limited to legal questions only.

Common Law Marriage and Divorce

Some states still recognize "**common law marriage**"—that is, acknowledgment of a formal marriage relationship carrying mutual obligations, even though there has been no ceremony of marriage. Such marriages are based upon specified periods of living in fact as husband and wife and after that fact has been acknowledged.

Generally speaking, a common law marriage may be ended in divorce only by pursuing the same process of dissolution as for civil marriages. In a common law divorce case, however, there may be an additional issue: whether there was, in fact, a marriage relationship. If the issue is contested, and if it cannot be proved that a marriage did exist, that ends the matter; a decree to that effect will be issued.

In recent years, some courts have awarded payments or other benefits to one member of a couple who has been living together, without formal or "common" law marriage, when the couple's relationship breaks down and they part. This is the so-called "Marvin rule," initiated in California. The award, in a slang expression, is sometimes called "palimony."

B. PROBATE COURTS

State law controls the protection of private property that is to be transferred when the owner dies, or property that is to be held for the present or future use of an owner or a person who has or will obtain rights to the property.

This is the field known, somewhat misleadingly, as "**probate** law." The word "probate" is taken from the Latin word *probare*, meaning "to prove." As used in the law of property transfer, it means testing the validity of a will or other document conveying property—proving it, in other words.

While much of probate law does, indeed, have to do with "proving" of wills, that is only one aspect of its overall scope. The field now generally includes many of the forms of protecting and transferring of property, not solely transfers upon the owner's death.

In general, this branch of the law is entrusted to a court or an agency of special jurisdiction. Part of the function of administering probate law is exercised by a "registrar of wills" and part is exercised by probate judges or courts.

As in the field of domestic relations, a great deal of the activity in probate law will be of little or no interest to the press. Much of it has to do with private matters within or among families, and a good part of this activity simply will never come to the attention of a legal reporter. Moreover, even if it does, the reporter will be guided by ethical restraints to ignore much of it in order to protect privacy.

Again, therefore, the reporter will become interested perhaps only when a prominent figure or family is involved. The protection and/or the transfer of the property of such persons is a matter of public interest where the amount or value of property involved is quite considerable.

Before analyzing the various forms of probate procedure, it would be useful to go over some generalizations about the law of probate.

As has been indicated, it is a matter within the discretion of the states. Seldom will a probate issue become a matter for federal courts to consider. There have been a few cases arising out of federal constitutional claims but, by and large, federal courts defer to state law in this field, because the states have jurisdiction over property and that, not persons, is the central focus of probate law.

Forms of Jurisdiction

A probate court, sometimes it is called an "orphan's court" or a "surrogate's court", may have three basic forms of jurisdiction:

- estate law administration, which includes overseeing the transfer of property in both **testate** and **intestate** situations—that is, with or without a will. This may also include a determination of the validity of a will, the scope of a will, the determination of heirs or legal successors, the allocation or recognition of rights in the heirs or successors, and the distribution of the estate.
- protection of the property of minors, missing persons, or persons who are incapacitated, in health, status, or law, so that they are incapable of looking after their own affairs.
- administration and supervision of **trusts.** A trust is a legal entity or arrangement created to hold property for the benefit of another person. Trusts may be set up simply to protect and manage property or to accomplish its transfer at a given point.

In general, probate courts sit without juries, although in some states a right at least to have an "advisory" jury may exist during a formal proceeding in estate law administration.

As another generalization, it is commonly understood that probate law exists primarily to give effect to the choices about property that are made by private persons. In other words, probate law is limited in the degree to which government may intervene in private property arrangements, and overturn or modify them. Much of the legal administration of property may, in fact, be done by a personal representative of the deceased, the person who owns the property or the one who holds a present or future interest in it. Such a personal representative very often is a private person.

This section will deal separately with the three major areas of probate jurisdiction.

Administration of Estates

Most of the time, the press' interest in probate law will be in the administration of property after its owner has died. This form of probate law is treated at somewhat greater length here than the others.

Forms of probate. There are two forms of so-called "probate administration" of the property of dead persons. Neither exists, however, until someone has invoked the power of a registrar or of a probate court. The two procedures, with exceptions in detail depending upon the jurisdiction, are:

- informal probate, a non-judicial form of putting into effect the will that a dead person has left to control succession to his property;
- formal probate, a judicial determination of property rights and distribution, but one which may in fact be limited to single issues in dispute rather than reaching the whole scope of rights to inherit.

Probate of a person's estate can only occur after the person's death, and one of the basic facts to be determined at the outset of probate is whether, in fact, the person has died. Usually, probate must be achieved through a personal representative of the deceased person, acting as "administrator" or "executor" of the estate.

Another fundamental fact to be determined by a public official, a registrar or a probate judge, is whether the person died with a will (**testate**) or without one (**intestate**). It should be noted that there may be **partial testacy**—that is, there may be a will covering some, but not all, of the property of the dead person.

Each state provides, by law, the standards for determining whether there is a will and whether it is valid. This will cover the age at which a person is legally able to make a will, the manner in which a will may be written, the means by which it may be changed or revoked, and the manner in which the intent of the **testator**—the one making the will—is to be construed.

State law controls the specific shares for heirs in cases where there is no will. These may vary according to whether the state is a **community property** state—that is, one in which a married couple owns property in common—or a **separate property** state—one in which property is held by a single person in his own name only. Some guarantee specific portions for spouses and/or children. These laws are called statutes of descent and distribution, or laws of "intestate succession."

If the owner of the property dies without a will, the property will be distributed among the heirs according to those laws. The task of the court in those situations is to determine that all bills or claims against the dead person or the property have been satisfied, to determine who the heirs are and to distribute the estate to them. If the estate is a small or modest one, the proceeding may be a highly informal one. If there is a contest over the rights of heirs, or if the estate is substantial in size, a more formal proceeding will be necessary.

In circumstances where there is a will, state law usually will require after a person's death that a will must be delivered to a court or to a personal representative who will take it to court to be probated. A will, in order to be legally binding in transferring property and thus conferring enforceable rights on the new owners, must be found to be valid either in informal probate, by a court officer such as a registrar, or in formal probate, by a court's action.

Method of informal probate. This is a procedure for putting a will into effect without extensive court proceedings. The process begins with the filing of an application for informal probate. In response, the registrar issues a statement to begin the proceedings, and then determines whether the will put before him has been executed properly. If he finds that it has, he will grant the application for informal probate, and the will is thus executed. If he finds that the will has not been executed properly, he will deny the application. Such a decision may not be appealed; the only recourse is to seek formal probate.

The press is likely to learn about informal probate proceedings because the registrar usually is obliged to keep wills offered for probate on public file and to give notice when a will has been offered for probate.

An informal probate normally will not be used if there is any contest over the will or the property involved. Nevertheless, the absence of a contest does not necessarily mean the press will have no interest in this type of proceeding. If the persons or estate involved is newsworthy, that will determine the press' interest.

Method of formal probate. The formal **testacy proceeding** is used for determining the validity and construction of a will where there are uncertainties or contests about those issues.

It begins with the filing of a petition seeking an order probating a will, an order to set aside an informal probate determination, or an order to determine heirs and property distribution when there is no will. After the filing, a notice and perhaps a hearing will be ordered by the probate court.

If the petition is unopposed, the court may order probate of a will or determination of rights in intestate property simply on the written pleadings before it without a hearing. If, however, proof seems to be required, the court will hold a hearing to gather evidence—perhaps by affidavits alone or by a combination of affidavits and oral testimony of witnesses. In some jurisdictions, a jury may be used to try such cases.

The burden of proof in a formal probate case rests on those who offer the will to be probated or those who seek an interest in intestate property. Those who contest a will or who challenge others' claims to property will have the burden of proving the lack of intent or capacity on the part of the owner, undue influence upon him before death, fraud, duress, mistake or revocation of a will.

At the close of formal probate, the court will issue an order determining that the owner is dead if that is certain legally, that the court has proper jurisdiction over the will and property if that is true, the identity and interests of the heirs, the presence or absence of a will, and the settlement of issues at stake including any conflicts where there is more than one will.

Such an order is final and binding on all parties but may be challenged either on appeal or by a petition to vacate the probate order.

Similar procedures may be followed in obtaining court appointment of the personal representatives of a dead person.

The press may well want to cover any open hearing, or pleadings, in formal probate—where, of course, the nature of the parties or the property justifies press attention. Obviously, the final probate order itself will make news in such cases.

Protection of Property

Procedures quite similar to those involved in estate administration will be followed in obtaining official protection of persons who are legally or otherwise incapacitated or incompetent. This will be a proceeding for "guardianship or protection."

The aim of such a case is to determine that a person cannot effectively manage or apply his own property, because of some form of incompetence. The court may determine that a **guardian** is to be appointed, or that a **conservatorship** is to be created to protect and manage the property.

This proceeding may be highly informal or formal. An informal proceeding that is quite well known is one, for example, in which a person is given **"power of attorney"**—that is, capacity to act in the interests of an incompetent or incapacitated person regarding his property.

Press coverage of a guardianship or protective proceeding will be quite rare. Sometimes these proceedings are sealed in order to protect the privacy interest of the person who is to be protected.

Administration of Trusts

Procedures quite similar to those for estate administration will often be used to provide judicial supervision of the internal affairs of trusts. These proceedings will result in ongoing administration of a trust, distribution of the property held in the trust, declaration of rights of those who are the beneficiaries of the trust, or determination of the role of trustees.

Trust administration procedures often will be spelled out in precise detail in state law, governing not only **inter vivos trusts**—those taking effect during the lifetime of those who commit property to the trust—but also of **testamentary trusts**—those taking effect after the death of the person committing the property to the trust.

Many matters involving administration of trusts are sealed because of the private nature of the interests involved. Where they are the object of public proceedings, press interest will be rare—unless, of course, the trust involves persons of prominence, well-known charities or property of major consequence.

C. MILITARY COURTS

The "military justice system" is basically a hybrid form of legal practice and procedure. Its aim is the simple one of maintaining discipline within the U.S. armed services. Part of it is civil in nature and part penal or criminal. Its civil side is a form of internal personnel administration, providing forms of "non-judicial punishment" for minor infractions in discipline. Its criminal side may and does include elaborate judicial forms and procedures, at times very much like a civilian criminal proceeding.

It is controlled—but only in part—by the same constitutional provisions that surround civilian criminal cases. Many of the constitutional guarantees are applied in lesser or diluted form for servicemen. The process of incorporating those guarantees into the military justice system is one left largely to the military courts themselves.

Civilian courts have given some review to the process of military justice, but that has been strictly limited. This is because, as the Supreme Court has said:

> The military is, by necessity, a specialized society separate from civilian society. . . . Military law is a jurisprudence which exists separate and apart from the law which governs in our federal judicial establishment. . . . Congress is permitted to legislate both with greater breadth and with greater flexibility when prescribing the rules by which the military shall be governed. . . .

Each of the military services conducts tens of thousands of disciplinary cases every year. The press is likely to be interested in only the merest fraction of these, the ones involving very conspicuous incidents in military life.

When, however, a celebrated case does arise—for example, the prosecution of Lt. William Calley for the My Lai massacre during the Vietnam war—

the press needs to know how the military justice system works. Moreover, this is a field of law that is still in the developing stage—the basic law on modern military justice dates only from 1950—and thus it provides a potential area for news and feature stories of interest to legal reporters.

Before moving into a discussion of the several forms of military court activity, it will be useful to go over some fundamental concepts.

The military justice system is, at its basic level, what may be called an *ad hoc* system—in other words, it is a system for processing a military case that comes into being only when there is a case to be handled. There are no permanent military courts sitting on the bases and stations of the armed services. Only at the appellate level is there a continuing court like those that exist in the civilian system.

A military case begins with a decision by the commanding officer of the individual serviceman involved. It is up to the commander to decide what kind of military tribunal is to be convened to deal with a serviceman who has become a disciplinary problem. The reasons for this have been stated by one commentator:

> The commander is responsible for maintaining an effective fighting organization. He still must promote and provide for the safety, welfare and morale of the personnel under his authority. Discipline is the ingredient that enables the commander to discharge all these responsibilities. In the maintenance of an effective fighting organization, and in promoting safety, the power to apply discipline is indispensable.

To be sure, the military justice system has been widely and increasingly criticized, primarily because its procedures do not imitate those of the civilian justice system. Even so, the tendency is still for the civilian courts—including the U.S. Supreme Court—to leave the development of military justice to Congress and to the military courts.

Non-Judicial Punishment

The simplest form of military court practice is not even a court proceeding. It is the direct disciplining of a serviceman by his commanding officer. This is confined to minor violations of disciplinary norms or rules. It is a highly informal procedure, primarily one of counseling, that leads to comparatively minor forms of punishment—maximums of 30 days in "correctional custody," 60 days restriction to base or quarters, 45 days of extra duties, loss of one-half pay for two months, postponement of half of pay for three months, reduction by one pay grade.

The press seldom if ever will become aware of non-judicial punishment within the military. This is a form of day-to-day personnel administration that rarely makes news.

Forms of Court-Martial

The Uniform Code of Military Justice, the basic law providing for the military court system, sets up three forms of "court-martial":

- summary court-martial
- special court-martial
- general court-martial.

The press will not often become aware of summary proceedings because they deal with minor offenses and provide for lesser penalties upon conviction. Only the special and general courts-martial are likely to have newsworthy cases before them. Their proceedings ordinarily will be open, thus permitting coverage.

Summary court-martial. Basically, this procedure is used to deal with enlisted men who commit offenses that would *not* violate the criminal law if committed by a civilian. It is convened by the commanding officer.

It usually consists of only a court officer who must be a commissioned officer and the accused serviceman, meeting in a conference room. A serviceman is allowed to have a lawyer whom he hires.

The proceeding is a form of trial, with the court officer examining witnesses, if any are called, and allowing the accused to cross-examine them. The court officer, however, is also required to help the accused examine witnesses who appear to give favorable testimony for the accused. If the serviceman is convicted, he has a right to make a plea to minimize the penalty.

The maximum penalties are: 30 days of confinement at hard labor, 45 days of hard labor without confinement, two months' restriction to base or quarters, reduction to the lowest enlisted man's pay grade, loss of two-thirds pay for one month.

An enlisted man is entitled to refuse summary court-martial. If he does, the charges against him either must be dismissed or referred to one of the two more elaborate forms of court-martial.

After conviction in a summary court-martial, an enlisted man has his case reviewed by the officer who convened the court, and then by an officer who supervises the convening officer. This is automatic. Beyond that, the convicted serviceman may ask the Judge Advocate General of his service to review the case; that is a discretionary form of review.

Special court-martial. This is one of two forms of court-martial with power to try military officers as well as enlisted men. (The other is general court-martial; see below.) It exists to try more serious crimes than those handled in a summary proceeding or to try a case in which a serviceman has refused summary court-martial.

Convened by the commanding officer, the special court-martial includes not less than three court members acting somewhat as a jury, or it may consist only of a single military judge, or it may have three members plus a military judge. A judge alone may try such a case only if the accused person asks for that and only if the judge approves.

If the court has only members and no judge, the senior officer among the members presides. There will be military officers who are lawyers by training acting as prosecutor (law officer) and defense counsel, and the accused may hire his own civilian defense lawyer as well, at his own expense. His military defense lawyer is free.

A special court-martial is limited to these maximum penalties: bad conduct discharge, six months of confinement at hard labor, forfeiture of two-thirds pay for up to six months.

This form of court-martial is a full courtroom proceeding, like a civilian criminal trial. A pre-trial hearing may be held, discovery procedures may be followed, the usual defense motions (such as suppression of evidence) are included, the jury—technically, the "court members" where the accused has not asked to be tried solely by a military judge—is selected by the usual method of **voir dire** and challenges (see Chapter 6), evidence is presented, and a verdict is reached.

Appeal procedures are discussed in a separate section, below.

General court-martial. This is the military trial court with the broadest power. It may try a serviceman—enlisted man or officer—for the most serious crimes provided under military law, and its power to punish includes all the possible sentences specified by military law, including dishonorable discharge and confinement beyond six months. Its jurisdiction actually includes all offenses covered by the military code.

Convened by the commanding officer, the general court-martial includes either a military judge and at least five members (the "jury"), or a military judge alone if the accused person asks for that and the judge approves. Note that there *must* be a military judge, unlike the procedure sometimes used in special courts-martial.

It is mandatory that there be legally trained prosecution (law officer) and defense lawyers, and the accused may hire his own civilian defense lawyer as well, at his own expense.

Like the special court-martial, the general court-martial operates as a fully judicial proceeding, much like a civilian criminal trial.

Military Appeals

The military justice system provides a two-tier system for review of convictions in special or general courts-martial.

Each service has its own Court of Military Review, with power to review convictions at the urging of the convicted serviceman.

At the top of the system is the U.S. Court of Military Appeals, which has power to review cases in which a general or flag officer was involved, cases sent to it by the individual Judge Advocates General of the military services or the Transportation Department's general counsel (acting for the Coast Guard), and cases in which the convicted person has received a sentence of a year or more of confinement, a punitive discharge or both. It must review the first two categories of cases and it has discretion to review the third category, if "good cause" is shown for its review.

The court has three civilian judges, serving terms of 15 years. Its decisions are limited to issues of military law; it has no power to review the scope of the sentence. It may reverse convictions and order charges dismissed or permit a rehearing, it may send a case back for further action by a Court of Military Review, or it may uphold a conviction.

It follows the usual procedure of appellate courts. Its decisions are binding on the military services. Beyond it, however, each secretary of military service has discretionary power to review a military conviction, and may approve or disapprove of it or grant clemency. The President also has authority to review military cases and to grant clemency.

Once a military case has gone all the way through the special military system—that is, up through the Court of Military Appeals—the convicted serviceman may attempt to file a petition for habeas corpus in a U.S. District Court seeking post-conviction review (see Chapter 7).

D. U.S. TAX COURT

The federal tax system has a pervasive impact on the nation's citizens, yet it works through a system of law that is astonishingly complex. Confronting it from his vantage, the legal reporter thus faces something of a dilemma: trying to find ways to deal with a subject of obvious interest to his audience, when that subject seems almost beyond description in a popular medium.

Occasionally the reporter might be able to handle that dilemma by covering some of the work of the U.S. Tax Court. Again though, he will find that his professional interest is likely to be restricted to those cases in which a well-known figure is involved. There will be a few of those and they do provide vehicles for stories about this branch of the judicial system.

The Tax Court was created to provide a means by which taxpayers could have their disputes with the federal tax collector resolved without the taxpayers first having to pay the tax they supposedly owe.

Under federal law, there are three courts to which a taxpayer may turn to obtain a ruling upon his duty—or the absence of a duty—to pay a deficiency that the Internal Revenue Service has assessed against him. The Tax Court is the one to which he may turn without first paying the disputed tax. If he is prepared to pay the tax first and then sue for a refund, he may do so either in a

U.S. District Court or the U.S. Court of Claims. The suit in a District Court will follow the procedures outlined in the discussion on civil cases (Chapters 10–12). Court of Claims procedures are discussed in the next section of this chapter.

The main difference between the Tax Court and the regular civilian courts is that it operates without juries.

Two Procedures

It has two levels of procedure:

For tax disputes involving $1,500 or less for any single tax year, the Tax Court may assign one of its "special trial judges" (formerly called commissioners) to try the case and make a decision. This is a procedure involving little formality, delay or expense. A decision in such a case is final, not subject to review in any other court. This procedure may be waived, however, in favor of the "regular" Tax Court procedure.

For tax disputes involving anything above $1,500, the Tax Court provides for the possibility of a full trial before a single Tax Court judge. Sometimes, the case may be assigned for trial by a special trial judge, who reaches a decision that will be reviewed by a Tax Court judge before it is issued in final form. When a case concerns a novel issue, resulting in a new precedent, it probably will be reviewed by the full Tax Court before it is issued. By far the greatest number of cases before this court are, however, factual disputes only, where the law is not in significant controversy.

The Tax Court has 16 judges, serving terms of 15 years. The judges and the special trial judges sit in various cities across the country to conduct trials.

Proceedings before the Tax Court follow the normal rules of civil procedure. The court's decisions result in orders stating the amount of tax due, or declaring that none is due.

Appeals from Tax Court decisions may be taken to the U.S. Court of Appeals for the circuit in which the taxpayer lives or has business headquarters. There, the appeal will follow the usual civil appeals process (see Chapter 12).

E. U.S. COURT OF CLAIMS

The Court of Claims is another federal tribunal of a special kind that processes large numbers of cases without generating much news. It has a very wide jurisdiction, often involving some very fascinating factual issues and, now and then, legal questions. At most, however, it provides the basis for intermittent feature stories about its caseload and about given cases of notable novelty.

Its jurisdiction includes cases in which individuals or businesses claim the U.S. government owes them money, disputes over the privileges, pay and allowances of federal civil service and military employes, disputes over government contract interpretation, controversies over federal tax deficiencies—*if* the taxpayer has paid the disputed tax and is seeking a refund—and such exotic disputes as those over Indian land rights, damages from oil "spills" at sea and damages to oyster growers from river and harbor dredging.

It also has some limited appellate or transfer jurisdiction: it reviews cases from the Indian Claims Commission and rulings by U.S. District Courts on suits against the government for breaches of its legal duties (**tort** cases), and it may receive, on transfer, cases filed in U.S. District Courts that should have been filed with the Court of Claims.

Finally, the Claims Court, on request by Congress, will conduct cases to establish the facts needed to enable Congress to act intelligently upon so-called "private bills"—those for the benefit of individual persons or entities.

Procedures

Cases before the Court of Claims are tried by "trial judges" (formerly called commissioners). They conduct normal trial-type proceedings, without a jury, and make findings of fact and recommendations on conclusions of law to the full court.

After a commissioner has reached a recommended decision, the parties in the case may file **exceptions** to the decision. These will then be determined and the case finally ruled upon, by the Court of Claims itself.

The court has seven members, a chief judge and six associate judges who serve for life.

Appeals from its decisions may be taken to the U.S. Supreme Court, with that court having discretion for or against review.

14

Covering
"Regulatory Law"

SOMEWHERE BEYOND THE THREE TRADITIONAL BRANCHES OF GOV-
ERNMENT, the legal reporter is sure to discover the regulatory agency. He will
find that it has its own brand of law and its own procedures, yet it is something
like a court, a legislature, an executive agency. Whatever it is like, this "other
branch" of government is bound to show up in one way or another on the
courthouse beat. It exists at all levels of government.

Increasingly, the regulatory agency finds itself in court as a party, as the
combined effect of the "rights revolution" and the "consumer revolution" generate more legal controversy over administrative justice.

Beyond that, the regulatory approach itself is burgeoning, with more and
more facets of life coming within the protection of what is called **"due process."** In constitutional theory, that means that a person or institution may not
have something important taken away by the government without some minimum procedural safeguards. In practical effect, that means that more problems
in life are being worked out in administrative forums.

A generation ago, Supreme Court Justice Robert H. Jackson commented:

> The rise of administrative bodies probably has been the most significant
> legal trend of the last century and perhaps more values today are affected by
> their decisions than by those of all the courts.

Since then, even more "values" have become affected by the regulatory
process. The entire welfare system, for example, is now immersed in due process cases for hundreds of thousands of persons who receive one form or an-

other of public assistance, ranging from Social Security to aid to dependent children. Environmental problems, behavior of children in public schools, on-the-job safety, scarcity of energy—an almost unending array of public policy activity is now drawn into the administrative process, resulting in what has been called "mass administrative justice." One observer has remarked: "The number of adjudicative determinations that have to be made in these areas is legion."

The legal reporter who covers a county or city courthouse or who has the statehouse as his "beat" will find himself covering several kinds of administrative justice.

At the state and local levels, these agencies exercise much of the basic "police power" of their jurisdiction. "Police power," in this, the constitutional sense, means the power to regulate "public health, safety and morals."

That, of course, takes in everything from issuing driver's licenses to monitoring medical practice, supervising barbers, beauticians and builders, operating public schools, making welfare payments, conducting elections, regulating beer and liquor sales, seeking to censor dirty movies and publications and to control massage parlors. It also takes in the whole field of regulating public utilities—direct and indirect controls over the companies or agencies that have a monopoly for providing mass transportation, electricity, gas, water, telephones.

At the federal level, it is quite common for a reporter to have as his whole beat a group of regulatory agencies. But sooner or later, almost all reporters covering news at the federal level will come into professional contact with some of these agencies. Legal reporters will encounter them often.

The still-growing number of regulatory agencies shares the exercise of the "commerce power" assigned to the federal government by the Constitution. There is no such thing, technically, as federal "police power" of the kind that state and local governments exercise. The "commerce power" embraces an almost limitless variety of activity that affects domestic and foreign commerce.

While the nature of this regulatory authority is economic, it obviously reaches much of the social life of the nation. Moreover, its reach is not confined to the massive industries and corporations, but also gets down to quite small businesses or professional entities at the community level.

Any list of federal regulatory agencies is soon out of date. Almost annually, Congress has added to the list as more and more social programs were created at the federal level or as existing government programs were expanded to reach new social problems and activity.

As at the state and local level, these agencies regulate not only specific kinds of activity—presidential campaign spending or factory safety hazards, as examples—but also entire utility industries: air, rail, truck, bus and barge transportation, for example.

It is plain, then, that the press will want to pay close attention to the development of "regulatory law" and to its application in multitudes of cases. The press will be able to do this quite easily, because one of the distinguishing features of the administrative process is that much of it is conducted in the open. Agency hearings are often public, records are open to public inspection, and the officials and employes who conduct agency affairs are usually very accessible, at least to the press, and so are attorneys involved in the regulatory process. The process also may become a conspicuous public issue in legislative hearings or investigations.

This chapter introduces the reporter to the regulatory process in two sections: first, the process itself and how and when it makes news; second, the process of judicial review of agency decisions and how and when that makes news. The usual approach of step-by-step, chronological analysis is followed.

A. THE REGULATORY PROCESS

The operations of regulatory or administrative agencies may be analyzed in two parts, somewhat arbitrarily divided for purposes of analysis.

First, the agencies may be examined according to the functions they are performing:

- Granting licenses or privileges, either in situations where there is competition for a limited number of licenses or privileges, or where anyone who can qualify may receive a license, certificate, or other form of authorization.
- Setting rates to be charged for a regulated activity.
- Directly supervising performance of a regulated activity, either where the activity goes on under a license or certificate or where it operates without a specific, advance grant of authority.
- Imposing sanctions for failure to meet standards of performance, including failure to charge appropriate rates.

Second, the agencies may be examined according to the methods they use in carrying out their functions:

- Investigating individuals, companies or institutions subject to regulation.
- Writing specific rules and regulations on how a regulated activity may or must be conducted. This may include setting of specific standards of performance.
- Adopting general policy statements dealing with the way in which an agency will use its powers or the way in which a regulated activity will be expected to operate.
- Applying rules, regulations and policy on a case-by-case basis to particular individuals, companies or institutions.

As has been implied, these two categories of agency operations are over-lapping. In exercising any one of its functions, the agency may use one or all of the methods available to it. In this discussion, however, the categories are kept separated as much as possible in order to illustrate the reasons why an agency does what it does and why the choices it makes are or may be newsworthy.

Functions of Agencies

Granting licenses. The process of permitting someone to exercise a "public" privilege may be as simple as having applicants report to one office, go through the simplest application and review process, and receive immediate approval or rejection of a license or certificate.

Examples of this kind of process are those used widely for issuing driver's licenses or registering autos.

In this form, the regulatory process may be said to be virtually automatic. It operates on a vast numerical scale and is subject to little supervisory review on a day-to-day or case-by-case basis.

The licensing and registration functions probably will be exercised entirely independently of the process of reviewing performance. For example, the agency that issues driver's licenses may have nothing to do with revoking them. That usually will be done as part of the criminal justice process—specifically, through traffic court cases.

Obviously, the chances that this form of regulatory activity will produce much news are somewhat remote. From time to time, however, reporters will want to monitor such licensing or registration programs for feature or investigative stories.

The more complex process of granting operating licenses or certificates for more substantial activity is likely to produce significant news, regularly.

Usually, the privileges that are involved in this process are competitive. Examples would be television station licenses or certificates to fly a given airline route. There are, of course, some forms of regulated "privilege" that are *not* competitive in the usual sense. An example of this would be authority to sell to the public a regulated product—a new medicine or medical device. Anyone who could meet official standards could expect to receive permission to offer the item.

This process begins with an application to carry on the activity or market the product that is regulated. Usually, such applications are available as public records and thus to the press. Competing applications are common. Even when there is no direct competitor, however, an applicant may face challengers who claim that the applicant is incapable of performing the activity. The right to challenge applications for many forms of public "privilege" has been expanded increasingly, particularly in situations where the activity has an impact on consumer interests or on environmental interests.

The mere filing of an application in a significant case will produce news. If there exists or is likely to be a challenge, the potential news value may be enhanced.

After an application is on file, the agency will conduct its own review of the sufficiency—in legal and policy terms—of the application and supporting documents or exhibits. The variety of procedures used for this is very broad, carried on under a maze of regulations.

Review may be through an agency's own staff, by referral to advisory or technical authorities outside the agency, perhaps by holding hearings. In a contested case, each of these steps will be much like the adversary process that goes on in a civil court case. Even where the case is not contested, the procedure may take on an adversary character, with the applicant bearing the burden of proof that it can satisfy policy or standards and the agency's staff or officials taking what may appear to be the "other side." Interested parties from outside may also be heard.

Quite commonly, an agency will act only after it has a staff recommendation before it. Senior agency officials—the members of the commission, board or agency—may conduct an independent review, or they may simply vote up or down on·the staff recommendation.

When the process is finished, the decision to grant or withhold a license, certificate or authorization will be announced, usually with a written decision seeking to justify the result. Agencies usually are obliged to "make a record," so that any review, in court or elsewhere, may proceed with a full understanding of the basis of agency action.

The standard often used for granting a license or certificate is that the applicant could be expected to serve "the public convenience and necessity." If the decision is one allowing a new product to be marketed, the standard may be one related to the safety or practical efficacy of the item.

Each of the steps in the license-granting process is likely to be open to the reporter, except, perhaps, the points at which the agency deliberates on its decision. He obviously will have repeated occasions to do both "spot" and feature stories on specific cases and on the agency's operation and performance in general.

Setting rates. The so-called "ratemaking" process of regulatory agencies can be exceedingly complex. By this method, the agencies determine whether an activity subject to regulation is charging what it ought to be for the public or quasi-public service it is offering. Much of the activity in public utility regulation has to do with the level of their rates.

Obviously, not all activities that are subject to regulation must have their rates approved by the regulators. Only those which by law are expressly subject to rate control or supervision need initial permission for their rate levels, or need agency authorization for any changes they seek to make in those levels.

Some of the most significant rulings made in the regulatory field have to do with rates, and thus reporters will want to take an active interest in this. Again, they usually will find that this part of the administrative process is open to the public.

The more common method of initiating a rate proceeding is for the regulated company or other entity to initiate a case, asking either for permission to charge a given rate for a new service or for authority to revise—up or down—a previously approved rate. The reviewing agency reacts to rate proposals, rather than making them itself in the first instance. A rate proposal technically is a **tariff.**

A rate application or tariff may be challenged, perhaps by competitors if any exist, perhaps by representatives of users of the service or of indirect users who would be affected by the rate proposal.

The agency's procedures may provide for some kind of staff review before the agency members themselves will act upon rates. Whatever the nature of review in a given agency, it is likely to be a more or less penetrating examination of the applicant's financial status and a search for justification, or the absence of it, for the proposal.

Depending upon the kind of powers the regulatory agency has, it may issue a final decision approving the rate proposal, rejecting it but with permission for the regulated entity to come back with a new and revised proposal, or modifying the rate structure as the agency deems appropriate.

In making its decision, the agency will be obliged in most jurisdictions to give a rationale for the result, providing the basis for possible review in court.

The usual standard for reviewing rates is that they must be "just and reasonable." This will take into account the operating needs of the regulated activity, its present and future financial circumstances, the level of profit or return that the activity is to be allowed, and the capacity of users to pay.

Rates may be calculated on a flat fee basis or may be keyed to some percentage of the "rate base"—the financial factors that determine the activity's current operating needs as well as its potential for growth and expansion.

The reporter will have considerable difficulty translating the rate-making process into popular language. The impact, however, of this process on the users of regulated services is very great and thus the reporter really has no choice but to find a means to cover it intelligibly. Perhaps the best way to do so is to calculate the actual dollars-and-cents impact on a typical user. Even if the rate is a "wholesale" one—the price to be charged to others who will resell to ultimate users at a "retail" price—the reporter still should attempt to translate the rate result to show its specific impact on an ultimate user.

Supervising performance. Once an individual, company or institution has entered (or has been given a license or other authority to enter) a regulated field, it can expect to be monitored regularly or periodically by the agency having jurisdiction in that field.

This may be done even on a day-to-day basis, somewhat less frequently or perhaps at specified intervals. Many activities that go on under a license or certificate are required to seek periodic renewal of their operating authority and this may trigger the review process.

The regulated activity may have to provide continuing reports on its performance and may have to submit to some form of inspection—scheduled and regular, or without advance notice.

If agency supervision is ongoing and continuous, there is not likely to be a specific review proceeding, as such, unless the regulated entity is accused of having violated its basic authority or obligation. Such review may be initiated by a complaint. If the regulated entity has a license that expires at a specified point, a proceeding will be initiated at or shortly before that point to determine whether the license should be renewed.

Typically a review proceeding, whenever and however it is begun, is a formal affair. Often, it involves some of the same investigative and review techniques used in initial licensing cases. But it also may have a punitive element to it.

The standard generally used to judge performance is whether the regulated activity has been conducted, in fact, in a way that serves "the public convenience and necessity" or the "public health, safety and morals."

Reporters clearly will have an interest in complaint proceedings or in license or certificate renewal cases. They may *not* find that the complaint procedure is as open as are other regulatory processes, but it *is* common for at least some aspects of these cases to be in public. Renewal cases, however, are almost routinely public matters, since they very often involve challenges by present or would-be competitors or by consumer or other "public interest" groups.

Final decisions in review proceedings probably will be in written form with justification for the result. This will be true especially if a regulated entity is punished or otherwise subjected to sanctions.

Imposing sanctions. Many regulatory agencies possess authority to impose sanctions on regulated individuals, companies or institutions that fail in their obligations. Sometimes these sanctions will be self-enforcing, with the agency itself acting directly. Sometimes, however, they may be only proposed sanctions that do not take effect until after some form of outside review has been held.

Among the sanctions that may be imposed, depending upon an agency's powers, are:

- Loss of license or certificate, permanently or for a specified period, by suspension or otherwise.
- Fines or other monetary assessments, perhaps including rebates to users.
- Referral of individuals or entities for possible prosecution in the regular criminal justice process.

- Referral for possible civil punitive action in the regular civil courts.
- **"Cease-and-desist orders,"** which are the regulatory equivalent of court-issued injunctions.
- Direct orders requiring a change in the regulated entity's mode or manner of operation.

As is obvious, some of these sanctions are fairly drastic. Thus, the reporter no doubt will often have a story out of the punitive actions an agency takes.

Methods and Procedures

Just as the functions of the agencies will be of interest to the press, the manner in which regulators carry out those functions will often attract press attention. This section deals with the more common techniques used by the agencies. Some combination of these may be used in any of the types of proceedings discussed in the preceding section.

Investigations. It is quite common for a regulatory agency to have investigative powers that are, or seem to be, as broad as or broader than those of prosecutors in the criminal justice system. This may include power to **subpoena** witnesses or documents, to conduct inspections, to require detailed reporting, to hold hearings (open or closed), to examine or audit books and records, and to conduct various tests or examinations.

This array of authority (it does vary from agency to agency) is designed to enable the agency to obtain full information to guide it in carrying out the functions it was created to perform. Because the agency usually is required to make specific findings of fact before it may take an action involving an individual, company or institution being regulated, the investigative technique is one of its most important.

An agency may use its own staff to conduct its investigations, or it may rely upon officers detailed to it from other organs of government. In some circumstances, an agency may have to obtain court approval of some investigative techniques—for example, inspections.

Investigations may be conducted as part of an agency's continuing supervisory activity, or they may be initiated only in response to a specific complaint against a regulated entity.

Sometimes an agency will start a special investigation, to develop information to be used in drafting rules and regulations (see below) or general agency policy (see below).

The reporter as a general matter will be more interested in special investigations or those conducted as part of complaint proceedings than in continuing investigatory activity that is part of an agency's normal review process.

Not all investigations, of course, are public proceedings. When an agency is supervising a private business or individuals, it often will feel obliged to protect privacy. It also may have its own administrative reasons for avoiding publicity about its investigations. The reporter, of course, need not necessarily feel bound by such considerations; his profession's own ethical obligation to respect privacy even when he is monitoring government activity should be his guide.

Occasionally, perhaps frequently, an agency's use of its investigative power may lead to a lawsuit in court, testing the scope of the regulators' authority. These agencies, like all other arms of government, are obliged to observe the constitutional restraints upon the use of their powers. The legal reporter will soon become familiar with test cases challenging the quality and nature of administrative justice.

Rule-making. Most regulatory agencies possess some power to act as "legislatures." In other words, the laws which create them may give the agencies the authority to write specific rules and regulations that have the force of law, and thus are as binding as if passed directly by the legislature.

Agencies use their rule-making power in order to develop standards for regulated entities to observe and standards to guide the agency's own officers and employes in carrying out their duties.

It is quite common for a regulatory agency to issue rules and regulations in proposed form, solicit public comment upon them and then issue them in final, perhaps revised form after the public reaction has been considered. (Such proposals are published, at the federal level, in the Federal Register and at other levels in similar formal documents or in official notices in newspapers.)

A great many agency rules and regulations are, naturally, of little interest to the press, because they deal with internal or highly technical matters with little news potential. On the other hand, there will be far-reaching rules and regulations, bearing immediately and directly upon those who are regulated by the agency, and having considerable impact as major public policy declarations. Those, of course, should be covered by the press.

An agency's rule-making authority is generally thought to be legislative in character, because the agency may take into account whatever it deems relevant in drafting its rules and regulations. It is not obliged, in this part of its work, to follow anything like rules of evidence as it does, more or less, in its quasi-judicial activity (discussed below).

However, the agency is obliged to observe some limits on its rule-making authority: it may not go beyond the powers given it by the law that created it, it is obliged to observe fundamental fairness, and it must have some convincing basis for the rules it makes.

Generally speaking, the rules and regulations it issues will be attempts to interpret, in detail, the basic powers that the agency has, as applied to the kinds of cases and proceedings that will come before it.

Declaring policy. Some agencies make declarations of general policy that may go considerably beyond what is normally stated in rules and regulations. Sometimes, these policy statements are made in the course of deciding specific cases (see below). When that occurs, the statements may not be subject to the kind of public comment that often is encouraged regarding proposed rules and regulations. Instead, such statements are used as ways to generalize about the policy considerations which lie beneath a given ruling in a specific case.

There will be times, however, when a general policy *will* be issued in a proposed form, much like any other rule or regulation. Then, public reaction may be solicited before the agency commits itself to the policy as a guide to its future intent.

Policy statements may encompass anything within the agency's jurisdiction. The agency usually considers issuing such a statement in order to try to reduce or control the amount of caseload it may confront on a recurring, centrally important issue. By stating quite clearly where it stands, in a general way, the agency puts its "client" entities on notice about the outcome of any cases that might arise which involve such an issue.

It goes without saying that the press usually will find much that is newsworthy in such a general declaration. It will tell much about the way an agency interprets its underlying powers, and it will show how an agency's current membership may be applying differently an authority which may have long existed.

Deciding cases. Much of the news that emerges from a regulatory agency will come out of the use of the agency's "adjudicatory power." This is its "quasi-judicial" activity, deciding how a set of facts involving specific individuals, companies or institutions fits within the regulatory policy of the agency.

These may be licensing proceedings, enforcement or review proceedings, or punitive cases leading to sanctions against an errant regulated entity.

Generally speaking, these cases will be handled much as civil cases in court would be. Normal rules of evidence, or something akin to that, will be followed. The proceeding often will be an "adversary" one, with two distinct sides seeking to "win."

Professor Harold J. Grilliot has noted, however, an important distinction between regulatory cases and court proceedings:

> The decisions of administrative tribunals in the adjudication process are made by administrators rather than judges. They perceive their function as that of implementing and administering a legislative purpose. Their judicial attitude is that of an executive wanting to get the job done rather than impartially deciding between two litigants.

It is in the case-by-case operations of the regulatory agencies, though, that the constitutional limitations that bear upon government in general are most vividly present in regulatory law.

The Constitution's guarantee of "due process" must be observed as faithfully by regulators as by judges. Generally speaking, this means that an agency may not take away or deny a privilege or impose a sanction without first giving the person or institution involved notice that that may happen, and then an opportunity to offer reasons why it should not happen.

In recent years, the U.S. Supreme Court has extended these "due process" guarantees to more and more circumstances in the regulatory field. Welfare benefits may not be taken away without some form of notice and hearing, and neither may jobs in public agencies (including schools), residence in public housing, and loss or interruption of many other forms of public privilege or benefit.

The strict rules of "due process" that apply in criminal cases—the right to call witnesses, the right to cross-examine opposing witnesses, the right to have a lawyer, the right to have an impartial decision-maker—do not necessarily apply in full to regulatory cases. The Supreme Court has permitted a good deal of flexibility in fashioning due-process methods in the administrative agencies.

A reporter who is accustomed to covering civil or criminal cases in court will have no difficulty covering regulatory adjudications, although administrative hearings often involve evidence and argument that goes well beyond the kind that could be considered or heard in a court trial. The reporter should be alert to the underlying differences between the processes of regulation versus litigation, and should try to make them plain to his readers or listeners.

Among the differences, one in particular should be noted: it is often true in regulatory agencies that the initial determination in individual cases is made by subordinate officers, not by the agency members themselves. In many federal agencies, this first review is by an "administrative law judge," who hears evidence and then recommends a decision to his superiors. The senior officials of the agency then may conduct their own proceeding, gather more evidence, and issue a ruling, or they may simply accept, reject or modify the recommendations of their subordinate.

Most case-by-case proceedings before regulatory agencies are public, in whole or in substantial part, and their records are open.

B. JUDICIAL REVIEW OF REGULATORY ACTION

Most of the time, statistically speaking, the actions that a regulatory agency takes are final. The process of judicial review exists for nearly all significant decisions emerging from the regulatory process, but in fact it is utilized only in a relatively few instances.

Standard of Review

At all levels of government, the standard of judicial review is more or less the same: an agency's findings of facts will not be second-guessed by the reviewing court if supported by "substantial evidence," and the agency's conclusions of law and applications of policy will not be overturned unless the court concludes that the agency acted in an "arbitrary" or "capricious" manner indicating that it "abused its discretion."

There is, then, only limited hope that a judicial test of an adverse agency ruling will give the disappointed regulated entity more satisfaction than he got from the agency. It may be said, as a generalization, that the only agency actions that are *likely* to be challenged in court are those that are of major dimensions, in cost or impact.

When judicial review of agency actions does exist, in state or federal courts, it usually exists at an appellate court level. This too reflects the general principle that it is the agency, not the court, that has the basic obligation to "try" the administrative case.

When a court does review a case, then, it is engaging in something very much like the appeal procedure within the judiciary itself. As has been noted, however, the reviewing court is likely to show even more deference to a regulatory agency decision than it would to a decision by a judge in a trial court. The regulatory agency, unlike the trial judge, is executing an underlying policy when it acts, and its choice of policy will be respected by the courts.

As U.S. Circuit Judge Harold Leventhal has said, the function of a reviewing court is to "combine judicial supervision with a salutary principle of judicial restraint." He remarked further:

> If satisfied that the agency has taken a hard look at the issues with the use of reason and standards, the court will uphold its findings, though of less than ideal clarity, if the agency's path may reasonably be discerned. . . . If the agency has . . . taken a hard look at the salient problems, and has genuinely engaged in reasoned decision making, the court exercises restraint and affirms the agency's action even though the court would on its own account have made different findings or adopted different standards.

When a regulatory case is challenged in court, the contest will be one between the party that lost or was disappointed with the agency result, and the agency itself, although the agency may be strongly supported by the winning party as an intervenor.

Such cases, however, will not even be considered in court if the agency decision is not yet final. A party must "exhaust" his remedies at the agency level before a court will provide any form of review of agency action.

Review Procedure

The case will proceed in court almost as if it were any other appeal: the petition for review will argue that the agency made "errors" in its legal judgment, the agency will reply in defense of its action, written briefs probably will be filed, an oral hearing will be held, and the judges of the court will deliberate to a decision.

A legal reporter will find much of interest to him professionally, both in the fact patterns and in the legal precedents that emerge in "appeals" from regulatory decisions. Sometimes, of course, there will even be fundamental constitutional issues at stake. Often they will have something to do with claims that "due process" was not observed by the agency.

The results of such cases, particularly when constitutional questions are involved, will reveal much about the nature of administrative justice in a state or at the federal level.

Because so much of the regulatory or administrative process does deal with matters affecting the everyday lives of common citizens, the reporter often will find a very wide audience and high popular interest in court decisions on significant agency actions.

15

Covering the Legislature in Court

LEGAL NEWS ABOUT LEGISLATURES EMERGES out of the dual nature of the relationship between legislatures and courts: they are partners at times and adversaries at other times. When working together or when working at odds with each other, the two branches of government frequently make news on the courthouse beat.

Covering a legislature is, of course, a beat of its own. The reporter assigned there, however, will sometimes be assigned also to cover a court. That is particularly true in covering state legislatures, since the statehouse reporter often covers the state supreme court, too.

This publication is not meant to deal with the legislative process as such. Here, the legislature is examined primarily for its potential as a source of news about the law. Thus, there is no discussion of even those legislative acts that bear directly upon court operations: the passage of codes of law, criminal or civil, governing both the substance and the processes of law in court, or the passage of appropriations bills to finance court administration and judicial salaries. There is, on the other hand, a limited discussion here of the legislature when it is acting like a court: trying direct contempts or trying cases of impeachment (see the final section).

The legislature figures in the judicial process through these relationships between the two branches of government:

- Those who make the laws depend, occasionally to a remarkable extent, upon courts to give detailed substance and meaning to laws by interpreting them to apply to specific cases and controversies.

- Courts, at both the state and federal level, have the authority to declare laws unconstitutional, and thus absolutely prevent their enforcement.
- Legislatures, at state and federal level, have the authority to initiate constitutional amendments and thus perhaps to "correct" constitutional rulings by the courts. Of course, legislatures also possess the power to draft and pass new laws to "correct" understandings by the courts of legislative intent in prior laws.
- Legislatures depend upon the criminal justice process in court to assist them in keeping order in legislative bodies or in enforcing their demands for information. This is done in criminal contempt cases.

Each of these relationships is examined for its news potential. The chapter closes with an examination of the quasi-judicial acts of legislatures in direct contempt and impeachment cases.

A. JUDICIAL INTERPRETATION OF LAWS

One of the most distinctive features of the American system of government—perhaps its most original contribution to the art and science of government—is **judicial review**. In its ultimate form, of course, this means the power to declare legislative acts invalid (see the next section). But it also means the power of courts to declare what the laws mean and to define their scope.

Statutory Construction

Most actions of courts in reviewing legislation are, in fact, decisions to construe the laws—that is, to interpret them in the context of a lawsuit involving a genuine "case or controversy." Numerically, little of the overall work of courts in **statutory construction** will result in decisions to nullify laws.

A court need not construe a law if its meaning and scope are clear. When the legislature speaks plainly and unambiguously, the court simply applies the result. It is only when the legislature has not spoken clearly that the process of construction must occur in a court.

This may occur when a legislature has passed a law that seemed to fit factual conditions put before the legislature in the first instance, but which in actual application reaches other, unforeseen circumstances. The "void" that results in interpretation may be filled by the courts.

Moreover, a legislature may pass a statute of fairly general scope with the understanding (explicit or implicit) that its details will be filled in by court decisions.

In using its powers of review, however, a court simply has no authority to make a law read to satisfy a court's own policy preferences, or to make it reach a situation that could not possibly have been within the intent of the legislature.

It is difficult, concededly, for the legal reporter or even for a professional in the law to know with certainty how far a court may go before it actually "legislates": doing the forbidden thing of applying a law beyond the will of the legislature. One of the tasks of the legal reporter, as a result, is to attempt to monitor just how broadly a court uses its powers of "construction."

The reporter should keep in mind, at a minimum, that the court may not act at all on legislation unless there is a genuine legal dispute before it. The only exception, and it is not very common in practice, would be a provision of state law or a state constitution allowing a court to give purely advisory opinions on the meaning or validity of legislation; federal courts are absolutely forbidden to give purely advisory opinions. It is the task of courts to decide lawsuits, not to make law independent of legal controversy.

Methods of Interpretation

A court may be drawn into interpretation of a law—local, state or federal—through either a criminal prosecution or a civil lawsuit. Its primary task in either circumstance is to determine what the legislature's intent was in passing the law. In doing this, it will look first at the language of the law and its normal meaning.

If, after that, it remains uncertain about legislative intent, the court will examine the **legislative history**—the testimony, if any, that the legislature had before it and the written reports and debates of the body on the legislation itself.

Sometimes if the law is of a kind that has been entrusted to an expert administrative or executive agency for enforcement, a court may examine that agency's experience and any legislative response to that experience for guidance.

In interpreting criminal laws, courts will be much more strict in insisting that the legislature's intent and the law's meaning be clear and unambiguous. Constitutionally, a person may not be required to guess, at his peril, what kind of actions will be criminal if he engages in them.

In interpreting any law, though, courts will defer as far as they reasonably can to the legislature's power to legislate. They will not lightly assume that a legislature has gone beyond its powers.

Disputes over the meaning and scope of legislation will be apparent to the legal reporter early in a lawsuit, perhaps at its very outset. In a criminal case, for example, the lawyer for the accused person may seek to have the case dismissed with the argument that the law simply did not cover the conduct involved. In a civil case, for example, the lawyer for either side may contend that the law, if properly understood, provides a conclusive answer in favor of his client in the legal dispute.

If a case is at all newsworthy, any underlying dispute over the meaning of a law will be worth covering as a central factor in the case. The reporter should make clear that there is a difference legally between disputes over legislative interpretation and disputes over facts, and should seek to show how each might affect trial strategies as well as the exercise of judicial power.

B. UNCONSTITUTIONAL LAWS

A legal reporter seldom will have a bigger story on his beat than one about a court ruling that finds a law to be unconstitutional. Such a ruling is a significant and usually rare use of judicial power, and it may be both bold and dramatic. In some circumstances such a ruling produces a hostile confrontation between the court and one of the other branches of government.

It should be stressed, again, that this is a rare occurrence. As a normal rule, a court will go far to avoid even facing constitutional issues in lawsuits. When such an issue is unavoidably before the court, it will seek to find a way in which the law could be interpreted to "save" it constitutionally. Only when such a "saving" would be plainly beyond the intent of the legislature will a court feel obliged to strike down a law.

Reasons for Invalidating Laws

Among the reasons upon which a court may base a decision to invalidate a law constitutionally are:

- The law goes beyond the constitutional power of the legislature to act.
- It represents an **"ex post facto"** action by a legislature—that is, it outlaws conduct retroactively.
- It is a **"bill of attainder"**—that is, it imposes punishment by a form of legislative "trial," with the accused having no chance to defend himself.
- It is too vague and thus does not specify the kind of conduct that is outlawed.
- It does not treat persons in like circumstances equally.
- It represents a use of legislative power that belongs to a different level of government (state versus federal, or vice versa).
- If a state law, it conflicts with a federal law on the same subject; the federal law is supreme.
- It imposes a form of punishment or a sanction without basic procedural safeguards to prevent arbitrary action.
- It voids a private contract that was validly made.

The process by which a court invalidates an executive or administrative action for constitutional reasons is little different from the process for invalidating a legislative act. Some of the same reasons may be used. For constitutional review purposes, many executive or administrative acts are treated as law.

Issues over constitutionality are raised quite routinely in criminal cases and frequently in civil cases. Although the challenges may be raised as the central feature of a lawsuit, they are in the nature of "last resort" legal thrusts, because of the judicial tradition of avoiding decisions on constitutional questions if at all possible.

If a court does reach a constitutional question, and decides that a law is unconstitutional or that an agency action is unconstitutional, it may issue an injunction barring enforcement or forbidding such action.

Decisions on constitutional questions may be made, customarily, at any level in a court system—trial or appellate. However, a decision striking down a law or an agency action is final only if not appealed and, if appealed, only if the result is upheld by the higher court. Once such a ruling has become final, there is no power in the legislature or the executive to restore the law or action to constitutionality by simply passing a new law of identical content or by simply taking the same action over again. Only a revision of the state or federal constitution, by the formal amending process, will "overrule" the court decision (see the next section).

C. LEGISLATIVE "CORRECTIVES"

Response to Statutory Rulings

It is fairly routine for legislatures to pass new laws to overcome court decisions that interpret prior laws, when a court ruling is limited to *statutory* construction.

A legislature may do so because it is displeased with the judicial result, or it may do so simply because it prefers a different interpretation than the one given a prior law in court. Sometimes, such legislative "correction" is done merely to take account of new information.

Those who make the laws need not feel bound by a court's understanding of past legislative intent. Legislators may act anew, stating or re-stating their current intent. In so doing, however, they may not change the actual result for the parties involved in a given court case. An interpretation of a law by a court is binding on the parties in the lawsuit which produced that interpretation. This is called the "**law of the case**" doctrine.

It is obvious that reporters covering the legislature will pay attention to at least some legislative attempts to alter a law that has been judicially construed. Sometimes the reporter on the legal beat may want to monitor such legislative action, too, perhaps because it may affect cases still pending in court or on their way to court.

Responses to Constitutional Rulings

When a legislature reacts to a constitutional ruling by a court, it may not necessarily engage the court in a major constitutional confrontation. It may simply yield to the court's decision, and pass a new law to cure the constitutional defect found by the court in an existing law. But there will be times, probably rare—especially at the federal level—when a legislature may attempt to have the constitution itself amended, an act producing news of major significance. If, however, a state is operating under a constitution that is vastly and precisely detailed, it may initiate constitutional change without creating much of a stir journalistically or politically.

At the federal level, Congress has succeeded only twice in efforts to have the Constitution amended to overcome a Supreme Court decision: the 11th Amendment, dealing with the scope of federal judicial power in lawsuits against states, and the 16th amendment, dealing with congressional power to impose an income tax. Perhaps the 13th Amendment, abolishing slavery, may also be said to be a response to a Supreme Court ruling.

The process of amending the U.S. Constitution is made deliberately difficult, legislatively and politically, to avoid frequent changes. An amendment must be proposed with the approval of at least two-thirds of the voting members of each house of Congress and may go into effect only if ratified by legislatures of at least three-fourths of the states. A constitutional convention may be called only if two-thirds of the states demand it.

The process of amending state constitutions varies considerably but it, too, is often difficult.

D. CONTEMPT PROSECUTIONS

A legislature, in order to be able to operate without disruption, depends upon laws making it a crime to interfere with orderly legislative procedure. Like all criminal laws, these may be enforced only through the criminal justice process in the courts. A legislature may have limited power to act, on its own, to punish contempts, as discussed in the final section of this chapter.

The most common form of legislative contempt cases involves actions before a legislative committee. A person may be accused of contempt for failing to respond, in person or with documents, to a subpoena or for refusing to answer questions at a legislative hearing. A person may face contempt action for actively disrupting a legislative proceeding, in committee or on the floor, by noise or other disturbances.

It is not universally true, but a case of legislative contempt in court almost always will be newsworthy. Such cases are unusual, statistically speaking, because a legislature seeks a contempt action only for the most serious affronts to its power and prestige or the most serious disturbances of its processes.

"Regular" Contempts

When a legislature seeks contempt action as a normal criminal prosecution, it will send the matter to the appropriate prosecutor. Technically, it usually is within his discretion to decide for or against prosecution. As a practical matter, however, the prosecutor ordinarily will proceed with the case in an attempt to satisfy the legislature.

Such a case will follow the usual steps in a criminal case (see Chapters 5–7). It probably will also include some issues that will be peculiar to contempt prosecutions. For example, if the contempt charge is based upon failure to respond to a demand to appear, give testimony or produce documents, the court may inquire into the authority of the committee or body to issue such a demand. The court may want to test the legislative body's need for the particular testimony, to be sure that that testimony is "pertinent" to a legislative purpose. Usually, however, the court will defer to the legislature as far as possible on such matters.

A legislature, it is clear, is subject to many of the same constitutional restraints that apply to other arms of government. Thus, courts will not lend their power to support legislative actions which violate a person's constitutional rights, and this includes attempts by legislatures to coerce a person to give testimony in violation of his rights by threatening him with contempt.

Once a legislature has turned to the criminal justice process for support, it may expect that its actions will be judged according to the rules and precedents that control that process. The prosecutor must prove that a crime has been committed by proving, beyond a reasonable doubt, every element of the offense against the person accused, to the satisfaction of a jury in a proceeding presided over by a judge and one in which the rules of evidence are controlling.

A person convicted in a criminal contempt case involving a legislature will be punished within the sentencing provisions specified by laws making such contempts a crime.

A legal reporter will cover a legislative contempt case as he does any criminal proceeding.

E. DIRECT CONTEMPT AND IMPEACHMENT CASES

State legislatures and Congress have authority, which is sparingly used, to take special actions that are almost judicial in nature.

Direct Contempt

One particularly drastic remedy for offenses to the legislative process is direct action by a legislative body against those who disrupt or interfere with its operations or functioning. Just as a court has authority to protect the administration of justice from those who would stop it or seriously disrupt it by acting summarily and quickly, legislatures have reserved power to remove serious obstacles to their functioning by swift, summary punishment.

This may mean—as at the federal level—that the legislature will order one of its officers to arrest the violator and hold him in custody. In Congress' case, the term of such detention may last at most only until the end of the session of Congress in which it began. The person arrested, of course, has the constitutional right to seek a **writ of habeas corpus** from a federal court, to test the authority to hold him. (See the discussion of this writ in Chapter 7.) After release, he may also file a damage lawsuit against officers of the legislative body, but *not* against its members in the case of Congress.

A legal reporter, and even a legislative reporter, will seldom encounter the use of direct contempt power in a legislature. It is an awesome use of legislative authority, and thus is politically risky to use except in the most aggravated contempt situations.

Sanctions Against Members

Another form of quasi-judicial activity available to a legislature is direct punishment of its own members for serious acts of misconduct. Courts do *not* have such power over judges, ordinarily, but it is considered to be a "quasi-judicial" function when a legislature disciplines legislators because it is done through a proceeding that has some of the attributes of a trial.

The sanctions available to a legislature after it makes findings of misconduct may include exclusion of a person elected to the body before he is allowed to take his oath, if the misconduct occurred before he assumed membership; suspension or expulsion, if the misconduct occurred while the member was serving.

Clearly this authority is an important supplement to the usual sanction that applies to misbehaving legislators: loss at the polls the next time they seek election. But the authority is likely to be used infrequently because it does interfere with the public service of a person elected by the voters to represent them in the legislature.

The procedures for implementing this authority vary widely between legislatures. In general, however, a legislature would not be likely to use such power without giving the accused member-elect or member full procedural protection along the way. The ultimate decision to punish will be sufficiently difficult to defend politically that a legislature's leaders would not be likely to add to the difficulty by risking charges of "railroading" an elected official.

More often than not, such proceedings would be covered by the reporter assigned to the legislature. A legal reporter could, of course, become involved in the coverage, too.

In covering such a case, the reporters would do well to keep the readers and listeners fully apprised of the procedures being used, compare them with the procedures that would exist in a true court proceeding, and explain the differences.

Impeachment

The special legislative technique that is most like that of a court's operations is an **impeachment** case. Congress has the power to impeach and so do some state legislatures.

This is the proceeding used by legislators to accomplish the removal from office of persons holding elected or appointed positions in the executive branch of government. Without such a proceeding, an errant executive official could continue to hold office until his term had concluded, if he is elected, or perhaps indefinitely if he is appointed, no matter how serious the error or misconduct with which he might be charged or even convicted.

A court customarily is without power to force an executive official out of office as a punishment even for a criminal conviction. That power is conferred, where it exists at all, upon the more popularly representative branch, the legislature.

An impeachment proceeding is not necessarily limited to cases in which the official is charged with misconduct that would constitute a crime under state or federal criminal law. Actual crimes may be classed as **impeachable offenses,** but other, non-criminal misbehavior may also be included.

The word "impeachment" is usually understood to mean, technically, the formal charging of an official with an offense. Loosely speaking, the word may cover the whole process of charging, trial, conviction, and removal.

The process. An impeachment proceeding begins with the submission of charges by one or more members of the legislature. The charges then are investigated, just as criminal charges would be except that the investigation is done within the legislature, not by an arm of the courts or the executive branch.

Formal charging of impeachable offenses usually comes on a vote of one house of a legislature, followed by a formal trial of the charges in the other chamber. This probably will be a trial in the fullest sense, with presentation of evidence according to some formal rules, safeguards to protect the personal rights of the accused official, a neutral magistrate or judge, deliberation by those possessing power to convict, and announcement of a verdict. Customarily,

conviction need not be by unanimous vote. Upon conviction, the official is removed from office; in some jurisdictions, he may also be made ineligible to
hold public office again.

This description generally follows the process as it unfolds in an impeachment proceeding in Congress. Where state legislatures have the power of impeachment, their procedures will vary considerably. The ultimate penalty,
though, is the same: removal from office. Sometimes removal from office may
be followed by criminal prosecution.

Like the other forms of direct action by a legislature, this one is used only
as a last-resort measure—as, for example, in the case of former President Richard Nixon.

Some observers tend to think that such a procedure actually reflects a
breakdown in government because it is such an extreme, disruptive and blunt
instrument. Other, however, are inclined to think that it is a valuable, "ultimate" tool to prevent the true breakdown of government because of grave misconduct by an executive officer who refuses to leave office voluntarily even in
the face of overwhelming evidence of guilt of an impeachable offense.

However it is viewed by specialists or theorists, it is a most fascinating
procedure for the legal reporter to cover. Few other proceedings that he may
encounter will so fundamentally test the values that public officials will seek to
apply in judging performance in public office, and the procedural values that
will be observed in a true legislative trial.

Beyond its fascination to the reporter as a professional, an impeachment
case is of profound importance to the public to whom both the news professional and the public official are accountable. Perhaps in covering no other act
of government does the reporter have so pervasive an obligation to provide the
fullest coverage, offer the fullest explanations for what is happening, and provide the most objective professional analysis at many critical points throughout
the proceedings.

A technique of such sweeping potential consequence, yet one that is so
rarely used that it is almost exotic, begs to be understood popularly. Only the
press is in a position to do that for a mass audience.

Glossary of Legal Terms

The law has a language of its own, much of which is not familiar to the lay public. A reporter should avoid use of legal terms unless they are routinely accompanied by a lay definition. The following definitions are written in that fashion.

Some words and phrases have more than one meaning in legal usage. Multiple definitions are given here as appropriate.

This glossary includes all of the words and phrases that are shown in bold-face type in the main text. They are in alphabetical order by key word; cross-references are indicated here in bold-face type. All of these terms may be located in the text by use of the index.

address—form of discipline of judges; formal charges are filed, followed by trial before a legislative body; conviction leads to a request for dismissal by the executive branch

action at law—technically, a **common law action**: a civil case in which the issues are determined by legal principles; a normal result would be an award of damages (differs from **suit in equity**)

admissible—evidence which a judge decides may be offered in either a civil or criminal trial because it satisfies **rules of evidence**

adversary system—legal process in which disputing parties pursue their case virtually from opposite sides, independently represented by their own lawyers (differs from **ex parte** proceeding)

affidavit—sworn statement; used by a policeman seeking to justify a request for court permission to make an **arrest** or a **search**

affirmative defense—assertion in either a civil or criminal case that the action taken by the person sued was justified in a legal sense

alimony—regular payment to be made to a spouse following **divorce**

"Allen charge" (also called **"dynamite charge"**)—judge's speech to a jury that is having difficulty reaching a verdict; the judge stresses the jurors' duty to agree, if possible, the individual juror's duty to listen to the others with sympathy and generosity, the interest of the state and of the accused person in having the matter settled

allocution—accused person's plea for mercy from the court

amici curiae, plural of amicus curiae—**"friend of the court;"** person or organization that is not a party to a lawsuit but nevertheless has interests at stake in it and formally notifies the court of those interests (differs from **intervenor**)

annulment—order to dissolve a marriage based on a conclusion that, because of a legal defect, the marriage never existed

answer—item-by-item, paragraph-by-paragraph response to points made in a **complaint**; part of the **pleadings**

appeal—plea to a higher court to alter or overturn a verdict or decision of a lower court because of error or injustice

appellant—party who takes an appeal to a higher court

appellate jurisdiction—authority in a higher court to take a case and decide it on appeal; may be discretionary

appellee—party against whom an appeal is taken

arraigned—reading of a criminal charge to the accused person, to which he is asked to plead

arraignment—first encounter of a criminal suspect with a court, at which he may be asked to plead to a charge (sometimes called **preliminary hearing** or **initial appearance**)

arrest—take someone into custody for committing a crime or on suspicion of a crime

"best evidence"—rule of evidence requiring the use, if available, of an original document, item or material rather than a copy or facsimile of it

beyond a reasonable doubt—standard in a criminal case requiring that the jury be satisfied to a moral certainty that the crime has been proven by the prosecution; applies to every **element of a crime**

bill of attainder—legislative bill that imposes punishment after a legislative trial, with the accused person having no chance to defend himself ("trial" in this sense means the usual process of legislating)

"blotter"—record kept at a police station of the first encounter of police with a crime or a suspected crime

"booking"—entering a person's name, address and other personal details in an arrest record indicating the possible criminal violation and the name of the arresting officer

brief—written argument on the legal issues, either at the trial level or on appeal

burden of proof—necessity of proving affirmatively a fact or a legal principle in dispute in a lawsuit; in criminal cases, the burden is on the prosecution; in civil cases, the burden may shift between the parties

calendar—list of cases with dates and perhaps times set for hearing, trial or argument

capital punishment—(also called **death penalty**)—sentence of death

case-in-chief—main body of evidence offered by each side in a civil or criminal case; includes offering of evidence, **direct examination, cross examination, re-direct examination, re-cross examination** (see **rebuttal**) (differs from **rejoinder**) case law—doctrines of law established by court ruling rather than by legislation or constitutional clause (differs from **law of the case**; differs from **common law**)

cause of action—legal basis for a lawsuit (differs from **jurisdiction**)

cease-and-desist order—requirement, usually by a regulatory agency, that a party stop an activity because of its probable or actual illegality

censure—form of discipline of a lawyer or a judge resulting in no loss of professional privileges or official authority (differs from **disbarment** and from **suspension**)

certification, certify—authorizing a party to file an appeal where there is no guaranteed right to appeal; also, referring a controlling issue of law to a higher court for decision before a lower court proceeds with a case

certiorari—order authorizing an appeal to proceed (see **writ of certiorari**)

challenge—objection to the seating of a particular person on a jury, civil or criminal; may be **for cause** or **peremptory**

challenge for cause—objection to the seating of a particular juror for a stated reason; the judge has discretion to deny the challenge (differs from **peremptory challenge**)

change of venue—transfer of a case from a court in one jurisdiction, geographical or governmental, to another

charge—accusation of crime; also, **instructions** to a jury on its duties and the law

choice of forum—selection of a particular court in which to file a case, when more than one court has jurisdiction or authority to decide it

circumstantial evidence—evidence which merely suggests something by implication (differs from **direct evidence**)

citation—reference to the volume and page number of an official report of a case or decision (differs from **style of a case**)

civil procedure—process by which a civil case is tried and appealed, including the preparations for trial, the rules of evidence and trial conduct, and the procedure for pursuing appeals

claim—assertion in a civil case that the suing party has been injured or wronged by the action of another

class action—lawsuit filed on behalf of many persons with a common legal interest at stake, where the number of such persons is so large that they could not be included as individuals

clear and convincing evidence—standard commonly used in civil lawsuits and in regulatory agency cases governing the amount of proof that must be offered in order to prevail

clemency (also called **executive clemency**)—act of grace or mercy by a President or governor to ease the consequences of a criminal act, accusation or conviction; may take the form of **commutation** or **pardon**

closing argument (also called **summation**)—summing up of a case by each side at the close of a trial

collateral attack (also called **post-conviction remedy**)—challenge to a criminal conviction after the conviction has become final; follows the conclusion of all steps in a **direct appeal**

common law—branch of law based upon a state's or nation's custom or long-standing assumption, rather than legislation or court decision; incorporated into legal doctrine through court ruling (differs from **case law**)

common law action (also called **action at law**)—civil case in which the issues are determined by legal principles; a normal result would be an award of damages (differs
from **suit in equity**)

common law contempt—power of the court, based on custom rather than statute or
constitutional provision, to punish for conduct that disrupts the operation of the
court

common law crime—crime defined by custom and traditional practice rather than by
legislation

common law marriage—legal relationship equivalent to marriage but without a formal
civil marriage by law; usually is found to exist after a couple has lived together, as if
married, for a specified period

common law privacy—enforceable right of privacy based upon custom and tradition
rather than legislation or constitutional provision

community property—joint ownership of property by a married couple, established by
legislation (differs from **separate property**)

commutation—reduction of a convicted person's sentence; a form of **executive clemency**

compensatory damages—form of money payment awarded at the end of a case to pay a
person for the actual losses he has suffered or will suffer because of a wrong done to
him; may take the form of **general damages** or **special damages**

complainant (also called **plaintiff**)—party filing a civil case; also, a person making a
complaint of crime to police

complaint—document by the suing party in a civil case identifying the parties involved
on both sides, reciting facts in the dispute, listing legal grievances and specifying
the remedies sought; in civil law, may be called **petition** or **declaration;** also, in
criminal law, the document by which a crime is alleged

compromise verdict—verdict reached by a jury on a charge less serious than the one
originally made by the prosecutor; usually refers to finding of guilt of a **lesser-
included offense**

conclusions of law—proposed or actual declarations of the legal bases for a court's ruling
in a civil case

concurrent sentences—two or more criminal sentences served simultaneously (differs
from **consecutive sentences**)

condemnation (also called **eminent domain**)—process of taking private property for
public use, with compensation to be paid

condemnation award—value to be paid in compensation for taking of private property
for public use

consecutive sentences—two or more criminal sentences served in succession (differs
from **concurrent sentences**)

conservatorship (may also be called **guardianship**)—legal right given to a person, perhaps a lawyer, to manage the property of a person deemed incapable of doing that
for himself

contemnor—person accused of contempt of court

contempt—intentional disregard or disobedience of a court order; also, disregard or disobedience of other public authority, as a legislature or regulatory agency; may be
civil or criminal, established by legislation or **common law**

continuance—postponement of civil or criminal proceedings

contract—agreement, written or otherwise established, that creates, modifies or destroys a legal relationship

controlling questions—decisive issues which a lower court refers to a higher court for a ruling before the lower court proceeds with a case; referral is by **certification**

counterclaim—assertion by the party that has been sued in a civil case that he has been injured or wronged by the party filing the lawsuit; may be a completely new **complaint**

counts—parts of a civil complaint claiming specific legal error or wrong done; also, the parts of a criminal charge, by **information** or **indictment,** alleging violations of law

court of last resort—final court to decide a case on appeal; may be **intermediate court of appeals** or **supreme court;** also, refers loosely to a supreme court

criminal information (also called simply **information**)—document, filed by a prosecutor, formally accusing a person of a crime (differs from **indictment**)

criminal intent—one of the **elements of a crime**; accused person must have intended to commit the act outlawed as a crime

cross-examination—questioning of a witness at a trial, hearing or during the taking of a deposition, by the party opposed to the one who produced the witness; the questioning is for the purpose of testing the truth of the witness' **testimony,** or for **impeachment** of his testimony

damages—payments of money to compensate for an actual or potential loss, or to punish a person for a wrong done; comes in various specific forms

death penalty (also called **capital punishment**)—sentence of death

declaration (also called **complaint** or **petition**)—statement in a civil case stating the bases for the lawsuit and the allegations of legal error or wrong

declaratory judgment—decision by a court identifying or defining legal or constitutional rights; may not include a binding order or award of damages

decree of divorce—decision at the close of a divorce case, perhaps awarding alimony, property, child custody or child support

default—failure to satisfy an obligation; also, a failure to respond to a lawsuit against one's self

default judgment—court order settling a case in favor of the person who sued because the other side did not respond to the lawsuit

defendant—person on trial for an alleged crime; also, may be the party sued in a civil case, sometimes called **respondent**

defense—the **defendant** and the attorney(s) representing his interests in a criminal case; also, refers to a specific form of legal argument answering a civil or criminal allegation

deliberation—process by which a jury considers a verdict at the close of a civil or criminal trial; also, a court's weighing of a case prior to decision

delinquency, delinquent—formal conclusion by a juvenile court that a youthful offender has committed the crime charged

demurrer—one form of a **motion to dismiss** a civil case; a formal request to bring a case to an end because of the legal insufficiency of a **complaint**

de novo—"anew" or "fresh;" usually refers to **trial de novo**

deposition—testimony given under oath outside a court trial or proceeding (differs from **interrogatories**) dicta, dictum—comments in a court opinion that are legal in nature but are not necessary to the legal **holding** of the decision

direct appeal—appeal pursued after the verdict has been issued in a criminal case (differs from **collateral attack**)

direct evidence—evidence which speaks for itself: eyewitness accounts, a confession, a weapon, an instrumentality of crime (differs from **circumstantial evidence**)

directed judgment—court decision in favor of one side because that side's evidence clearly prevails, or because the other side has not clearly prevailed; may be issued in a civil or criminal case; may be issued despite a jury's verdict to the contrary, as in **judgment of acquittal** or **judgment n.o.v.**; may be issued at the close of one side's evidence or at the close of all evidence (sometimes called **directed verdict**)

directed verdict—*see directed judgment*

direct examination—questioning of witnesses at a trial, hearing or deposition by the party producing the witness, to elicit **testimony** favorable to that side

disbarment—form of discipline of a lawyer resulting in his loss (often permanently) of his right to practice law (differs from **censure** and from **suspension**)

discovery—process, before or during trial, by which one side seeks to determine the evidence in possession of the other side that could affect the outcome of the case

dismiss—*see motion to dismiss*

diversity of citizenship—legal basis for proceeding with a civil case under state law but in federal court because the parties are from different states

divorce—process or result by which a marriage relationship is dissolved, totally or by **separation agreement**

divorce a messa et thora (also called **separate maintenance**)—legal separation of a married couple without dissolution of the marriage; translates "divorce from bed and board"

divorce a vincula—complete divorce or dissolution of a marriage

docket—court record in which cases are listed or formally entered; also, a record in which a judge makes entries about the progress of a case before him

double jeopardy—putting a person on trial more than once for the same crime

due process—doctrine that a person may not lose rights or have his interests compromised unless he has had an opportunity to defend his interests; may be by procedural guarantee or by protection of his rights in their substance

"dynamite charge" (also called **"Allen charge"**)—judge's speech to a jury having difficulty reaching a verdict

elements of a crime—specific factors that define a crime; the prosecution must prove every element **beyond a reasonable doubt** in order to obtain a conviction

eminent domain (also called **condemnation**)—process of taking private property for public use, with compensation to be paid

en banc—all judges of a multi-judge court sitting jointly to decide a case, perhaps but not necessarily on **rehearing**

equity—the spirit and habit of fairness and justness in law; the inherent power of a judge to correct an injustice; pursued in a suit in equity as opposed to a **common law action** or **action at law**

error coram nobis—method by which a court may correct its own error (*see writ of error coram nobis*)

estate—property, real or personal, owned by a person; usually refers, in law, to property which may succeed to other persons evidence—assertions, by **testimony**, document or **exhibit** by which a party seeks to prove its case, in civil or criminal proceedings; may be **circumstantial** or **direct**; the process is governed by **rules of evidence**

evidentiary hearing—hearing in a divorce case to determine whether some form of **temporary relief** is to be ordered

exceptions—declarations by either side in a civil or criminal case reserving the right to appeal a judge's ruling upon a motion; also, in regulatory cases, objections by either side to points made by the other side or to rulings by the agency or one of its hearing officers

exclusionary rule—a judge-made doctrine that convictions based upon illegally obtained evidence must be reversed, and that such evidence be excluded from use in any re-trial (differs from **suppress**)

exculpatory—evidence or information that could help an accused person demonstrate his innocence (opposite of inculpatory, meaning evidence suggesting guilt)

execution—carrying out of an act or course of conduct to its completion; may refer to implementation of an order in a civil or criminal case; also may refer to act of carrying out a **death penalty**

executive clemency (also called **clemency**)—act of grace or mercy by a President or governor to ease the consequences of a criminal act, accusation or conviction

exemplary damages (also called **punitive damages**)—order to pay money as a form of punishment or deterrence from future error of the same kind that has caused legal injury or wrong

exhaustion of remedies—requirement that procedural rights before one tribunal must be pursued before another tribunal may hear a complaint or challenge; required as a premise for filing a **writ of habeas corpus** in federal court, for example

exhibit—evidence in a physical form, including an object or a document

ex parte proceeding—one in which only one side is represented (differs from adversary system or proceeding)

ex post facto—the doctrine that establishes an act to be a crime after the act has been completed

expungement—official and formal erasure of a record or partial contents of a record

extradition—detention of a person followed by his transfer from one state to be tried for a crime charged against him in another state

fact-finder—role of the jury (or of a judge in a non-jury case) in determining which party's evidence is to be accepted as fact

felony—class of more serious crimes; often refers to a crime for which the sentence may be a year or more in jail or prison (differs from **misdemeanor**)

"felony crime"—a crime committed during the course of another crime; persons involved in the first crime may be charged with the secondary crime even if they were not personally and directly involved in its commission

final hearing—proceeding by a judge in a divorce case to canvass all issues before issuing a **decree**

finding—formal conclusion by a judge of a fact or a principle of law; also, such a conclusion by a regulatory agency; also, a conclusion by a jury regarding a fact; a finding on a legal principle becomes part of the **law of the case**

friend(s) of the court (also called **amicus, amici curiae**)—person or organization that is not a party to a lawsuit but nevertheless has interests at stake in it, and notifies the court of those interests general appearance—notice by the party who has been sued that he is aware of the lawsuit, concedes the court's authority to decide it and is ready to let the case proceed to a decision (differs from **special appearance**)

general damages—form of **compensatory damages** ordered paid when the injury done was a natural and necessary consequence of the wrong or error done (differs from **special damages**)

general verdict—jury's **finding** for or against a **plaintiff** or **petitioner** after determining the facts and weighing them according to the judge's instructions regarding the law (differs from **special verdict**)

"good cause"—kind of proof that must be offered to justify an exceptional use of a court's authority

"good-time" credit—allowance of time reducing a criminal sentence for good behavior as a prisoner

grand jury—jury with authority to conduct criminal investigations and to charge a crime by **indictment**; also may have power to issue a report, or **presentment**, without charging a crime; may act as a **runaway grand jury**

greater weight of the evidence—standard used in civil law to govern the amount of proof needed for one side to prevail

guardian, guardianship—person, perhaps a lawyer, appointed to look after the interests of a person incapable of doing that for himself

habeas corpus—field of law dealing with release of persons from custody if they are wrongly held; *see writ of habeas corpus*

hearing—any form of judicial, quasi-judicial or legislative proceeding at which issues or questions are canvassed

hearing on the merits (also called **oral argument**)—hearing before a court, usually on appeal, on the legal questions at issue

hearsay—form of evidence, not **admissible**, based on what one person has heard from or about another person; something that the witness himself has not observed directly

holding—legal declaration or principle that forms a court's decision and provides the basis for its **judgment** and **mandate**

"house counsel"—lawyer on the staff of a company, corporation or other organization (differs from **outside counsel**)

"hung" jury—jury that is unable to agree on a verdict

immaterial—form of evidence, usually not **admissible,** that is not essential to the case

immunity—grant by the court of immunity to prosecution in return for providing criminal evidence (differs from **sovereign immunity**)

impeachable offenses—categories of crime or misconduct upon which **impeachment** may be based; do not necessarily have to be crimes punishable by criminal prosecution

impeachment—process by which a public official outside the legislative branch is tried for misdeeds related to official duties and resulting, upon conviction, in removal from office; also, the process of discrediting a witness' testimony

incompetent—form of evidence, not **admissible,** that is not properly offered or has been illegally or improperly obtained; also, a person ruled incapable of managing his own property or affairs

indictment—formal accusation of a crime, by a grand jury (differs from **information** and from **presentment**)

inferences—truths or propositions drawn from evidence or facts

information—(also called **criminal information**) formal accusation of crime by a prosecutor (differs from **indictment**)

informer—one who provides information about actual or potential crime to the police

initial appearance—first encounter of the suspect with a court; the function of this proceeding varies, sometimes having the characteristics of an **arraignment** or a **preliminary hearing**

injunction—*see temporary* and *permanent injunction*

instructions (also called **charge**)—judge's directions to the jury regarding its authority to determine the facts and to draw inferences from the facts in order to reach a verdict; instructions include legal guidance

integrated bar—organized state bar to which every lawyer in a state must belong

intent—*see criminal intent*

interlocutory appeal—appeal to test a decisive issue (**controlling question**) of law that has arisen during the course of a trial

intermediate court of appeals—court with authority to decide initial appeals, civil or criminal, from the trial court

interrogatories—written questions put, under oath, to parties in a civil case (differs from **deposition**)

intervenor—interested party who joins a civil case as a party after the case has been filed, perhaps supporting one side or the other, perhaps taking an independent position (differs from **amici curiae**)

inter vivos trust—legal arrangement for the management or protection of property during the lifetime of the person committing property to the trust (differs from **testamentary trust**)

intestate—without a will (differs from **testate**)

irrelevant—evidence, not **admissible,** which does not relate to the specific crime charged in a criminal case, or does not support the point for which it was offered in a civil or criminal case

judgment—formal order of a court embodying its decision (differs from **holding** and from **mandate**)

judgment of acquittal—form of **directed verdict** in which the judge decides that the evidence will not support a criminal conviction; may be made at the close of the evidence before a case is submitted to a jury

judgment n.o.v.—literally, judgment non obstante veredicto, which translates as judgment "notwithstanding the verdict;" judge's decision to decide a case contrary to the verdict, whether the verdict has been made by a jury or by the judge in a non-jury case; may be made in a civil or criminal case

judicial review—authority of a court to review the official actions of other branches of government; also, authority to declare unconstitutional the actions of other branches

jurisdiction—court's authority to hear and/or decide a case (differs from **cause of action**)

justiciable claim—claim of legal error or wrong that is capable of being resolved in the courts

law of the case—**findings** and **holdings** of a civil or criminal case, binding upon the parties even if the law or legal principle upon which the case was decided is later changed (differs from **case law**) legal aid—professional legal services available usually to persons or organizations unable to afford such services

legislative contempt—punishment for interfering with the legislative process; may be imposed by the legislature itself or by a court in a regular criminal case

legislative history—background of action by a legislature, including testimony before committees, written reports and debates on the legislation

leniency—recommendation by the prosecutor to the judge regarding the sentence that may be imposed in a criminal case

lesser-included offense—less serious crimes that are incorporated in the category of a **felony**; a jury's unwillingness to convict on the felony may lead it to consider conviction on a lesser offense; sometimes this is called a **compromise verdict**

lineup—procedure to display one or more criminal suspects to victims or witnesses to a crime for possible identification

liquidated damages—form of money payment in an amount specified in advance by agreement of the parties as the sum that would be paid if a contract or agreement were violated

long-arm statute—state law giving a court jurisdiction to try civil cases in which persons from other states have been sued

magistrate—lesser judicial officer exercising some of the functions of a judge; also, refers in a general way to a judge, as in the phrase "neutral magistrate"

malpractice—professional misconduct or negligence, providing the basis for a suit against an attorney

mandamus—*see writ of mandamus*

mandate—document which implements a court's **judgment,** directing that the judgment be applied

mandatory injunction—*see permanent injunction*

material—evidence that may be essential to the case, and thus is **admissible**

memoranda of law—formal written arguments in support of motions filed in a civil or criminal case (sometimes called **briefs**)

merits—issues of legal substance at stake in a case, as opposed to procedural considerations that may affect it

"Miranda warning"—requirement that police tell a suspect in their custody of his constitutional rights before they question him

misdemeanor—minor or lesser crime, punishable by a limited fine or reasonably short jail term (differs from **felony**)

"Missouri plan"—method of selecting judges on merit rather than political acceptability; the official with power to appoint judges must make his selection only from lists of recommended candidates; a judge must submit to periodic voter referenda on whether he is to remain on the bench

mistrial—a trial that has been ruled invalid because of some essential error; also, ending of a trial because of the inability of the jury to agree upon a verdict— **"hung" jury**

motion to acquit, or motion for a judgment of acquittal—formal request that the judge declare the accused person acquitted of the charge (*see judgment of acquittal*)

motion to dismiss—formal request for the judge to dismiss criminal charges or a civil complaint, for various reasons of error or insufficiency of evidence

motion for a new trial—formal request that the judge nullify a guilty verdict and grant a new trial because of a fundamental error motion for non-suit—formal request that the judge refuse to let a criminal case go to a jury because the evidence is insufficient; may be offered at the close of the prosecution's evidence, or later in the trial, before a jury has begun **deliberations**

motion to strike—formal request that the judge expunge or remove evidence or briefs offered in a civil or criminal case

no contest plea (also called **nolo contendere**)—a refusal to challenge a criminal charge, thus bringing a case to an end without a formal **finding** or **verdict** of guilt; constitutes an admission of the crime for the purposes of ending the case only

"no-fault" proceeding—civil case, as in divorce, in which parties may resolve their dispute without a formal finding of error or fault

nolle prosequi (also loosely called "nolle pros")—decision by a prosecutor not to go forward with a charge of crime; translates "I do not choose to prosecute"

nolo contendere—*see no contest plea*

nominal damages—payment of an insignificant amount, perhaps $1, when there is no basis for establishing a set amount of **compensatory** or **punitive damages** for the wrongdoer's action

non-suit—*see motion for non-suit*

notation of jurisdiction, note jurisdiction—formal order of an appeals court (U.S. Supreme Court, for example) declaring that it has authority to decide a case appealed to it

note probable jurisdiction—order of an appeals court declaring that it will hear an appeal and will decide later whether it has authority to decide the case

notice—formal notification to the party that has been sued in a civil case of the fact that the lawsuit has been filed; also, any form of notification of a legal proceeding

notice of appeal—short formal document indicating that an appeal will be filed from a **judgment** or **verdict**; it may state the grounds for the **appeal**

nunc pro tunc—a form of appeal pursued after a convicted person or the losing party in a civil case has failed to file an appeal during a required period; translates "now for then," meaning figuratively the erasure of time considerations

objection—challenge by one side in a trial to questions put by the other side to witnesses, or to the introduction of evidence; if a judge **overrules** an objection, an **exception** may be taken

ombudsman—public official, perhaps a lawyer, monitoring governmental action on behalf of the public in general

omnibus hearing—single proceeding in advance of a criminal trial, at which all pre-trial motions will be heard and disposed of

"on his own recognizance"—release of a person from custody without the payment of any money bail or posting of bond

opening arguments, statements—oral declarations by each side at the start of a trial, discussing the points each side expects to establish

oral argument—formal hearing in court, perhaps on motions made during trial, perhaps on the legal issues at stake in an appeal (sometimes called **hearing on the merits**)

original jurisdiction—authority to try a case in the first instance; may refer to trial court or, in some circumstances, to an appeals court

outside counsel—lawyer retained from outside an organization (differs from "**house counsel**")

overrule—judge's decision not to allow an **objection**; also, decision by a court finding that an earlier decision was in error; also, decision by a higher court finding that a lower court decision was in error

panel (of a court)—several judges, less than the whole membership of a court, sitting to decide a case

pardon—form of **executive clemency**, removing or extinguishing a criminal conviction, or preventing criminal prosecution

parole—release of a prisoner prior to the expiration of his sentence

partial testacy—will that provides for the disposition of part, but not all, of the property of a person after his death

per curiam—"by the court"; a means by which a court speaks in its own name rather than through an opinion signed by a specific judge

peremptory challenge—right to exclude a person from service on a jury for no stated reason (differs from **challenge for cause**)

permanent injunction—court order requiring that some action be taken, or that some party refrain from taking action (differs from forms of **temporary relief**, as a **temporary** or **preliminary injunction**)

"person in need of supervision"—juvenile found to have committed an offense that would not provide a basis for a finding of **delinquency**

petition—written form of a plea to a court, used either to initiate a case or to request some action by the court; also, in civil cases, called a **complaint**

petitioner—one who asks a court to act, or one who files a case

plaintiff (also called **complainant**)—party filing a civil case or bringing a criminal complaint

plea—entry of an admission or a denial of guilt in a criminal case; also, any form of request to a court (differs from **pleading**)

"plea bargaining"—negotiation between the prosecution and the defense over a possible guilty plea thus closing a case without a trial or before a trial is concluded

pleading(s)—written documents, as **complaint, answer** and **reply** in a civil case, informing the court of the claims at issue; also, refers to the manner of making an argument in court (differs from **plea**)

pool—list of persons eligible for jury duty, from which a **venire** will be drawn for a **term** of court

post-conviction remedy (also called **collateral attack**)—challenge to a criminal conviction after the conviction has become final; follows the conclusion of all steps in a **direct appeal**

"power of attorney"—formal authorization of a person, perhaps a lawyer, to act in the interests of a person incapable of managing his own affairs or property

precedent—controlling **holding** of a court decision, binding in that court's jurisdiction until changed or **overruled**

prejudicial publicity—news about a criminal case that may tend to interfere with an accused person's right to be tried by an impartial jury

preliminary hearing—one of the first, and perhaps the first, encounters of a criminal suspect with a court; sometimes may include the function of an **arraignment**, including entry of a plea by a person charged with crime (also sometimes called **initial appearance**)

preliminary injunction—court order requiring action or forbidding action in order to preserve the status quo until a decision can be made whether to issue a **permanent injunction** (differs from **temporary restraining order**)

preponderance of the evidence—standard used in civil law to determine which side's offer of evidence has been sufficient to allow it to prevail

presentment—declaration or document issued by a **grand jury** that either makes a neutral report or notes misdeeds by officials charged with specified public duties; ordinarily does not include a formal charge of crime (differs from **indictment**)

presumption of innocence—the doctrine that a person accused of crime is innocent until proven guilty in a court of law

pre-trial conference—meeting of attorneys, customarily with the judge, in advance of a trial to seek to narrow the issues in a case or to arrange procedures for the case's determination

pre-trial motion—any form of legal request filed in advance of a civil or criminal trial

privilege—form of legal immunity from compelled disclosure in court; ordinarily refers to confidential communications between husband and wife, attorney and client, doctor and patient, etc.

probable cause—justifiable belief that a crime has been or may be committed, providing the basis for keeping a person in custody prior to trial, or for issuing a **warrant** for an **arrest** or a **search**

probare—"to prove"; used in **probate** law

probate (also called **testacy proceeding**)—process by which a person's will is tested for authenticity and legal sufficiency and the property distributed under the terms of the will; also, refers more generally though loosely to the law governing **estates**

probation—form of sentence not involving jailing or imprisonment; includes supervision by a probation officer

pro bono publico—"for the public good"; refers to the lawyer's offering of services, probably without legal fees, in a case of notable public significance

prohibitory injunction—*see permanent injunction* and *temporary injunction*

proposed findings of fact—recommended **findings** prepared for a judge's approval in a civil case

pro se—person acting as his own attorney, whether or not he is a lawyer

public defender—governmental official who provides free legal defense services to an indigent accused of crime

public interest law—branch of law involving broader questions of public policy that may be determined by the courts; also, refers, loosely, to some forms of **pro bono publico** representation

punitive damages (also called **exemplary damages**)—order to pay money as a form of punishment or deterrence from future error of the same kind that has caused legal injury or wrong

quash—withdraw or nullify a subpoena issued to obtain witnesses or evidence

rebuttal—presentation of evidence by the opposing side after the side which opened the case has concluded; includes all of the opposing side's **case-in-chief**: offering of evidence, direct examination, cross-examination, re-direct examination, re-cross examination (differs from **rejoinder**)

recall—summons for a judge or other elected official to go before the voters in a special referendum to determine his right to remain in office record—all of the documents and **evidence** plus **transcripts** of oral proceedings in a case

re-direct examination—opportunity to present limited supporting evidence after one's evidence has been subjected to **cross-examination**

rehearing—second oral hearing by an appeals court on a case; also, reconsideration of a case once decided; also, consideration of a case by a court sitting **en banc** after a **panel** has decided it

rejoinder—opportunity for the side which opened the case to offer limited responses to evidence presented during the **rebuttal** by the opposing side; responses may be limited to new matters brought up on **rebuttal**

relevant—**admissible** evidence which relates to the specific crime charged in a criminal case; also, evidence in a civil case which may or does support the point for which it was offered

remedy—legal or judicial means by which a right or privilege is enforced or the violation of a right or privilege is prevented, redressed or compensated

remove—transfer a state case to federal court for trial—in civil cases, because the parties are from different states; in criminal and some civil cases, because there is a significant possibility that there could not be a fair trial in state court

reply—item-by-item response to the statements or assertions made in the **answer** to a **complaint** in a civil case; if the **answer** has made **counter-claims,** the reply will serve as an **answer** to those

res judicata—legal question that has been "settled before"—that is, by a prior court **precedent;** also, a prior settlement of facts in a continuing legal dispute between particular parties

respondent—party who has been sued in a civil case; sometimes called **defendant**

rest—notice to the court that one side has completed its entire case

retire—departure of the jury from the courtroom to **deliberate**

return—report to a judge by police on the implementation of an **arrest** or **search warrant;** also, a report to a judge in reply to a **subpoena,** civil or criminal

reverse—action of a higher court in setting aside or revoking a lower court decision

right to treatment—claim by a juvenile offender regarding the inadequacy of some aspect of the juvenile justice system; also, a claim by a prison inmate regarding the inadequacy of medical services in a prison facility

rules of evidence—standards governing whether **evidence** in a civil or criminal case is **admissible**

rules of procedure—guidelines or specific requirements imposed upon pre-trial, trial and appellate proceedings, civil or criminal

"runaway" grand jury—**grand jury** that seeks to charge a crime despite contrary wishes of the prosecutor

search—examination by a police officer of a person or property in pursuit of criminal evidence

search incident to an arrest—search made without a warrant at the time of arrest and in the same location

self-defense—claim that a criminal act was legally justifiable because it was necessary to protect a person or property from the threat or action of another

sentence—**judgment** imposed upon a person after his conviction of a criminal offense, stating the punishment to be inflicted sentencing report—document containing background material on a convicted person, prepared to guide the judge in the imposition of a **sentence**

separate maintenance—**decree** in a divorce case providing that the husband and wife are free in all legal respects except they cannot remarry (similar to **separation agreement**)

separate property—property held by a person in his name only (differs from **community property**)

separation agreement—private agreement between a husband and wife to free each other from the marriage relationship without a dissolution of the marriage; may or may not be entered in court (*see separate maintenance*)

sequester—in a criminal trial, to require the members of the jury to reside under a court officer's supervision during the trial

serve—issue a legal document, such as a **complaint, summons** or **subpoena**; service constitutes formal legal **notice**

sever—separate persons who have been charged jointly with crime for separate trials

solitary confinement—form of discipline of a prison inmate placing him in a restricted cell with loss of normal privileges

sovereign immunity—the doctrine that the government, state or federal, is immune to lawsuit unless it gives its consent

special appearance—notice by the party who has been sued that he is aware of the lawsuit, but contests the court's authority over him or over the case; serves to avoid losing a case by **default** (differs from **general appearance**)

special damages—form of **compensatory damages** ordered paid when the injury done resulted from the other side's wrong but was not a natural or necessary consequence of that (differs from **general damages**)

special verdict—jury's **findings** in answer to questions of fact put by the judge, forming the basis upon which the judge will make his **judgment** (differs from **general verdict**)

specific performance—carry out a duty undertaken by agreement or imposed by law, to obey a **mandatory** or **permanent injunction**

standing—legal right to sue or to enter a lawsuit, based upon an assertion that one's interests have been threatened or injured

statutory—created, defined or required by legislation

statutory construction—process by which a court seeks to interpret the meaning and scope of legislation

stay (also called **stay of enforcement** or **stay of execution**)—temporary order issued by a court forbidding or postponing enforcement of a court order or **sentence** until the issuing court or another court may act further

stipulation—statement of agreement between opposing sides in a civil or criminal case on facts or legal questions thus removing them from contest

strike—remove from the **record** of a case **evidence** that has been improperly offered

"style" of a case—title of a lawsuit, by the names of the parties (for example, Jones v. Smith) (differs from **citation**)

subpoena—order issued by a judge or magistrate, grand jury or prosecutor requiring a person to appear and give **testimony** or produce documents

suit in equity—civil case in which a judge determines whether a person's right to be treated with fairness and justice, under general principles of **equity,** has been violated; a normal result would be an order forbidding or allowing another person to take an action (differs from **common law action**)

summary judgment—court order deciding a case in favor of one side on the basis of the **pleadings,** before trial and before or after a hearing

summation (also called **closing argument**)—summing up by each side of its case at the close of a civil or criminal trial

summons—formal **notice** to a person that he has been sued; it constitutes a notice that he must defend himself or lose by **default**

suppress—forbid the use of evidence at a trial because it is improper or was improperly obtained (differs from **exclusionary rule**)

suspension—form of discipline of a lawyer resulting in the temporary loss of his right to practice law (differs from **censure** and from **disbarment**)

sustain—court order allowing an **objection** or motion to prevail

tariff—formal schedule of a regulated company's rates for its service; may include terms and availability of service

temporary injunction—court order requiring that some action be taken, or that some party refrain from taking action, until the court may decide whether to issue a **permanent injunction** (differs from **temporary restraining order**)

temporary relief—any form of action by a court granting one side or the other an order to protect its interests pending further action by the court

temporary restraining order (also called TRO)—court order forbidding or requiring action until the court may hold a hearing; usually of short duration (differs from **temporary injunction**)

term of court—period of time for a court's regular session or sitting; also, a description of the class of cases a court will consider during a specified sitting

testamentary trust—legal arrangement for the management or protection of property after the death of the person committing property to the trust (differs from **inter vivos trust**)

testacy proceeding—*see probate*

testate—conveying property by a will (differs from **intestate**)

testator—one who makes a will

testimony—**evidence** given by a witness under oath; does not include evidence from documents and other sources

timely (untimely)—an appeal is timely if it has been filed as required by rules of procedure, including time requirements and restrictions on the issues that may be raised; an appeals court may not rule upon a case that is untimely

tort—private or civil wrong or injury subject to redress by legal action

transcript—verbatim record of an oral proceeding (differs from **record** of a case)

trial de novo—second trial in a trial court with broader jurisdiction than that in which the initial trial was held; the second trial is completely new ("de novo")—that is, the outcome of the initial trial is ignored

trial memoranda (also called **briefs**)—documents discussing points of law at issue in a civil or criminal trial

trust—legal entity or arrangement created to hold property for the benefit of a person (see **inter vivos trust** and **testamentary trust**) venire—set number of potential jurors drawn from a jury **pool**; a trial jury will be selected from those on a given venire

verdict—conclusion, as to fact or law, drawn in a jury or non-jury civil or criminal case that forms the basis for the court's **judgment**

voir dire—process of questioning potential jurors so that each side may decide whether to accept or oppose individuals for jury service

waive—abandon or relinquish a right or privilege

warrant—court order authorizing police to make an **arrest** or a **search**; an **affidavit** seeking a warrant must specify the **probable cause** upon which the request is based

writ of certiorari (often abbreviated simply "cert")—court order accepting a case for review on appeal (may differ from **certification**)

writ of error coram nobis—error "before us"; an order by a trial court to release a convicted person due to an error committed in the trial

writ of habeas corpus—a court's formal demand that a person in custody be released if continued detention is not justified; issued on a showing that the person's rights have been violated in the case leading to his conviction

writ of mandamus—order issued summarily by a court, to a lower court or to some non-judicial official, requiring the performance of an official duty

writ of ne exeat—court order issued during a divorce case requiring one spouse to post bond assuring that he or she will not flee and that he or she will obey any orders of the court; may involve the spouse's detention

writ of prohibition—court order stopping the proceedings of a judge or other court, or other public official, when the proceedings are beyond established authority

Selected Readings

The materials here are arranged in three categories: books, special reports and studies on the free press-fair trial issue, and significant Supreme Court rulings dealing with the press.

BOOKS

Listed alphabetically by title, with a brief description by this author of their contents.

American Bar Association Project on Standards for Criminal Justice. 18-volume analysis of the criminal justice system with recommendations for change and reform. Available from the American Bar Association, Chicago. (Many of the standards are revised from time to time to take account of changing law.)

Anglo-American Criminal Justice. by Delmar Karlen. Oxford University Press, New York. (1967) A comparison of the American and British systems of criminal law, illuminating both systems for the layman.

The Brethren. by Bob Woodward and Scott Armstrong. Simon & Schuster, New York. (1979) Probably the best book there is on how the Supreme Court actually works, and a brilliant illustration of how courts could be covered by investigative reporters.

The Constitution and What It Means Today. by Edward S. Corwin. Princeton University Press, Princeton, N.J. (1958) A classic, now noticeably dated, on the Constitution as interpreted in Supreme Court cases.

Constitutional Law. Selected essays reprinted from the Harvard Law Review. Harvard Law Review Association, Cambridge, Mass. (1967) Some of the most notable, and now truly historic, essays on the subject.

Court and Constitution in the 20th Century. by William F. Swindler. Bobbs-Merrill, Indianapolis. (1969, 1970, 1974) A classic and very well written survey of constitutional history and law in three volumes: covering the period of 1889–1932 and the period of 1932–1968, with the concluding volume offering a commentary on all of the provisions of the Constitution.

Courts. A Report of the National Advisory Commission on Criminal Justice Standards and Goals, Task Force on Courts. (1973) A thorough review of the criminal justice process, with recommendations for reform. U.S. Government Printing Office, Washington, D.C.

The Courts, The Public and The Law Explosion. ed. by Harry W. Jones. An American Assembly book. Prentice-Hall, Inc., Englewood Cliffs, N.J. (1965) Step-by-step description and analysis of the realities of court functions and procedures, for the lay reader.

Crime and Publicity. The Impact of News on the Administration of Justice. by Alfred Friendly and Ronald L. Goldfarb. Twentieth Century Fund, New York, N.Y. (1967) A closely reasoned analysis from case studies of the actual impact of news on criminal cases.

Gideon's Trumpet. by Anthony Lewis. Random House, New York, N.Y. (1964) Perhaps the best one-case casebook in legal literature. Analyzes the growth and Supreme Court history of the case leading to the establishment of the indigent's right to a lawyer.

The Good Guys, the Bad Guys and the First Amendment. Free Speech vs. Fairness in Broadcasting. by Fred W. Friendly. Random House, New York. (1975) One of the best studies of the legal history of government regulation of broadcasting.

Introduction to Law. Selected essays reprinted from the Harvard Law Review. Harvard Law Review Association, Cambridge, Mass. (1968) As good a basic reader on law's basic premises and functioning as there is.

Introduction to Law and the Legal System. by Harold J. Grilliot. Houghton Mifflin Co., Boston. (1975) A basic primer on the law, written for the layman, with helpful case studies.

Law and the American Future. ed. by Murray L. Schwartz. An American Assembly book. Prentice-Hall Inc., Englewood Cliffs, N.Y. (1976) An attempt, quite successful, to take the measure of the future of law in America.

Law in a Changing America. ed. by Geoffrey C. Hazard Jr. An American Assembly book. Prentice-Hall Inc., Englewood Cliffs, N.J. (1968) A forward-looking analysis, in varying essays, on the problems of the legal profession.

Lawyers' Ethics in an Adversary System. by Monroe H. Freedman. Bobbs-Merrill, Indianapolis. (1975) A lively treatment of a difficult subject; appendix provides complete texts of the Canons of Professional Ethics and the Code of Professional Responsibility.

Mass Communications Law in a Nutshell. by Harvey L. Zuckman and Martin J. Gaynes. West Publishing Co., St. Paul, Minn. (1977) Extended, up-to-date and lucid analysis of First Amendment protections and of regulatory supervision of advertising, copyright and broadcasting.

The Media and the Law. ed. by Howard Simons and Joseph A. Califano Jr. Praeger Publishers, New York, N.Y. (1976) Edited transcripts of the Washington Conference on the Media and the Law; useful as a survey of a wide range of responses to specific hypothetical cases on press-law issues.

Milestones! 200 Years of American Law; Milestones in our Legal History. by Jethro K. Lieberman. Oxford University Press, New York/West Publishing Co., St. Paul. (1976) A beautifully illustrated, exceptionally well written description of the biggest cases and constitutional events in American history. Especially good for the perspective in which it puts these developments.

The Nature of the Judicial Process. by Benjamin N. Cardozo. Yale University Press, New Haven. (1921) Probably the best single essay in American legal literature on the subject.

Supreme Courts in State Politics. An Investigation of the Judicial Role. by Henry Robert Glick. Basic Books, Inc., New York. (1971) A volume in the Studies in Federalism project sponsored by Temple University. A fascinating and revealing analysis of the way state judges approach and do their work.

SPECIAL REPORTS ON FREE PRESS-FAIR TRIAL

Listed alphabetically.

Fair Trial and Free Expression. A background report prepared for the U.S. Senate Committee on the Judiciary, Subcommittee on Constitutional Rights. Available from the Superintendent of Documents, U.S. Government Printing Office, Washington, D.C.

Fair Trial/Free Press Voluntary Agreements. A report of the American Bar Association Legal Advisory Committee on Fair Trial and Free Press. Available from the American Bar Association, Chicago.

Freedom of the Press and Fair Trial: Final Report with Recommendations (the "Medina Report"). A report of a committee of the Association of the Bar of the City of New York. Available from the Association of the Bar of the City of New York, New York, N.Y.

Free Press and Fair Trial. A report of the American Newspaper Publishers Association, Special Committee on Free Press and Fair Trial. Available from the American Newspaper Publishers Association, Reston, Va.

Guidelines of the U.S. Department of Justice, relating to release of information about criminal and civil proceedings. Reported at 28 Code of Federal Regulations 50.2 (1975). Available from the Justice Department, Washington, D.C.

Prejudicial Pre-Trial Publicity ("Policy 212"). A report of the American Civil Liberties Union. Available from the American Civil Liberties Union, New York, N.Y.

Recommended Court Procedures to Accommodate Rights of Fair Trial and Free Press. A report of the American Bar Association Legal Advisory Committee on Fair Trial and Free Press. Available from the American Bar Association, Chicago.

Report of the Committee on the "Free Press-Fair Trial" Issue (the "Kaufman Report"). A report of the U.S. Judicial Conference Committee on the Operation of the Jury System. Available from the Administrator of U.S. Courts, Washington, D.C.

Rights in Conflict. A report of the Twentieth Century Fund Task Force on Justice, Publicity and the First Amendment. Available from the Twentieth Century Fund, New York, N.Y.

Standards Relating to Fair Trial and Free Press (the "Reardon Report"). A report of the American Bar Association's Advisory Committee on Fair Trial and Free Press.

Available from the American Bar Association, Chicago. (In 1978, the Standards were substantially revised and liberalized by the ABA. The new version is titled "Fair Trial and Free Press, second edition," and is popularly called "the Goodwin Report." It, too, is available from the ABA in Chicago.)

The Courts and the News Media: Fair Trial-Free Press: A Compromise Proposal for Procedural Due Process on Judicial Restrictive Orders. A report by the Reporters Committee for Freedom of the Press. Available from the Reporters Committee, Washington, D.C.

SIGNIFICANT SUPREME COURT RULINGS ON THE PRESS

Brief summaries of the most significant decisions on law as it affects the press directly. Cases listed chronologically within each category. Citations are to volume numbers, pages and year in the official United States Reports (abbreviated "U.S.").

Advertising

Valentine v. Chrestensen, 316 U.S. 52 (1942)
   "Purely commercial advertising" is not protected by the First Amendment against prior restraint. (Precedent much in doubt because of Virginia Board of Pharmacy v. Citizens, **see below.**)

Pittsburgh Press v. Commission, 413 U.S. 376 (1973)
   States or cities may ban classified advertising for jobs where sex qualifications are listed. (Precedent somewhat in doubt because of Virginia Board of Pharmacy v. Citizens, see below.)

Lehman v. Shaker Heights, 418 U.S. 298 (1974)
   Car card space on city transit may be limited to non-controversial commercial advertising.

Bigelow v. Virginia, 421 U.S. 809 (1975)
   States may not impose prior restraints on advertising of a non-commercial nature, provided the subject matter is of clear public interest and provides the public with information about such issues.

Virginia Board of Pharmacy v. Citizens, 425 U.S. 748 (1976)
   First Amendment protects communication (advertising) which merely proposes a commercial transaction.

Linmark v. Willingboro, 431 U.S. 85 (1977)
   Local governments may not impose a total ban on public advertising displays even though they may reflect adversely on the community.

Carey v. Population Services, 431 U.S. 678 (1977)
   States may not ban advertising of products even though it may be offensive or embarrassing to those exposed to the ads. (Expands constitutional protection recognized in Virginia Board of Pharmacy case, see above.)

Bates v. State Bar of Arizona, 433 U.S. 350 (1977)
   States may not impose a total ban on advertising lawyers' fees and availability.

First National Bank v. Bellotti, 435 U.S. 765 (1978)
   Corporations have a constitutional right to spend their funds to influence the outcome of referenda elections.

Broadcasting

Red Lion v. Federal Communications Commission, 395 U.S. 367 (1969)
"Fairness doctrine" requiring broadcasters to provide free time for reply or response by those criticized by or taking an opposite view of a broadcast program does not violate the Constitution.

CBS v. Democratic National Committee, 412 U.S. 94 (1973)
Broadcasters may refuse to sell television advertising time for discussion of controversial political issues.

Zacchini v. Scripps-Howard, 433 U.S. 562 (1977)
States may create a "right of publicity" for performers, allowing them to sue for damages if a broadcaster shows their entire act on a news show. Limits scope of Time v. Hill (see Privacy, below.)

Federal Communications Commission v. National Citizens Committee, 436 U.S. 775 (1978)
The federal government may limit the right of a newspaper to obtain a broadcast license in its own city.

Federal Communications Commission v. Pacifica, 438 U.S. 726 (1978)
The federal government may regulate the times during which vulgar language may be used on radio or television broadcasts.

Federal Communications Commission v. Midwest Video, 440 U.S. 689 (1979)
The federal government has no authority to require cable television systems to give the public some free use of their channels. (Expands broadcaster freedom under CBS v. Democratic National Committee, see above.)

Controls on Publication, Contempt

Gitlow v. New York, 268 U.S. 652 (1925)
States are required, by the Fourteenth Amendment, to respect freedom of the press as protected by the First Amendment.

Near v. Minnesota, 283 U.S. 697 (1931)
Prior restraint upon publication, especially that which deals with official misconduct, is forbidden except in extreme or emergency situations—for example, war or public emergency. However, the First Amendment is not an absolute prohibition on prior restraint.

Bridges v. California, 324 U.S. 252 (1941)
Courts may not use contempt power to punish out-of-court publications unless there is a "clear and present danger" of serious and imminent threat to the administration of justice.

Pennekamp v. Florida, 328 U.S. 331 (1946)
Courts may not use contempt power to punish out-of-court publications directly criticizing the conduct of judges unless there is a clear and imminent threat of obstruction of fair and impartial trial of pending cases.

Craig v. Harney, 331 U.S. 367 (1947)
Trials are public events and what happens in the courtroom is "public property." Judges may not use contempt power to punish out-of-court publications directly criticizing the conduct of a judge during the trial of a pending case. (Limited by Gannett v. DePasquale, see below.)

N.Y. Times v. United States, 403 U.S. 713 (1971)
> The federal government failed to justify prior restraint on publications of the secret "Pentagon Papers." (Legal rationale for the result varied among the Justices.)

Branzburg v. Hayes, 408 U.S. 665 (1972)
> First Amendment does not protect reporter from obligation to respond to grand jury subpoena and answer questions about sources or information obtained from them.

Pell v. Procunier, 417 U.S. 817 (1974) and *Saxbe v. Post,* 417 U.S. 843 (1974)
> News organizations and reporters have no more right of access to prisons for interviews with inmates than does the public at large. Access is subject to prison regulations.

Miami Herald v. Tornillo, 418 U.S. 241 (1974)
> First Amendment protects news media from state-imposed right to reply to news stories.

Nixon v. Administrator of GSA, 433 U.S. 425 (1977)
> Congress has power to seize former President's records and hold them for screening for possible future public, including press, access.

Nixon v. Warner Communications, 435 U.S. 589 (1978)
> The "common law" right of access to evidence admitted in court does not apply to the "White House tapes" played in the Watergate cover-up trial.

Landmark v. Virginia, 435 U.S. 829 (1978)
> The press may not be prosecuted for publishing truthful confidential information about investigations of judges' fitness in office.

Zurcher v. Stanford Daily, 436 U.S. 547 (1978)
> The 4th Amendment provides no special protection for the press against police searches of newsrooms or news files.

Houchins v. KQED, 438 U.S. 1 (1978)
> The press has no more right than the general public to enter or tour prison facilities to investigate conditions (Expands Pell and Saxbe decisions, above).

Free Press-Fair Trial and "Prejudicial Publicity"

Stroble v. California, 343 U.S. 181 (1952)
> Lapse of time after publicity about a defendant's confession may significantly reduce the chance that his right to a fair trial will be impaired, even though the publicity involved a confession given at the time of arrest.

Marshall v. United States, 360 U.S. 310 (1959)
> In **federal** cases, the mere fact that jurors saw and read news stories about a defendant's criminal record may be sufficient to void conviction. Ruling based on Supreme Court's "supervisory power" over lower federal courts. (Compare with Murphy v. Florida, below.)

Irvin v. Dowd, 366 U.S. 717 (1961)
> Protection of defendant's right to fair trial in a **state** case does not require that all jurors be totally ignorant of the facts or issues in the case before trial begins. Jurors may serve if it is clear that they may put aside preconceived notions about a case and decide fairly.

Beck v. Washington, 369 U.S. 542 (1962)
> Lapse of time after news revelations may be sufficient to cure "prejudicial publicity" problem.

Rideau v. Louisiana, 373 U.S. 723 (1963)

Change of venue should be allowed where local television station has broadcast an interview by a sheriff with the defendant, during which the defendant admitted he committed the crime.

Estes v. Texas, 381 U.S. 532 (1965)

Televising of criminal trial may violate right to fair trial.

Sheppard v. Maxwell, 384 U.S. 333 (1966)

Specifies the steps judges must take to protect a defendant's right to a fair trial before resorting to direct prior restraint on the press. Empowers judges to control conduct of the press in the courtroom.

Murphy v. Florida, 421 U.S. 794 (1975)

In **state** cases, jurors' advance knowledge of defendant, of the crimes, and of defendant's prior conviction of another crime does not automatically void a conviction. (Compare with Marshall v. U.S., above)

Nebraska Press Association v. Stuart, 427 U.S. 539 (1976)

Judges must try all other alternatives to protect a defendant's right to a fair trial before they may resort to direct prior restraint on the press, and even last-resort use of such power is extremely limited.

Oklahoma Publishing v. District Court, 430 U.S. 308 (1977)

Judges may not restrain news media from publishing information about juvenile cases obtained in open court proceedings. (Also see Cox Broadcasting v. Cohn, Privacy, below.)

N.Y. Times, Farber v. New Jersey 439 U.S. 997 (1978)

Supreme Court refused review of first state court decision that "shield law" protecting reporter's and newspaper's files from disclosure must always yield to 6th Amendment guarantee of fair trial.

Gannett v. DePasquale 443 U.S. 368 (1979)

The public, including the press, has no constitutional right, under the Sixth Amendment's "public trial" guarantee, to attend pre-trial proceedings in criminal cases. The right of a "public trial" is the defendant's right. (A sequel to the Gannett decision, testing the authority of judges to close criminal trials, was reviewed by the court in the 1979–80 term: Richmond Newspapers v. Virginia.)

Smith v. Daily Mail 443 U.S. 97 (1979)

The press may not be prosecuted for disclosing the names of juveniles who commit crimes, provided that the information was obtained by lawful means.

Libel

N.Y. Times v. Sullivan, 376 U.S. 254 (1964)

Public official may win libel lawsuit only on proof that the publication was false and that it was published with "actual malice"—that is, publication with knowledge that it was false or with reckless disregard of whether it was true or false. (Publication in this case was an advertisement.)

Garrison v. Louisiana, 379 U.S. 64 (1964)

Times-Sullivan rule applies to libel lawsuits based on news stories regarding official conduct of public officials.

Rosenblatt v. Baer, 383 U.S. 75 (1966)

Times-Sullivan rule applies to persons, not public officials but in a position to influence outcome of public activity; also applies to subordinate government employes with significant control over official action. (Precedent in doubt because of Gertz v. Welch, see below.)

Curtis Publishing v. Butts, 388 U.S. 130 (1967)

Times-Sullivan rule applies to persons who are "public figures." (Precedent in doubt because of Gertz v. Welch and Time v. Firestone, see below.)

St. Amant v. Thompson, 390 U.S. 727 (1968)

In proving "actual malice" under Times-Sullivan rule, must show that the person responsible for the story entertained serious doubts as to the truth of the story.

Greenbelt Publishing v. Bresler, 398 U.S. 6 (1970)

Times-Sullivan and Curtis-Butts apply to truthful stories about public hearings before governmental agencies.

Monitor Patriot v. Roy, 401 U.S. 265 (1971)

Times-Sullivan rule applies to candidates for public elective office.

Time v. Pape, 401 U.S. 279 (1971)

Times-Sullivan rule applies to some news media paraphrasing of contents of official government documents.

Rosenbloom v. Metromedia, 403 U.S. 29 (1971)

Sought to apply Times-Sullivan rule to news stories dealing with "issues of public interest." Decision did not have support of a Court majority. (Precedent of no force because of Gertz v. Welch, see below.)

Gertz v. Welch, 418 U.S. 323 (1974)

Limits full protection of Times-Sullivan rule to public officials and to other persons who are obviously public figures. Requires less proof of injury for private persons, unless they seek punitive damages.

Time v. Firestone, 424 U.S. 448 (1976)

Restricts use of Times-Sullivan rule when libel lawsuit involves news stories based on judicial proceedings of private persons. Restricts Times-Sullivan and Curtis-Butts definition of "public figures." (Ruling expanded in Wolston v. Reader's Digest, see below.)

Herbert v. Lando, 441 U.S. 153 (1979)

In "public official" and "public figure" libel cases (see Times-Sullivan, above), lawyers for the suing person may compel a reporter or editor to explain every step of the news-gathering process, including the "state of mind" of the reporter or editor as a story was planned, reported and written.

Hutchinson v. Proxmire, 443 U.S. 111 (1979)

A person is not a "public figure" for libel lawsuit purposes (see Times-Sullivan, above) merely because the person has achieved publicity by receiving public funds.

Wolston v. Reader's Digest, 443 U.S. 157 (1979)

A person is not a "public figure" for libel lawsuit purposes (see Times-Sullivan, above) merely because the person has been charged with or convicted of a crime. (Expands Time v. Firestone, above.)

Privacy

Time v. Hill, 385 U.S. 374 (1967)

Times-Sullivan rule (see Libel, above) regarding "actual malice" applies to privacy lawsuits involving newsworthy persons or events.

Cantrell v. Forest City Publishing, 419 U.S. 245 (1974)

Time-Hill rule followed, but implies that Gertz v. Welch (see Libel, above) theory might be applied to privacy cases involving private persons.

Cox Broadcasting v. Cohn, 420 U.S. 469 (1975)

States may not impose damage liability on the press for accurate reports of judicial records or judicial proceedings, provided they were open to the public. (Also see Oklahoma Publishing v. District Court, Free Press-Fair Trial, above.)

Index